Creative Machine Knitting

Creative
Machine
Knitting

Ruth Lee

THE GUILD OF MASTER CRAFTSMAN
PUBLICATIONS

First published 2003 by
Guild of Master Craftsman Publications Ltd,
166 High Street, Lewes,
East Sussex, BN7 1XU

ISBN 1 86108 311 4

A catalogue record of this book is available
from the British Library.

Cover design by Oliver Prentice
Book design by GMC Studio and John Hawkins
Photography by Martin Palmer
Diagrams and pattern editing by Carol Chambers

Typeface: Franklin Gothic and Novarese ITC

Colour origination by Articolor Italia srl, Italy

Printed and bound by CT Printing

Contents

Foreword

It is with great pleasure that I introduce this volume of Ruth Lee's recent work. As Editor of *Machine Knitting News* I am well placed to confirm Ruth's exceptional design talent and we are extremely fortunate that she has chosen machine knitting as her forum.

It is a rare set of skills that enables any craftsperson to also become an author, and requires an ability to convey through writing the making process, always keeping in mind what might present problems to the reader. Sometimes the effect can be to imagine that the reader does not wish to be challenged with learning new and interesting techniques, but Ruth, always ambitious to make knitting exciting, avoids this and still manages to use some of the most basic techniques available.

All of Ruth's work sizzles with colour, texture and style, if not all three. In the true spirit of the artist, her work is a reflection of her personality and creative nature; why be satisfied with two colours when you can use four!

For the creative machine knitter, the real magic of Ruth's work is that you can 'unpack' tiny parts of each design and still have something really different, because from her colour palette to her shaping, Ruth is an original.

I do hope you enjoy making these designs as they are published, but I know that Ruth thinks of each one as only the beginning, and would encourage you to do the same.

Christine Richardson,
Editor of *Machine Knitting News*

Acknowledgements

The following companies are to be credited
for supplying yarns and trims for the garment patterns
and samples for the Style Files:

Yeoman Yarns Ltd,
36 Churchill Way, Fleckney,
Leicester, LE8 8UD
www.yeomanyarns.co.uk

Texere Yarns,
College Mill, Barkerend Road,
Bradford BD1 4AU
www.texereyarns.co.uk

Empress Mills (1927) Ltd,
Hollin Hall Mill, Trawden, Colne,
Lancashire, BB8 8SS
Telephone +44 (0) 1282 863181

Streamers,
7 Castlesteads, Bancroft,
Milton Keynes, MK13 0PS
www.streamers.co.uk

Brother UK for the loan of the
KH90 electronic knitting machine and ribber.

Finally and not least of all a big thank you to my partner,
Mick Pearce, for checking my text and dubious grammar,
usually at short notice when deadlines are looming large!

Abbreviations

alt	alternate(ly)	MT+1,	one, (two), (2), (3) (three) full sizes looser than main tension
BB	back bed		
beg	beginning	MT+4,	four, (five) (5) full sizes looser than main tension
CAL	carriage at left		
CAR	carriage at right	MT+9	nine full sizes looser than main tension
ch	chain		
cm	centimetres	MY	main yarn
Col 1	colour one	N(s)	needle(s)
Col 2	colour two	NRL(s)	needle return lever(s)
Col 3	colour three	NWP	non-working position
cont	continu(e)(ing)	0	no stitches or rows worked
dc	double crochet	P	purl
dec	decreas(e)(ing)	patt	pattern
FB	front bed	RB	ribber
ff	fully fashioned	RC	row counter
FNR	full needle rib	rem	remain(ing)
fig	figure	rep	repeat
foll	following	SS	stitch size
g	grams	st(s)	stitch(es)
HP	holding position	st st-	stocking stitch
inc	increas(e)(ing)	SYG	second yarn guide
K	knit	tog	together
LC	lace carriage	T	tension
MB	main bed	TD	tension dial
MC	main colour	UWP	upper working position
mm	millimetres	WK	waste knitting
MT	main tension	WP	working position
MT-1,	one, (two), (2), (3) (three) full sizes tighter than main tension	WY	waste yarn
		A/ B,	contrast C & D colours
MT-4,	four, (five), (5), (6) (six) full sizes tighter than main tension		

Introduction

I don't believe I have ever followed a knitting pattern as written. As a child, the creative versions I produced of the egg cosies and kettle holders in my mother's knitting books bore witness to this fact, as did some of my more outrageous outfits from college days.

I was always drawn to mixing unusual colours, patterns, textures and yarns to make a strong statement, crossing or ignoring conventional boundaries. Thus, for me, the knitting machine was a means to an end. It enabled me to have a certain freedom in the way I designed.

My experimental approach is evident in my articles for *Machine Knitting News*, now reproduced here. No apologies are offered for the fact that my published patterns are quite often time consuming to knit, since great satisfaction can be had from a beautifully crafted piece that will stand the test of time. An imaginative use of hand-manipulated techniques may not be quick to produce, but will add value to your work and set it apart from off-the-shelf knitwear.

On a purely practical level, another favourite hobbyhorse of mine is the encouragement of the greater use of the visual charting device. This immediately frees you from following the pattern as written and allows you to re-interpret it in many different ways. Simply make an outline copy of the published measurement diagrams onto your charter paper. Choose your own colours and yarn, or even a different stitch pattern. Make a tension swatch for each new variation and set the charter mechanism accordingly, then follow the diagram to see where to shape. It's that simple.

Creative machine knitting opens so many doors for the adventurous practitioner. Break the rules. Push your boundaries. Never be afraid to try out new ideas, however far-fetched they might seem at the time. Not all will succeed. That is the very nature of experimental work. For every experiment that moves your work forward there will be many discarded pieces. But for the one that does work it will be something to be proud of, and will provide a real sense of achievement.

Ruth Lee

Use your charting device and intarsia carriage to knit this fabulous dress. A designer look for a knitter with some experience of both devices

Lady Stardust

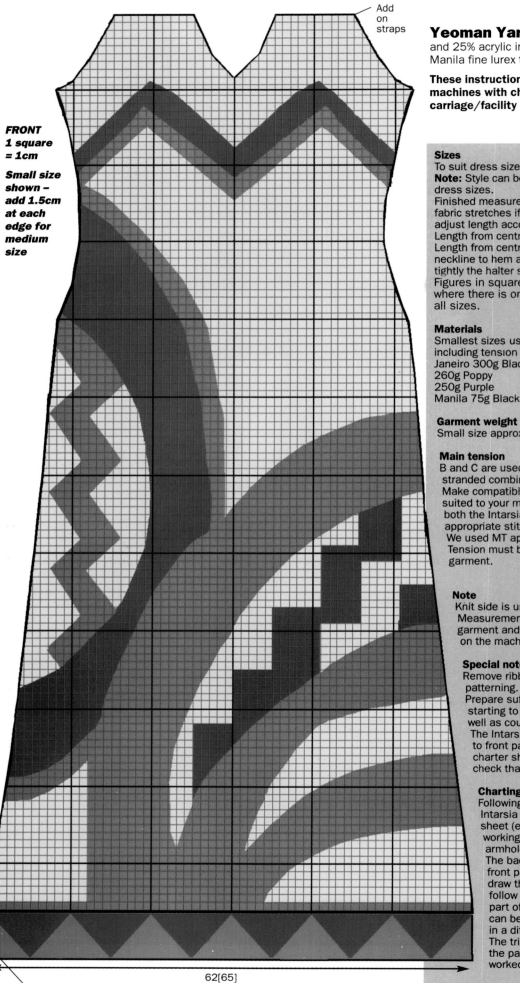

Add on straps

FRONT
1 square = 1cm

Small size shown – add 1.5cm at each edge for medium size

8cm   **Diagram 1**   62[65]

Yeoman Yarns Janeiro 50% viscose, 25% linen and 25% acrylic in Black (A), Poppy (B) and Myrtle (C), Manila fine lurex thread in Black

These instructions are written for standard gauge machines with charting device and intarsia carriage/facility

Sizes
To suit dress sizes small[medium]
Note: Style can be adapted on the charter to suit most dress sizes.
Finished measurement 88[94]cm (please note the fabric stretches if hung for storage and when worn, so adjust length accordingly)
Length from centre back to hem 113cm
Length from centre front measured from top of vee neckline to hem approx 138cm, depending upon how tightly the halter straps are tied.
Figures in square brackets [] refer to larger sizes; where there is only one set of figures, this applies to all sizes.

Materials
Smallest sizes used the following amounts approx including tension swatches:
Janeiro 300g Black
260g Poppy
250g Purple
Manila 75g Black

Garment weight
Small size approx 550g

Main tension
B and C are used 2 stranded throughout. A is used 2 stranded combined with 1 strand Manila throughout. Make compatible tension squares in the manner suited to your make and model of charting device for both the Intarsia and the main carr. Select appropriate stitch rule and set row counting.
We used MT approx 7 and intarsia carriage approx 6 Tension must be matched exactly before starting garment.

Note
Knit side is used as right side.
Measurements given are those of finished garment and should not be used to measure work on the machine.

Special note
Remove ribber before commencing intarsia patterning.
Prepare sufficient separate balls of yarn before starting to knit (see tensions requirement as well as counting colours across the work).
The Intarsia pattern on back is a mirror image to front pattern. It may be possible to insert charter sheet back to front. If you try this, check that the sheet is still feeding correctly.

Charting garment and pattern shapes
Following measurement diagrams and outline Intarsia pattern, convert same to charting sheet (excluding triangular border patt if working this by partial knitting) and up to armhole shaping.
The back pattern is a mirror image of the front pattern so you may wish to simply draw the top back detail on the charter and follow mirrored front pattern for the lower part of the dress. Front vee and halter neck can be drawn on a separate sheet, or draw in a different colour over main diagram. The triangle border can be knitted using the partial knit technique or it can be worked as an intarsia pattern if preferred.

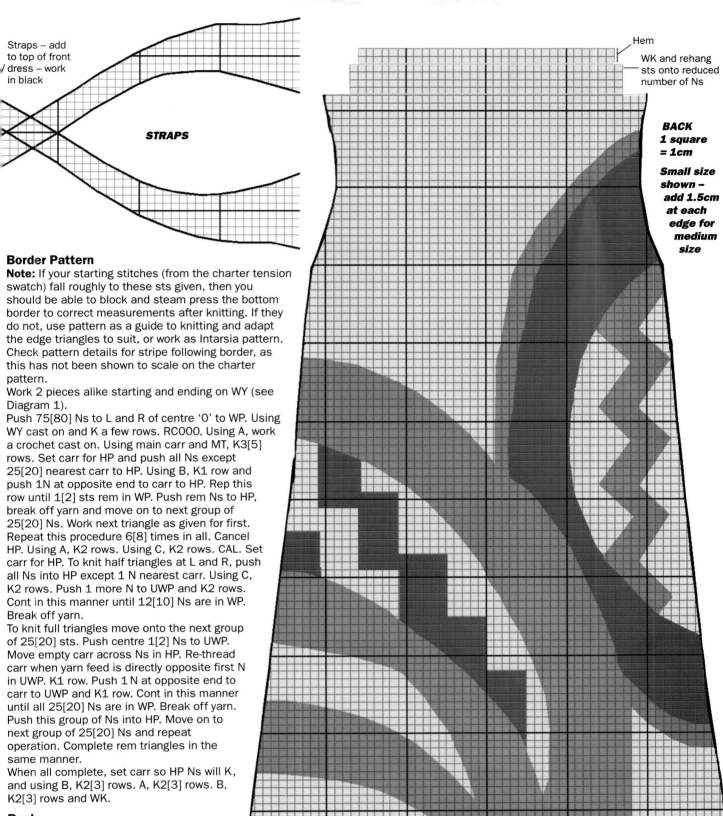

Straps – add to top of front / dress – work in black

STRAPS

Hem

WK and rehang sts onto reduced number of Ns

BACK 1 square = 1cm

Small size shown – add 1.5cm at each edge for medium size

Border Pattern

Note: If your starting stitches (from the charter tension swatch) fall roughly to these sts given, then you should be able to block and steam press the bottom border to correct measurements after knitting. If they do not, use pattern as a guide to knitting and adapt the edge triangles to suit, or work as Intarsia pattern. Check pattern details for stripe following border, as this has not been shown to scale on the charter pattern.

Work 2 pieces alike starting and ending on WY (see Diagram 1).

Push 75[80] Ns to L and R of centre '0' to WP. Using WY cast on and K a few rows. RC000. Using A, work a crochet cast on. Using main carr and MT, K3[5] rows. Set carr for HP and push all Ns except 25[20] nearest carr to HP. Using B, K1 row and push 1N at opposite end to carr to HP. Rep this row until 1[2] sts rem in WP. Push rem Ns to HP, break off yarn and move on to next group of 25[20] Ns. Work next triangle as given for first. Repeat this procedure 6[8] times in all. Cancel HP. Using A, K2 rows. Using C, K2 rows. CAL. Set carr for HP. To knit half triangles at L and R, push all Ns into HP except 1 N nearest carr. Using C, K2 rows. Push 1 more N to UWP and K2 rows. Cont in this manner until 12[10] Ns are in WP. Break off yarn.

To knit full triangles move onto the next group of 25[20] sts. Push centre 1[2] Ns to UWP. Move empty carr across Ns in HP. Re-thread carr when yarn feed is directly opposite first N in UWP. K1 row. Push 1 N at opposite end to carr to UWP and K1 row. Cont in this manner until all 25[20] Ns are in WP. Break off yarn. Push this group of Ns into HP. Move on to next group of 25[20] Ns and repeat operation. Complete rem triangles in the same manner.

When all complete, set carr so HP Ns will K, and using B, K2[3] rows. A, K2[3] rows. B, K2[3] rows and WK.

Back

Pick up border section on to equivalent Ns. Using intarsia carr, set Ns for Intarsia knitting. Follow charter for shaping and patt until first WK line and WK. Replace sts onto equivalent Ns doubling up approx every 8 Ns 13 times (dependant upon your own tension requirements). Cont to knit from charter to second WK line and WK. Replace sts onto equivalent Ns doubling up approx every 10 Ns as before. Complete back with hem working 2 rows C prior to knitting hem and the fold rows.

Front

Work as given for back using front charter patt until vee neck. WK.

Pick up sts at L and use ff shapings on vee neck so shaping takes place on 3rd N from edges. Complete R neckline to correspond with L.

To make up

Neaten all ends. Block and steam pieces to correct measurements. Mattress stitch side seams together taking care to match Intarsia pattern. Give final press to side seams.

Style File

Designing 'Lady Stardust'

This is the story of the intarsia dress from initial ideas through to the finished piece.

I always think of the design process as a journey. At each stop along the route certain decisions have to be made, alternative solutions weighed up and either discarded or refined further. Unexpected blips have to be dealt with, wrong turnings righted, until you arrive at your destination. Designing is all about problem-solving. In this case:

• the design and realisation of a glamorous patterned party frock in intarsia knitting
• using the charting device
• in at least two sizes
• to be produced as a printed pattern
• in a sensible number of colours

Having established the nature of the problem, the next step is to look at a range of possible answers, selecting the most promising avenues of enquiry to pursue further.

First things

For this design I had a fairly clear idea of the style I wanted to develop; definitely a dress for the party season. Long, slinky, glamorous and sophisticated with bold, asymmetrical patterning in big blocks of colour, and a deep 'V' neck. My initial thoughts were either for a backless number with a halter neckline, or with back and cut away armholes.

The dress shape came first, then the surface pattern. I wanted the pattern to complement the shape, so it seemed logical to decide on the shape first. Several quick sketches were made to establish the style lines. I tend to work on layout paper so that I can trace off ideas quickly and make minor adjustments. (Layout pads can be purchased from most good art suppliers; they consist of sketchbooks of semi-transparent paper in various qualities suitable for felt-tip markers, pens, ink, brush etc). I like to work fairly quickly at this stage, using black and white and simple line drawings. My initial sketches started me thinking about strong geometric shapes in bold blocks of colour that recalled the kind of patterns you might find in Art Deco buildings.

Second things

I quickly realised that some of the many photos of Art Deco buildings taken on my trip to New Zealand last year would be a

fine source of inspiration for pattern. With the dress shape in mind, I examined the pictures for suitable shapes I could play around with, in this case circles, sunburst patterns and ziggurats. The latter were sourced from photographs of a number of different buildings. I then tried different possible placements of the patterns and their relationship to the dress shape, while simplifying them to the minimum so that they would not be too complicated to knit in Intarsia. I decided on the most successful for further development, choosing four ideas that looked different enough to refine further.

At this point I was still working in black and white only.

More Decisions

Having decided on favourites, I thenthought about potential colour schemes, choices and availability of yarn and looked at any other problems that might need solving. The main unresolved issue with the dress at this stage was how best to design different sizes so that the pattern was not changed substantially. More on this later.

Choosing yarns and colours

Since this was to be a party frock, yarns were chosen to give slinky, sexy, glamorous qualities with style and sophistication. Viscose was an obvious choice here for my main yarn, possibly

mixed with some glitz for a festive sparkle. The colour palette was selected to tie in with one of the season's main colour stories, rather than being sourced from the Art Deco influences. This is a common way of working in fashion /textile design; inspiration and influences are drawn from a number of different reference points. The design could, of course, be interpreted in Art Deco colours or colours derived from another, quite different source.

Once I had decided on a broad colour range, I needed to check the yarn suppliers shade cards to find a close match in suitable yarns, and to narrow my colour palette down to no more than four shades to keep the cost reasonable. I decided that the rich purple would probably be the hardest colour to match in the type of yarn I was looking for. I found just what I wanted in Yeoman Janiero, shade Myrtle. I chose the other colours so that one would stand out against the other when translated into individual blocks of pattern (and, importantly, different enough in hue and tone for photography purposes). I arrived at two distinct groups of colour which would have worked equally well together, either black, purple and red, or purple, gold and red. Having resolved the colour palette, I made coloured versions of the designs selected for further development, tracing quickly over the original black and white drawings using more layout paper. As you can see from the illustrations, many permutations are possible; for example the same pattern in the same colours but placed differently one against the other, or variations of the intarsia pattern perhaps using 3 out of the 4 chosen colours.

Sampling

Sampling and full colour visualisations must take place in order to test how colours react and work next to each other. Intarsia knitting is a time-consuming business, so it is vital that everything is resolved beforehand. There can be nothing worse that spending many hours knitting an outfit only to find that the colour looks completely wrong in a certain place. To resolve the colour balance, I knitted up tension square-sized swatches in each of the colours I intended to use, to compare the colours and their proportions.

Full scale development

I then decided to make a full size paper pattern to test out the most successful design in colour. Drawing out the Intarsia pattern like this was far quicker than knitting samples in Intarsia. I used dressmakers dot-and-cross paper first to plot out the dress shape and then draw in the surface pattern. For me, full scale

visuals on pattern drafting paper are a must at this stage of the process. I also find I get a much better feel for the overall effect of the design and shape combined. I like to make a back and front, and pin or tape them together to see the design in 3 dimensions. Working large-scale lets me see if I can simplify the pattern down even further without losing the essence of the design. I used oil pastels to block in rough areas of colour quickly to get a feel for the design as a whole. If you want to try this yourself, you can always work with jumbo-size felt-tip pens, or cut out shapes of coloured paper and stick them in position. Think of the outline dress shape as a blank canvas to work on in the same way as if you were composing a picture or photograph within a certain sized format.

Knitting the design

My choice of working method for intarsia knitting has to be from a drawn charter pattern rather than a graph. It is a quicker and more versatile working method, letting you change the tension, colour and quality of yarn simply by knitting new tension swatches and selecting the appropriate stitch ruler and row counter setting.

Matching side seams on different sizes proved awkward, until I realised that a mirror image of the pattern would match exactly, and because the pattern was large in scale, the differences between the two sizes are imperceptible.

As to matching the tension of all the yarns used in the dress, I confess to using a little creative licence by adding a fine glitz thread to the 2 strands of black Janiero, but not to the red and purple, because an exact match of colours couldn't be found. The differences in tension were small, and on the plus side the black knitted up into a firmer fabric than the purple and red, and worked well on the dress straps and bodice.

Sampling was necessary to arrive at the

correct tension for the garment, and to check the differences in tension between the main knitting carriage and the intarsia carriage. I had already decided that it would be quicker to knit the triangle-patterned border using the main carriage and the partial knitting technique, whilst the bulk of the dress would require the use of the intarsia carriage. I found that my intarsia carriage needed to be set at one whole tension lower than the main carriage to achieve a compatible tension.

The only major miscalculation of the whole project was the fit of the back of the dress. I didn't find this out until I had completed the back and the front, sewn it together and tried it on the dress stand. The back bagged out slightly, confounding my aim of a dress that fitted like a glove. It needed additional shaping, which meant unravelling a small amount of knitting that was fortunately on the plain section of the back. The yoke shaping method was the ideal solution, and I can't think why I hadn't done this to start with!

Result!

Intarsia can be time consuming, but worth all the extra effort once you see the finished piece. I have to admit that this commission took longer to knit than I had initially calculated, simply because I found that I needed to take regular breaks from the machine to give my back/neck a rest. Do please give yourself enough time to complete the project over, say, a week. If you need your machine for another project you can always strip off on waste yarn. I find that the first few rows at the start of knitting seem to go slowly, but once you get into a rhythm of working, intarsia can become quite therapeutic.

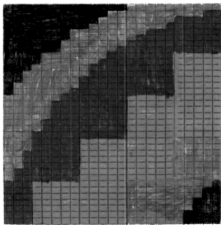

Design for Intarsia, graph format or 4 colour Jacquard (double bed techniques)

Lilac

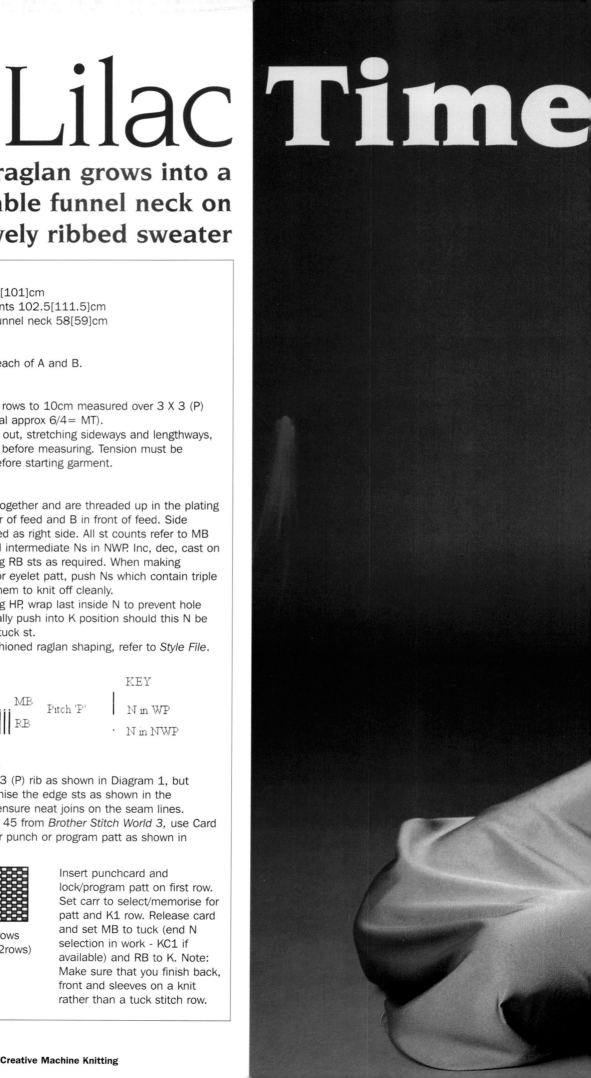

Time

The raglan grows into a fashionable funnel neck on this lovely ribbed sweater

Sizes
To fit bust sizes 91[101]cm
Actual measurements 102.5[111.5]cm
Length excluding funnel neck 58[59]cm

Materials
1 x 500g cone in each of A and B.

Main tension
29.6 sts and 45.4 rows to 10cm measured over 3 X 3 (P) tuck rib (tension dial approx 6/4= MT).
Pin tension swatch out, stretching sideways and lengthways, lightly steam press before measuring. Tension must be matched exactly before starting garment.

Notes
A and B are used together and are threaded up in the plating feed using A in rear of feed and B in front of feed. Side facing knitter is used as right side. All st counts refer to MB only and include all intermediate Ns in NWP. Inc, dec, cast on or off corresponding RB sts as required. When making manual transfers for eyelet patt, push Ns which contain triple sts to HP to help them to knit off cleanly.
When shaping using HP, wrap last inside N to prevent hole forming and manually push into K position should this N be programmed for a tuck st.
To knit the fully fashioned raglan shaping, refer to *Style File*.

Pattern note

KEY
| N in WP
· N in NWP

Diagram 1

Tuck rib pattern
Arrange Ns for 3 X 3 (P) rib as shown in Diagram 1, but taking care to organise the edge sts as shown in the INSTRUCTIONS to ensure neat joins on the seam lines.
Program stitch patt 45 from *Brother Stitch World 3,* use Card 1 from basic set, or punch or program patt as shown in Diagram 2.

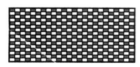

Repeat 24sts x 16rows
(Electronics 2sts x 2rows)

Diagram 2

Insert punchcard and lock/program patt on first row. Set carr to select/memorise for patt and K1 row. Release card and set MB to tuck (end N selection in work - KC1 if available) and RB to K. Note: Make sure that you finish back, front and sleeves on a knit rather than a tuck stitch row.

Yeoman Yarns

Janiero 50% Viscose, 25% Linen and 25% Acrylic, in shade Lavender (A) and Brittany 2ply 100% Cotton in shade Lavender (B)

These instructions are written for standard gauge punchcard or electronic machines with ribber

Back and front

With RB in position, set machine for a 1 X 1 rib. Push 77[83] Ns at L and 76[82] R of centre '0' on MB to WP. 153[165] Ns. Push corresponding Ns on RB to WR. Using WY in a contrasting colour, cast on and K tubular rows. MT, K approx 24 rows. Transfer sts from RB to MB, dec 1 st at L. 152[164] Ns.
Thread up A + B and make a chain cast on using the latch tool over the existing WY sts. K2 rows at T8.

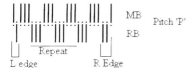

Diagram 3

Re-arrange sts for a 3 X 3(P) rib, making sure that the L, R and centre sts are as shown in Diagram 3. CAR. Using MT K1 row. Insert punchcard and lock/program patt on first row. Set carr to select/memorise for patt and K1 row.
RC000. Release card and work in tuck rib (see patt note)**. K20 rows.

Eyelet section

Transfer all RB sts to MB and vice versa except L and R end sts on MB. Reset Ns for patt using the slip setting on MB and RB (without actually knitting a row).
K4 rows tuck rib. RC shows 24.

Diagram 4

*To make the eyelet patt work on each group of 3 Ns in WP on the RB in turn, transferring sts 1 and 3 to st

2, as shown in Diagram 4. (3 sts rem on N2). Return empty Ns 1 and 3 to WP. Push N2 to HP. K4 rows in tuck rib *. RC028. Repeat from * to * until RC shows 044. Re-transfer MB sts to RB and vice versa except end sts on MB. Reset Ns for N patt using the slip selling on MB and RB (without actually knitting a row). RC44. K in tuck rib until RC shows 056.

Eyelet section 2

Transfer and work as given for first eyelet section only K36 rows in eyelet patt. RC shows 092.
Re-transfer MB sts to RB and vice versa except end sts on MB. Reset Ns for patt knitting using the slip setting on MB and RB (without actually knitting a row). RC92. K in tuck rib patt until RC shows 158.

Diagram 5

Armhole shaping

CAL. Dec 1 st and K1 row. CAR. Dec sts and K1 row. 149[161] sts. Realign edge sts for raglan shaping, as shown in Diagram 5.
Set RC000. Cont in tuck rib patt throughout and dec 1 st at each end of every alt row 21 times in all. K until RC shows 42. Dec 1 st at each end of next and every 3rd row 19 times in all. 69[81] sts. K until RC shows 100[106].

Shape saddle shoulder

Set RC000. Set both carr for HP. Cont in tuck rib patt throughout and push 2 Ns opposite carr HP on next 6 rows. Push 3 Ns opposite carr to HP on next 4 rows. RC10.

Diagram 6

Transfer sts to MB and WK on separate lengths of WY, 12 sts L and R for saddle shoulder and 45[57] sts for neck edge.
Ns for neck sts are arranged as shown in Diagram 6.

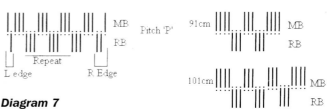

Diagram 7

Sleeve

With RB in position, set machine for a 1 X 1 (P) rib. Push 35[38] Ns at L and 34[37] R of centre '0' on MB to WP. 69[75] Ns. Push corresponding Ns on RB to WP. Work as given for back to ** noting 68[74] sts after dec and re-arranging sts for a 3 X 3(P) rib, making sure that the L, R and centre sts are as shown in Diagram 7. Shape sleeve by inc 1 st at each end of every 6th row throughout and working in the sequence shown below until 108[114] sts and RC shows 120.

RC000. K20 rows tuck rib patt. K20 rows eyelet patt as for back. RC shows 40. K150 rows of tuck rib patt. RC shows 190.

Diagram 8

Shape raglan

CAL. Cont in patt throughout. Dec 1 st L and K1 row. Dec 2 sts R and K1 row 105[111] sts. Transfer sts at L and R edges for fully fashioned raglan shaping, as shown in Diagram 8 (size 91cm).

NOTE that there are 8 sts on the RB initially, meaning there will be 2 extra dec in the first set of shapings, then work as given for back.
RC192.

Diagram 9

Working as before, dec 1 st at each end on alt rows until RC shows 280. 1 7[23] sts rem. See N arrangement, Diagram 9. K 8[14] rows. RC288[294]. Place a marker at edge to denote start of saddle shoulder. K until RC shows 302[308]. Transfer sts to MB and WK.

Interim make up

Neaten all ends. Block and press as for tension swatch. Join three out of four of the raglan seams using mattress stitch. Link saddle shoulder sts held on WY on front and back to extended trapping on sleeve head on three out of the four seams only.

Funnel neck

With right sides facing, pick up 45[57] front neck sts, 17[23] L raglan sleeve sts, 45[57] back neck sts and 17[23] R raglan sleeve sts onto the MB. 124[160] sts.

With RB in position, carefully transfer MB sts to RB to correspond with tuck rib pattern. Weight evenly. CAL. Set carr to select/memorise for patt without K (slip) and take to R.
RC000. Using MC and MT, start and work in tuck rib patt (see patt note). K30 rows. Transfer sts to MB. T8 K2 rows. Cast off behind the gate pegs.

To make up

Join remaining raglan and saddle shoulder seam. Join side and sleeve seams using mattress stitch. Carefully join funnel neck. Give a final press.

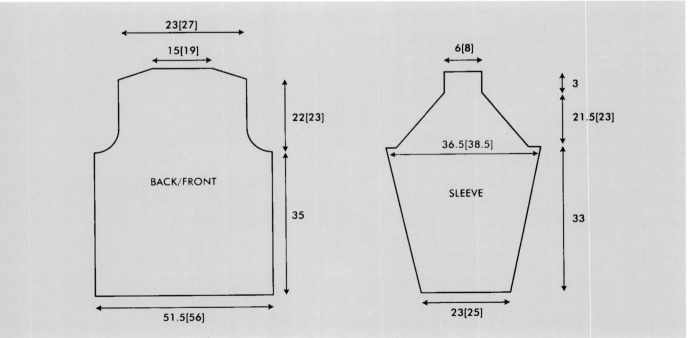

23[27]

15[19]

22[23]

35

BACK/FRONT

51.5[56]

6[8]

3

21.5[23]

36.5[38.5]

SLEEVE

33

23[25]

How to achieve funnel necks and raglan sleeves

Funnel neck patterns

If you have a set of basic pattern blocks and the use of a Knitleader (or similar visual charting device) you should be able to quickly and easily make the necessary adjustments to your pattern for any number of interpretations of the style, in various stitch patterns. The charting device gives you so much freedom when developing new ideas from scratch, without the hassle of complicated mathematics. The main difference between the funnel neck and the standard roll neck is that the body of the former continues on up into the high straight collar but without the seam line at the neck edge. This style can either be developed from a classic set-in sleeve pattern or from the raglan pattern block.

The raglan style offers much potential for decorative shaping, both to emphasise style and to give that extra added value to your own designs. Although these techniques are more time consuming than a standard decrease, they give your knitwear the designer look and allow you to show off your knitting skills.

Decorative raglan shaping techniques

Cables and eyelets patterns, or bands of stocking stitch worked in a broad continuous strip on the edge of the raglan shaping, are especially effective, as can be seen in Samples 1-6. To do this, you must decide on the number of stitches reserved for the edging, then keep constant throughout the decreasing. This, in turn, takes place on the stitches inside the decorative edging. An adjustable, multi-pronged transfer tool is most useful for this technique.

Ribs may, of course, be knitted plain or patterned. Sample 4 illustrates a plain, knitted border contrasted against a main body of purl facing tuck rib.

Forward planning

It is advisable to calculate for at least one extra stitch for seam allowance on the outermost edge. This should be on the side of the knitting to be used as the front of the fabric if possible. In the case of broad tuck ribs, where the purl face of the main-bed tuck stitch pattern is used uppermost, the end stitches also need to be on the main bed to ensure that they knit off cleanly. This will vary from machine to machine and in relationship to the end needle rule.

You will find limitations regarding the number of stitches worked adjacent to each other on either the main bed or the ribber when using double-bed techniques on machines with a ribbing attachment, such as Brother or Silver Reed machines. If you are using a true double-bed machine (the Pfaff for instance) then these limitations are not so apparent. You just need to choose your strippers with care. In the case of the Pfaff, patterning is possible on both beds if you use manually operated pusher patterns in conjunction with the arrow keys. This opens up many more possibilities for decorative rib structures.

Initial sampling

If you aren't familiar with double bed shaping techniques, practice making fully fashioned decreases on a 1 x 1 (P) or a 2 x 2 (P) rib first. Sample A shows a practice sample in 1 x 1 (P) ribbing knitted at MT4/4. Decreases are made firstly every 2 rows and latterly every 4th row. Continue the knitting to form a thin shoulder strap for a halter neck design.

The main samples

All my examples are knitted on the Brother KH970 with 850 ribber. The plating feed is used on most of the samples to emphasise the difference in textures between two close-coloured yarns. Here I have chosen to contrast 2ply Brittany cotton, mall in appearance, in combination with the lustrous Janiero, in close tints of pale mauves and blues.

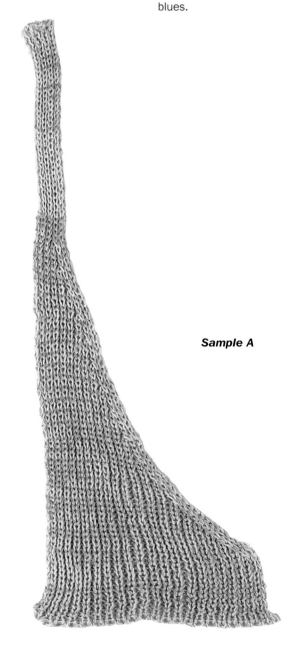

Sample A

Sample 1
Sample 2
Sample 3

Sample 1

Cast on 42 stitches in a 1 x 1 (P) rib and knit several rows straight at MT 4/4. Transfer the left end stitches, as shown below, before starting the raglan decreases.

X = Working position
O = Non working position
KH = Main bed
KR = Ribber

```
1 2 3 4 5 6
X X X X X X O X O X O X O X          O X      KH
O O O O O O X O X O X O X O          X O      KR
```

Row counter 000. Decrease 2 stitches on row 004 and every following fourth row over stitches marked ..... as described above. At the same time make eyelets on row 002 and every following fourth row by transferring stitches 3 and 5 to needle 4. Remember to push the empty needles back into WP.

Sample 2

Commence this sample as a 2 x 2 (P) rib and knit several rows straight at MT4../4.. using the plating feed. Transfer the left end stitches as shown below before starting the raglan shaping.

```
1 2 3 4 5 6
X X X X X X O O X X O O X X etc.       KH
O O O O O O X X O O X X O O etc        KR
```

Row counter 000. Make decreases as described above for a 2 x 2 (P) rib on every 4th row. At the same time make an eyelet on every other row over by transferring stitch 3 to needle 2 and pushing the empty needle back into WP. Always make the decrease first and then the decorative eyelet. This sample has been decorated with small, silvery tap washers, as sold by your local hardware shop.

Sample 3

In this sample 2 x 2 (P) plain knit rib is worked against a border of six edge stitches. Decreases are made every 4th row, a 2 over 2 cable pattern is made every 16 rows. It is easier to transfer stitches for the cabling once you have made the decreases.

Sample 4

In this example a tuck rib is worked in a 3 x 3 (P) rib with a border of 6 edge stitches plus 1 extra stitch (A) on the main bed for seaming purposes. The tuck stitch pattern is Stitch Pattern 45 from *Stitch World Pattern Book 3* from Brother. The purl face of the tuck stitch pattern is right side. Commence the swatch with a 1 x 1 (P) rib at MT4/4. Knit a few rows and then rearrange the stitches to form a 3 x 3 (P) rib following the needle diagram shown below, and with particular reference to the end stitches on the LHS.

```
A              1 2 3
X O O O O O O X X X O O O X X X O O O etc   X KH
O X X X X X X O O O X X X O O O X X X etc   O KR
   1 2 34 5 6
```

Knit several rows at MT4../4.. in plain knit rib. Program stitch pattern 45 and set carriage for patterned knitting and MT6/4. Always arrange to make the raglan decreases on the rows where there are no tuck stitches, in this case on even-numbered rows. To knit the raglan shaping, follow the steps outlined below.

1 Using a multi-pronged transfer tool, shift needles marked 1-6 on the KR one full position to the right. Do the same to edge stitch A on the KH. Transfer stitch 6 on the KR up to needle 1 on the KH. You have decreased 1 stitch. The new needle arrangement is shown below. Knit 2 rows, for example, depending upon shaping details.

```
A              1 2 3
X O O O O O X X X O O O X X X etc          KH
O X X X X X O O O X X X O O O etc....      KR
   1 2 3 4 5
```

2 Shift needles marked 1-5 on the KR one full position to the right. Do the same to edge stitch A on the KH. Transfer stitch 5 on the KR up to needle 1 on the KH. You have decreased 1 stitch. The new needle arrangement is shown below. Knit 2 rows, for example:

```
A              1 2 3
X O O O O X X X O O O X X X etc....        KH
O X X X X O O O X X X O O O etc....        KR
   1 2 3 4
```

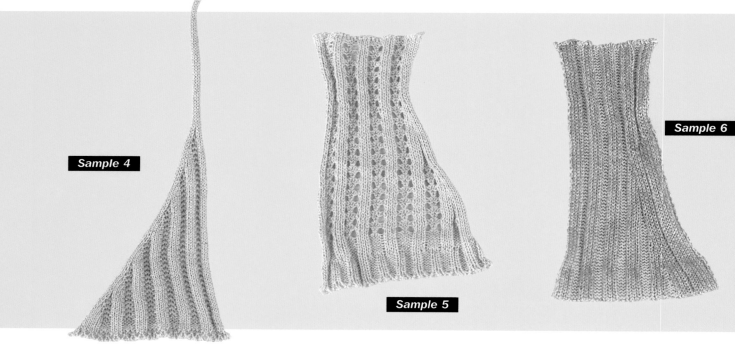

Sample 4

Sample 5

Sample 6

3 Shift needles marked 1-4 on the KR one full position to the right. Do the same to edge stitch A on the KH. Transfer stitch 4 on the KR up to needle 1 on the KH. You have decreased 1 stitch. The new needle arrangement is shown below. Knit 2 rows, for example:

```
A         1 2 3
X O O O X X X O O O X X X etc        KH
O X X X O O O X X X O O O etc        KR
   1 2 3
```

4 Working on the KH first, move stitch 3 to needle 2 and then move the double stitch back to needle 3. Shift stitch 1 and end stitch A one full position to the right. Now move stitches 1, 2 and 3 on the KR one full position to the right. The new needle arrangement is shown below. Knit 2 rows, for example:

```
A         1 2
X O O O X X O O X X X etc        KH
O X X X O O X X X O O O etc        KR
   1 2 3
```

5 Working on the KH first, move stitch 2 to needle 1 and then move the double stitch back to needle 2. Shift end stitch A one full position to the right. Now move stitches 1, 2 and 3 on the KR one full position to the right. The new needle arrangement is shown below. Knit 2 rows, for example:

```
A         1
X O O O X O O O X X X etc        KH
O X X X O X X X O O O etc        KR
   1 2 3
```

6 Working on the KH first, shift end stitch A one full position to the right. Now move stitches 1, 2 and 3 on

the KR one full position to the right. Transfer stitch 1 on the KH down to stitch 3 on the KR. The new needle arrangement is shown below. Knit 2 rows, for example:

```
A
X O O O  O O O X X X etc        KH
O X X X X X X O O O etc        KR
   1 2 3 4 5 6
```

Repeat steps 1-6 until 8 stitches remain thus:

```
X O O O O O O X        KH
O X X X X X X O        KR
```

Continue knitting on these needles for a shoulder strap for a halter neckline or continue into a funnel neckline, as described below.

Sample 5

Here the 3 x 3 (P) rib is knitted plain and the lace transfers are on rib bed. A band of 6 edge stitches on the main bed separate the shaping from the edge.

Sample 6 - Funnel neckline construction

This sample illustrates the front section of a fully fashioned funnel neck design idea based on the samples shown above. Here a 3 x 3 (P) plain rib is knitted. The needle arrangement for the eight left and right edge stitches is shown below.

```
1 2 3 4 5 6 7 8                                        8 7 6 5 4 3 2 1
X O X X X X O X X X O O X X X ..............................O O O X X X O X X X X X O X
O X O O O O X O O O X X X O O O..........................X X X O O O X O O O O O X O
```

It is important to note that the decreases on the left and right edges of the front (for example) should be mirror images of each other and symmetrical. The same process as knitting paired decreases by hand. In my example, the broad edge strip is gradually decreased into a straight 3 x 3 (P) rib for the funnel neck (top section of swatch).

Woven Magic

A Tshirt shaped dress, combines simple 'e' wrapped stripes with bands of stocking stitch

Yeoman Yarns
Brittany 2ply 100% cotton in Clematis (A) and Spring Green (B), Cannele 100% cotton in Emerald and Papillon 100% polyamide in Jade (D).

These instructions are written for standard gauge Brother electronic machines - alternative stitch pattern (and selection technique) is given so that it may also be worked on any electronic or punchcard machine with weaving facility

Back
Push 160[180:200] Ns to WP. Arrange for alt Ns in WP and rem Ns in NWP. Work a chain cast on using 2 strands A over all Ns in WP. Change to 1 strand A and MT, K1 row. Push rem Ns into WP and K4 rows. RC000. Working from patt and colour sequences throughout K until RC shows 466.

Shape armholes
Cast off 2 sts at beg of next 2 rows. Dec 1 st at each end of next and every foll 4 rows 6 times in all. RC492. 144[164:184] sts. K until RC shows 597[605:613].

Shape shoulders
Cont in stripe patt (rows 16-28). Set carr for HP and push 6[7:8] Ns at opposite end to carr to HP on next 12 rows. Set carr so HP Ns will K. Using A, K2 rows across all sts. Set carr for HP. Push all but 42 Ns nearest carr to HP and WK. Take carr to opposite side and push 42 Ns nearest carr to UWP and WK. Set carr so HP Ns will K and WK over rem 72[80:88] sts (for back neck).

Front
Work as given for back until RC shows 565.

Sizes
To suit dress sizes 10-12[14-16:18-20]
Finished measurement 107[120:133]cm
Length 118.5[120.5:122.5]cm
Sleeves seam 12cm
Figures in square brackets [ ] refer to larger sizes; where there is only one set of figures this applies to all sizes.

Materials
1 x 500g cone in each of A and B
1 x 250g cone of C
10 x 50g balls of D
2.50mm crochet hook
A chunky gauge latch tool (optional)

Garment weight
Size 14-16 weighs approx 700g

Main tension
30 sts and 51 rows to 10cm, measured over one complete repeat of the knitweave patt (109 rows and after pressing using a slightly damp cloth and a warm iron. (TD approx MT3..=MT). Tension must be matched exactly before starting garment.

Note
Purl side is used as right side. Measurements given are those of finished garment and should not be used to measure work on the machine.

Special note
You will find it easier to knitweave if you remove the ribbing attachment from your machine.
When knitting the stripe patt keep the stitch patt moving on one row at a time even if the row to be knitted is plain rather than lay-in or "e" wrapped.

Pattern note
Brother 970 machines:
Program stitch patts 45 and 283 from *Brother Stitch World 2*. 283 is used on reverse setting.
Other electronic machines: Program patts before starting to knit.
Punchcard machines: Use card 1 from basic set as patt 45 and punch card from punchcard diagram for patt 283 before starting to knit.

Pattern sequence
RC000 - 060. Two full repeats of stripe patt. RC060 - 091. Three full repeats of triangle patt plus first row of patt. RC091 - 109. Repeat rows 012 - 030 of strips patt. These 109 rows form the main knitweave patt.

Colour sequence of stripe pattern
Stitch patt 45.
(Knitmaster/Silver machines see note). These 30 rows form the main stripe pattern

Row Counter	Main knitting yarn	Weaving yarn
000 - 002	A	D 'e' wrap
002 - 004	A	–
004 - 008	A	D weave
008 - 010	A	–
010 - 012	A	D 'e' wrap
012 - 016	A	–
016 - 018	C	–
018 - 020	B	–
020 - 022	B	C weave
022 - 024	B	–
024 - 026	C	–
026 - 030	A	–

Knitmaster/Silver Reed machines only: As your machine does not select Ns forward, the 'e' wrap selection will need to be done manually. Use the 1 x 1 ruler to push alt Ns forward and 'e' wrap using 'D' over these Ns. The birds-eye patt can be left rotating throughout and the woven (lay-in) section of the stripe patt worked conventionally.

Triangle pattern
Stitch patt 283 on patt reverse setting for 31 rows (3 full repeats plus first row of patt). Main/knitting yarn is A, 'e' wrap using D over selected Ns.

Knitmaster/Silver Reed machine only: As your machine does not select Ns forward, this 'e' wrap can also be done manually. Use the punchcard/electronic diagram shown (whichever you prefer) to push alt Ns forward in triangle patt and 'e' wrap using '' over these Ns.

All machines: The knitweave triangles are each knitted from a separate ball of yarn which is 'e' wrapped around Ns programmed/selected into upper working position. You do not need to break off the yarn between rows of triangles.

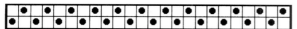

Pattern 45 card 1 from the basic punchcard set, reproduced courtesy of Brother UK

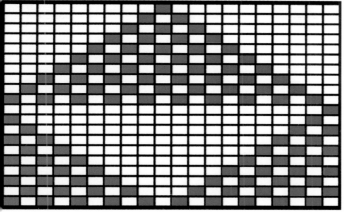

Electronic pattern 20 sts x 20 rows. Reversed version of Patt 283 Stitchworld 3, reproduced courtesy of Brother UK

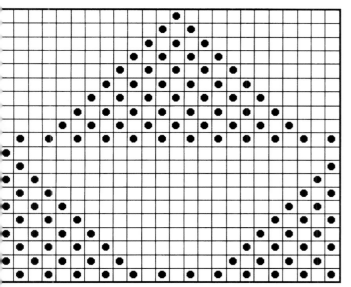

Punchcard pattern 24 sts x 20 rows

Shape neck

Note patt row and position in stripe sequence. Using nylon cord, K98[112:126] Ns at R by hand (loosely) taking Ns down to NWP. Use an old tension swatch or waste piece of knitting and hang this onto sinker gates in front of work held by NWP Ns. This will protect the fabric from brush marks whilst knitting first part of neck. Cont over rem 46[52:58] sts at L for first side. K1 row. Dec 1 st at neck edge on next and every foll alt row 10 times in all 36[42:48] sts. K until RC shows 605.

Shape shoulders

Cont in stripe patt (rows 16-28). Set carr for HP and push 6[7:8] Ns at opposite end to carr to HP on next and every foll alt row 6 times in all, K1 row. Set carr so HP Ns will K. Using A, K2 rows and WK. CAL. Remove swatch from sinkers in front of nearest 52[60:68] sts (i.e. centre neck sts). Unravel nylon cord over these sts bringing Ns down to WP and WK. CAR. Remove swatch from sinkers completely and unravel nylon cord over these sts bringing rem 46[52:58] Ns down to WP. Reset RC at 46[52:58] and, keeping patt and colour sequence correct from noted position, work R side to correspond with L.

Sleeves

Push 146[150:154] Ns to WP. Using WY, cast on and K several rows. Using MT and A, K4 rows. RC000. Start and work in stripe patt. Inc 1 st at each end of next and every 6 rows, 10 times in all. RC060. 166(170:174) sts.

Shape top

Cont in stripe patt. Set carr for HP. Push 4[4:3] Ns at opposite end to carr to HP on next 4(40:28) rows. Push 5(0:4) Ns at opposite side to carr to HP on next 26(0:20) rows. 10 sts rem in WP. Cancel HP. Reselect Ns. K1 row A. K2 rows A (knitting yarn) and 'e' wrap using D. K1 row A and WK.

Sleeve edge

Push 123(125:126) Ns to WP and with purl side facing, pick up first row worked in MC, dec evenly along the row by doubling up on every 5th N. *Using MT and A, K1 row. Make a row of eyelets by transferring every alt st to adjacent N and pushing empty Ns back into WP. K2 rows A. Cast off using 2 strands A.

Front neckband

Push 82[94:107] Ns to WP and with purl side facing, pick up 20(23:26) sts from L neck edge, 52(60:68) sts from below WY at centre front but doubling up on every 5th needle (42[48:55] sts) and a further 20[23:26] sts from R neck edge. Work as given for sleeve edge from * to end.

Back neckband

Push 58[64:71] Ns to WP. With purl side facing pick up sts from below WY at back neck and hang on to Ns dec C evenly by doubling up on every 5th N. Complete as given for front neckband.

To make up

Neaten all ends. Carefully block to correct measurements and press on reverse side, taking care not to touch the ribbon yarn with the iron (I used a slightly damp cloth and a warm iron). Link shoulder and sleeve head seams on the knitting machine by replacing stitches, right sides together, and using A and MT to K1 row and cast off. Mattress stitch side and under arm seams. Carefully press seams on inside, as above.

Neck sleeve and hem edging

Using crochet hook and D, make a row of double crochet using the eyelets as a spacing guide. A further optional row of chain st can be made in between the eyelets on the neck edging (I used the chunky gauge latch tool to do this).

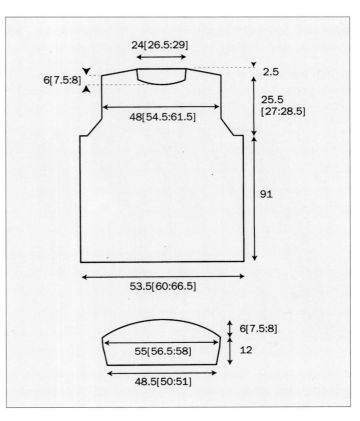

Knitweave for glamour

In this article we explore variations on the knitweave dress *Woven Magic*, and also look at accessory designs for beach and resortwear based around the same stitch patterns as the dress, but knitted in various unusual yarns. Design ideas cover a mix of stylish, slinky, glamorous and fun pieces. The main focus is on bags, but purses, belts, shawls, scarves and evening gloves can all be developed from the sampling shown below.

Accessories are a good way to show off your knitting skills and creativity, giving you the satisfaction of making unique and intricate pieces of work, even though you may have a limited amount of time to indulge in your favourite craft.

Colours and yarns

The bright colours of the South Seas and lush tropical foliage inspire this sample collection. Sparkling blues, intense greens, jades and turquoise are worked together using a mix of thick and thin yarns in the same piece. Fine sewing cottons, lurex, ribbon yarns, natural and shiny synthetic raffia, invisible nylon thread and sewing and mercerised cotton all add interest.

Stitch Patterns

The examples shown combine purl-facing plain knitted stripes with knitweave that

is either hand-wrapped over selected stitches or worked using the standard lay-in method. The latter will need a small-scale stitch pattern, unless you are incorporating cut floats into the design as shown below, or you decide to hook up the long floats as an integral element of the design. You could also choose a stitch pattern that contains larger geometric shapes, broken down into birds-eye format and alternating with solid blocks of foreground or background colour. The former relate to the knitweave element of the design, whilst the latter equate with the plain knitted areas.

The triangle pattern used on the knitweave dress is a good example of a suitable stitch pattern. Remember to program the pattern on reverse setting so that the needles selected to knit the background only are all in lower working position. You will need a separate bobbin of yarn for each triangle to be knitted (which is why I always refer to this method of working as intarsia style knitweave). You will also need to work on a machine that has visible needle selection, the Brother for instance.

Bags of Style

Recent fashion pages have featured bags in diverse shapes, sizes and colours. Colourful, decorative and ethnic inspired designs proliferate. Examples include small brocade drawstring bags, which can be worn around the wrist; shoulder bags in knitted stripes; brightly coloured cotton bags decorated with large and exotic flowers in raffia and ribbons; felted bags; baguette shaped bags; bags of handcrafted appearance, trimmed with

marabou feather edging; patched and embroidered shoulder bags; circular bags; bags with a retro feel, such as fifties florals, or 1980s' plastic see through bags with matching inner purse.

Knitted and decorated bags

Knitted bags in semi-sheer knits combining areas of transparent nylon filament with ribbon or raffia 'e' wrap or lay-in stitch patterns give you the chance to experiment further with the stitch patterns for the knitweave dress. You could line the knitting with a contrasting fabric; for example, a shimmering shot silk, sparkling lurex, or even brightly coloured plastic. A lining will help your bag retain its shape, as well as adding a contrasting element to the design. Decorate the bag with over-the-top knotted, plaited and braided fringes. Try incorporating beads, sea shells and pebbles, buttons or crochet flowers into the fringing. Alternatively, make a series of knitted add-ons, as shown in Sample 4. Handmade paper beads can be designed to complement the knitting and are lightweight enough not to affect the fabric's hang. Roll small paper shapes around a knitting needle or similar. Use PVA glue to stick the paper down. Decorate with acrylic paint. Try using non-traditional materials, such as fine wire, to give a contemporary twist to your work. Fine-gauge wire can be combined with thin lurex sewing threads and decorated with ribbon or raffia. Handles and straps can be made from twisted and plaited knitted cords. Alternatively, trawl the charity shops for old handbags, recycling and revamping closures and handles to give your bag unique appeal by mixing the old and new together. Simple styles and shapes for bags will do the most justice to decorative fabrics, as shown in the design sheet Fig 1. Let the knitting speak for itself.

Variations on a theme

Returning to the knitweave dress, why not try knitting it in various lengths and degrees of complexity. Different options include a short T-style dress, a sleeveless beach top or below-the-knee dress with three-quarter length sleeves. For a more instant result, keep the hand wrapped knitweave pattern for borders around the cuffs hem or neckline only.

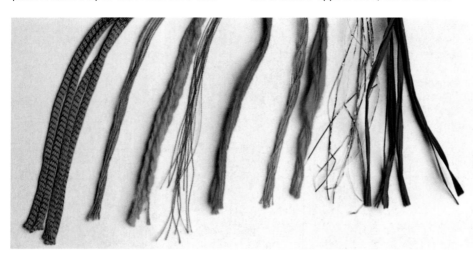

From left to right: Ribbon yarn, 2/16's mercerised, Cotton slub, Plain dyed machine embroidery thread, Brittany 2ply, 2/16's mercerised, Fine cotton slub, Lurex thread, Raffia.

Fig 1

Replacing the remainder with discreet slip stitch, ripple stitch patterns in a self colour. Alternatively, incorporate semi-sheer inserts into the sleeves or as a yoke, based on Sample 3.

Sample 1

Stitch pattern and knitting details as for the dress. Simply attach large wooden beads at the points of the triangles. Add fringing or tassels and develop into a small drawstring bag for the wrist or a more functional shoulder bag.

Sample 2

A variation on Sample 1 but knitted in a mix of fine machine sewing cotton contrasting against hand wrapped triangles in ribbon yarn and the purl facing stripes which were knitted in 2ply Brittany cotton and an oddment of ultra-fine mercerised cotton. The final section of the sample is knitted in slip stitch and the bottom edged with a row of double crochet in ribbon yarn. This swatch could be developed into a simple T-shaped top with borders of semi-sheer knitting on the cuffs, neckline or hem, or perhaps a lightweight shawl to throw over other outfits.

Sample 3

As for Sample 2, but replace the sewing cotton with fine nylon filament thread. This example was knitted at MT2. The beaded edge helps to weigh the knitting down. Line with an intensely coloured and contrasting silk Dupion or other contrasting fabric for a small evening purse.

More swatches

The two main samples develop the south sea island look further. Cropped cardigans or tops with wide, boat-shaped necklines and simple, purl-faced, rolled edges are suggested, although the same samples have much potential for beach bags or shoulder bags.

Sample 4

The main knitweave pattern is 'e' wrapped in either a medium weight slub cotton or Raffia in two different shades of turquoise. The background is knitted in a combination of a fine mercerised cotton and Rayon sewing thread in jade and mid-blue. The stripe pattern alternates a fine slub cotton in turquoise with 2ply Yeoman Brittany cotton in Clematis. Brass tap washers are used for decoration.

The knitweave add-ons were knitted separately over 10 stitches and 30 rows. 'E' wrap the raffia alternate rows and stitches only. Strip off on individual lengths of waste yarn until sufficient pieces are knitted. Hook up individual add-ons through the first row of stitches above the waste yarn and onto equivalent needles before continuing with the knitting. You could of course introduce add-ons at any point in the knitting.

Sample 5

In this example, the knitweave pattern utilises the standard lay-in method of working. A birds-eye pattern is programmed for every alternate group of 12 stitches and for 20 rows. You could of course decide on a different number of rows and stitches. Using a medium weight slub yarn for the weaving yarn and a mix of matt and mercerised cottons, rayon sewing thread and fine lurex for the stripe pattern, this knitweave design is knitted with a continuous end of yarn. Carefully cut through the long floats with a sharp pair of embroidery scissors to reveal the base fabric. Choose a slub or textured yarn for the lay-in yarn. Smooth yarns will easily pull out when using the cut float technique, unless you use the 'e' wrap method to anchor the yarn in place. Attach brass tap washers, tassels and crochet flowers in two tones of blue raffia for added decoration.

Further information

Raffia can be obtained mail order from **Fred Aldous** (Tel 0161 236 2477) or **Home Crafts Direct.** PO Box 39, Leicester LE1 9BU (Tel 0116 251 3139). Ring for current catalogue and price list.

Dancing Queen

Bring on the dancing queens in this sequins and bead trimmed shift in two layers. Texture is maximised with transfer lace and release stitch using four yarns

Sizes
To suit bust 87-92[97-02:107-112]cm
Finished measurement 94[104:114] cm (approx due to the nature of release stitch).
Back length taken from top of back bodice is approx 67cm to give a full length measurement of 85cm approx
Figures in square brackets [ ] refer to larger sizes; where there is only one set of figures, this applies to all sizes.

Materials
Yarns:
1 X 500g cone in A
1 X 250g cone in B
1 X 200g cone in C
1 X 50g ball in D
Beads and sequins:
Flat round sequins, single hole, 24mm in red 1 packet (100) (used approx 40).
Flat oval sequins, single hole, 26mm in red 1 packet (100) (used approx 50).
2mm glass beads in red 1 packet.
2mm glass beads in gold 1 packet.
Elasticated sequin braid, 2m x 20mm wide in red.
1 x 6mm metal crochet hook.

Garment weight
Approx 450g for size 97-102cm.

Main tension
Block and lightly steam press all swatches before taking measurements. Pin out the release stitch swatch as for single bed knitting.
Stocking stitch: 27 sts and 42 rows to 10cm, TD approx 8.
Transfer lace: 28 sts and 38 rows to 10cm, TD approx 7.
Release Stitch: (It is only possible to give an approx average tension). 23 sts and 33 rows to 10cm. TD approx 2./2. with fine knit bar in place.
Knitweave border (A + B): 27 sts and 41 rows to 19cm. TD approx 7. Tension must be matched exactly before starting garment.

Note
Knit and purl sides are used as right side. Use WY or garter bar to turn work at points specified in the pattern. Measurements are those of finished garment and should not be used to measure work on machine.

Special notes
Yarns: St st and transfer lace is knitted in A + B. Release st knitted in B + C. C in rear of plating feed and B to the front.
Brother machines: Use the fine knit bar for the release st patt and the end stitch presser plates to ensure that end sts K off cleanly.
Casting on: Use a double bed waste yarn cast on throughout. 1 X 1 (P) rib will be fine.
Order of work: Please follow the order of working as laid out in pattern.
Making up and care: Do not let the iron touch the sequins. You should do all blocking and pressing including side seams prior to attaching sequins. Remove sequins before washing, as they may melt or lose their colour. Store flat.

Pattern note
Punch card or program patt before starting to knit. Patt 1 transfer lace is 119 from Brother Stitch World patt book 3 (for the KH970). You could select a similar patt from existing patterns for your own make and model of machine.
See Diag 1 for release st N settings which refer to the point after FB sts have been transferred to BB to make the barrier for release st.

Yeoman Janiero 4ply 50% viscose, 25% linen, 25% acrylic in Seville (A)
Manila Lame, 2ply 86% viscose 5% nylon 9% polyester in Ruby (B)
Fine Cannele 1ply 100% mercerised cotton (C)
Citadella 4ply 100% viscose tape in red (D)

These instructions are written for standard gauge electronic machines with ribber, plating feed and lace transfer carriage

Underskirt
Section A Border: Work 2 alike.
Push 148[162:176] Ns to WP. Using WY, cast on and K a few rows. Using T7 and A + B work a crochet cast on over WY. CAR K1 row. *K1 row. Using C 'e' wrap every alt N*. Rep from * to * twice in all. RC3 **K1 row. Make an eyelet on every 5th N. K1 row. Insert beads alternating bead cols A and B along the row **. Rep from ** to ** 3 times in all. RC9. Rep from * to * twice in all. RC11. K1 row. RC12 CAR. Program machine for patt A. Set up lace carr as applicable to your make/model of machine. T7. K2 full rep of patt. RC40. Rep from * to * twice in all. RC42. K2 rows. RC44. WK.
Section B: Work 2 alike.
Push 132[146:160] Ns to WP. With knit side of border facing, re-hang sts onto equivalent Ns doubling up every 8th N, 12[0:0] times, every 9th N, 4[16:0] times and every 10th N 0[0:16] times in all. 132[146:160] sts rem. Using T8 and A + B, K184 rows and WK.
Block and press both pieces foll the measurements as given.

Overskirt
Section C Border: Work 2 alike.
Push 153[162:171] Ns to WP. Using WY, cast on and K a few rows. Using T7 and A + B work a crochet cast on over WY. CAR K1 row. * K1 row. Using C 'e' wrap every alt N*. Rep from * to * twice in all. RC3 **K1 row. Make an eyelet on every 5th N. K1 row. Insert beads alternating bead cols A and B along the row **. Rep from ** to ** 3 times in all. RC9. Rep from * to * twice in all. RC11. K1 row. RC12 CAR. K8 rows st st. RC20. Rep first 12 rows again. K2 rows. RC34. WK, leaving cast on comb in place.
Push 132[146:160] Ns to WP.

Re-hang knitting on equivalent Ns doubling up on every 6th N, 15[0:0] times, every 7th N, 6[0:0] times, every 9th N, 0[16:0] times, every 14th N, 0[0:5] times and every 15th N, 0[0:6] times in all. 132[146:160] sts. Leave on machine.

Main section D: Work 2 alike.
With RB in position, insert fine knit bar on MB (see note). Push 132[146:160] Ns into WP on RB. Thread up plating feed with B and C. Pitch lever H. T 2./2. K2 rows. Pitch lever P. Transfer all RB sts to MB, returning all Ns to NWP. Pitch lever H. Re-align RB Ns as shown in Diag 1. Insert end stitch presser plates. K108 rows. Release all sts on RB. Using T7 and A + B K2 rows on MB only. WK.

Front bodice
CAR. *Push 126[140:154] Ns to WP. Re-hang sts thus:
With back of knitting of main overskirt facing knitter, re-hang sts onto equivalent Ns doubling up on every 21st N, 6[0:0] times, every 23rd N, 0[4:0] times, every 24th N, 0[2:0] times, every 25th N, 0[0:2] times and every 26th N, 0[0:4] times in all, 126[140:154] sts. Now do the same with the underskirt so that the two pieces are both hanging together from the same Ns.
RC000. Using A + B and T8, K18 rows.

Shape armholes
Cast off 3[4:5] sts beg next 4 rows. RC22. 114[124:134] sts. Dec 1 st at each end of next and every foll alt row 8[13:18] times in all. K2 rows and dec 1 st at each end of next and every foll 3 rows, 7[5:3] times in all. 84[88:92] sts. RC59 [63:67].* At the same time, when RC 27[31:35].

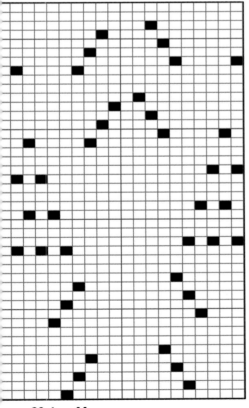

20sts x 44rows

Shape neck
Set carr for HP. Push all Ns to R and 6[8:10] Ns to L of centre '0' into HP. Always taking the yarn around the first inside N in HP, K2 rows. Cont in this manner pushing 4 Ns at neck edge to HP once, 3 Ns 3 times and 2 Ns 11 times on alt rows. Push any rem sts to HP. All sts in HP.
CAR. Leave all Ns to L and 6[8:10] Ns to R of centre '0' in HP and push rem Ns to UWP. Work R side to correspond with L. Set carr so HP Ns will K and K1 row. WK.

Back bodice
Work as given for front bodice from * to *. At the same time, when RC 41[45:49].

Shape neck
Push all Ns to R and 7[9:11] Ns to L of centre '0' to HP. Set carr for HP. K2 rows. Push a further 7Ns to HP on neck edge and K2 rows. **Push a further 4 Ns to HP on neck edge and K2 rows **. Rep from ** and ** 7 times in all. Push any rem sts to HP. All sts in HP.
Leave all Ns to L and 7[9:11] Ns to R of centre '0' in HP and push rem Ns to UWP. Work R side to correspond with L. Set carr so HP Ns will K and K1 row. WK. Cancel HP. K1 row. WK.

Front bodice facing
Pick up 126[140:154] sts from the point where the front bodice meets the skirt section, with the purl face of front bodice facing knitter. Work as given for front bodice. Pick up sts from front bodice from just below WY 2 sts on each N. K1 row. WK.

Back bodice facing
Pick up 126[140:154] sts from the point where the back bodice meets the skirt section, with the purl face of back bodice facing knitter. Work as given for back bodice. Pick up sts from back bodice from just below WY 2 sts on each N. K1 row. WK.

Neck bands
Work two alike. Push 72[76:80] Ns to WP, Double up sts every 6th N 12 times in all. Using T6 and A + B, K10 rows. T8 K2 rows, T6 K10 rows. Make hem and cast off.

Shoulder straps
K approx 100 rows single bed tubular (K in one direction/slip opposite direction) at T4. Stitch loosely under elasticated shoulder strap and attach to top edge of neckband.

To make up
Neaten all ends. Block and press pieces to correct measurements. Mattress stitch side seams of underskirt and over skirt. Stitch back bodice facing to back bodice. Do the same for the front bodice. Block and press all seams before attaching sequins.

Diagram 1   9st repeat

Sequin decoration: Attach sequins after blocking and pressing. (I found it easier to determine the correct length and stretch of the shoulder straps by working onto a dress stand and carefully pinning into place before loosely stitching onto neck bands.) Do not iron or press sequins or immerse in hot water. They may melt or lose their colour. It is advisable to remove sequins if you need to launder the dress.

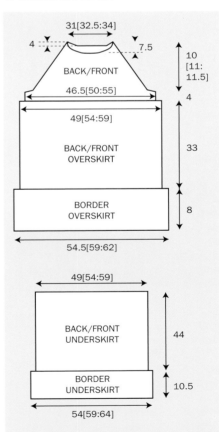

Note: measurements are approximate due to the variability of the stitch patterns (see patt notes)

Style File

Let's Party

The festive season means party time, and the opportunity to put on the glitz and glamour. How about slinky, open-work knits in hot reds, decorated with beads and BIG sequins? Read on, but first, as always, the techniques.....

Stitch structures

There are many different ways of creating open-work stitch patterns. For example, a fine yarn on a loose tension; needle-out patterns in single and double bed tuck-stitch and plain-knit ladder laces; manual and automatic transfer lace (fine and normal gauge eyelets if you have a Brother lace carriage) and manually worked double-bed release-stitch patterns. Pfaff E6000 knitters have the added advantage of automatic release stitch patterns using knitting technique 185.

I'm going to describe ways of combining different open-work patterns to create changes within the texture of the knitting, working with very close colours so as not to detract from these structural elements. The sampling focuses on release-stitch. Successful open-work patterns need a balance between the open spaces and the solid areas of knitting. Further contrasts can be made by knit and purl-facing stitches, the introduction of a new technique such as the hand-wrapped ribbon yarn, and by combining different sized areas of open-work patterns in which the orientation of the design lines are also varied. For example, patterns might have strong vertical, horizontal or diagonal directions. Sample 2, for instance, shows columns of vertical stripes in release-stitch, with the horizontal bands of transfer lace used in the narrow borders to divide up the vertical stripe patterns.

Colours

Choose to work with a single colour story, such as red on red, where the differences between colours are subtle shifts between darker, deeper, warmer, cooler or brighter versions of one key colour. It is also best to keep the contrast of tone to a minimum in the main body of the work. If reds don't appeal, consider pinky mauves through to purples or deep indigo blues moving through to violets. A single colour used in this way can pull together a design made up from a number of different patterns and textures. If you want a higher degree of contrast than this will give, try using a different colour for the under layer, such as the gold lining of Sample 5.

Yarns

Look for contrasting textures, such as matt, shiny, glitzy, smooth or rough in the same colour. You might want to use machine embroidery threads as a mixer. Empress Mills is a great source for a wide range of shades in both cottons and floss. Sewing thread would work well mixed in with the same colour of fine Cannele or Manila, giving a subtle shaded effect if you chose to work around the colour spectrum from hot reds through to purply reds and back again. Texere Yarns carry an excellent range of qualities and textures, and often have fine cottons, silks and fancy yarns suitable for open-work knitting.

Knitting release stitch

Release stitch is a double-bed knitting technique that allows you to produce knit or purl facing, elongated stocking stitch. The second needle-bed is used to knit stitches that will later be unravelled to form ladders in between the stitches that remain on the other needle bed. The latter form the solid areas of the stitch pattern. In knitting release stitch, there is one very important rule to follow. A barrier of stitches must be put in place on the opposite needle bed to the one carrying the release stitches. To understand this principle try a few simple experiments.

Cast on for a full needle rib. Knit a few rows tubular. Transfer all the front bed stitches to the back bed, leaving the empty needles in working position — I find it easier to do this if I temporarily move the pitch lever to full pitch — return the pitch lever to half pitch and knit 12 rows full needle rib. Using the straight edge of a needle pusher or a ruler, move the front bed stitches up and down to release the stitches. They should unravel as far as the tubular hem, which is the point at which the front-bed stitches were initially transferred to the back bed.

You could continue in this manner, alternating tubular knitting with bands of release stitch. Try transferring all the back-bed stitches to the front bed and releasing stitches from the back bed instead.

For further developments, knit and release only selected stitches from one or other of the needle beds (the opposite one to the barrier) to form alternating columns of open-work and solid stitches — Sample 1. The main stitch patterns in the samples below are all variations on this technique, combined with fine and normal gauge transfer lace, worked on a brother machine with lace carriage.

Decoration

Sequins and beads are an obvious choice for party decoration. Supplies can be obtained mail order from a company called Streamers, either online or regular post (see acknowledgements for address). They have an absolutely brilliant selection of stock, including shaped sequins with top (rather than centrally) placed holes.

Applying sequins to knit can be done in a number of ways, but all require some forward planning. Since sequins can easily cut through thread, the Streamers catalogue suggests that the sewing-on thread is passed first through a bead or series of beads before going through the hole in the sequin, then back up through the bead again. Also, on stretch fabrics such as knit, they suggest that each sequin is secured separately so if there is a break it doesn't mean the loss of a whole row of sequins. You can do this on the knitting machine in the same way as the beads were attached for my wedding dress design *Crystal* but there is a snag in using this method — once you have attached the sequins you can't block and press the work (we won't talk about who managed to melt her sequins into the first sample!).

You will need to knit the main body of the dress, then hand stitch the decoration onto the knitting after blocking and pressing, using the lace patterns as a guide. Obviously you can knit-in beaded decoration that is not attached to sequins. You could try incorporating tie markers into the knitting at the point where a sequin should go, then using this to attach some once the work is off the machine.

Knitting tips

Forward planning is important if you are designing from scratch with a number of stitch patterns in the same piece of knitting or complete outfit. Remember, they will all knit up to a different tension and possess different properties of handle, drape and elasticity. Always make a separate tension swatch for each stitch pattern to determine how they will work together and, for example, any adjustments that need to be made to the number of rows and stitches per 1cm.

Making up ribbed release-stitch patterns: release stitch elongates the knitting when compared to the solid areas of the pattern. Avoid drop stitches on the outer edges where they are to be seamed. You will get a neater finish if you split a solid column of stitches on either side of the seam line, remembering to add an extra stitch for the actual seam. Use a fine needle bar if knitting on tight tensions and with fine yarn, and use a waste yarn cast on.

The samples
Knitted with Yeoman Yarns on a Brother KH970 with 850 ribber with plating feed.

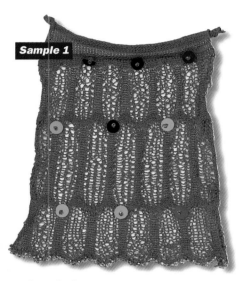

Sample 1
1. Waste yarn cast on. Change to main colour (Fine Cannele cotton and Manila). Tubular cast on.
2. Move all front bed stitches to back bed.
3. Push alternate groups of 4 needles either up into working position or leave in non working position on the front bed. Tension approximately 2/2 Knit 20 rows. Release front bed stitches.
4. Push all front bed stitches into working position.
5. Knit 4 rows full needle rib.
6. Pitch lever P. Transfer all front bed stitches to back bed. Pitch lever H.
7. Repeat step 3, offsetting the starting point for the groups of 4 needles. Knit 30 rows. Release front bed stitches.
8. Repeat steps 4 and 5.
9. Repeat steps 2 to 8 as required and decorate with beads and sequins.

Sample 2
Purl facing columns of release stitch knitted as for sample 1 combine with hand wrapped single bed knitting knitted thus. Tension approximately 5. Knit 2 rows Grigna shade Ruby, 1 row main colour, E wrap alternate needles with red Citadella ribbon yarn. Knit 1 row main colour. Knit 2 rows Grigna. Push up all equivalent needles on the ribber into working position, pitch lever H, knit 4 rows full needle rib at tension 2/2 refer to sample 1 for release stitch section. Alternate hand wrapped sections with release stitch varying the number of rows to suit.

Sample 3
This stitch pattern is the forerunner to the main pattern in *Dancing Queen*.

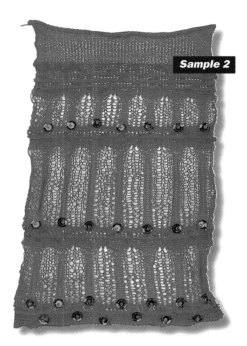

The single bed section is a development of the previous sample with knitted-in 2mm glass beads on every 4th needle, using the technique described in *Crystal* and decorated with 24mm sequins.

Sample 4, under layer to sample 3
Stitch pattern 119 was chosen from the Brother *Stitch World Pattern Book* 3 to contrast against the strong vertical lines of the drop stitch pattern in sample 3. The border begins and ends with 10 rows of hand wrapped and beaded pattern similar to sample 3.

Sample 5
A double layered sample. The top layer is knitted in Poppy Janiero plied with red Manila and combines a border of purl facing knitweave, and lace pattern 133 from the same source as sample 4 on the normal carriage setting, incorporating gold beads, followed by another band of knitweave and ending with 2 rows of stocking stitch. Strip off on waste yarn and turn the knitting. Using stitch pattern 185 and the lace transfer carriage set for fine lace knit as many rows as required. Finish with a border of knitweave, lace pattern 133 and a further band of knitweave followed by two rows of stocking stitch. The bottom layer is knitted in stocking stitch using Gold Janiero plied with gold Manila. Re-hang the top layer above the first row of knitweave, the purl side is the right side, and knit to the bottom of the first layer, change to the red colourway as for the top layer and finish with a border of knitweave, lace pattern 133, incorporating gold beads, and a further band of knitweave followed by two rows of stocking stitch.

Attach sequins to samples after pressing.

Spot of Relaxa

Fully fashioned fitted dress with intarsia spot detail that spirals down the front and back with contrasting stripes

Sizes
To suit dress size 10[12:14]
Finished bust measurement 102[107:112]cm
Finished hip measurement 108[113:118]cm
Length 96cm

Figures in square brackets [ ] refer to larger sizes; where there is only one set of figures, this applies to all sizes.

Materials
1 x 500g cone MC
100g in A
Small amounts (approx 50g) in B and C
The contrasting colours can be knitted in oddments of suitable yarns, so long as the tensions and weights are compatible. You might like to use more or less colours in the spot pattern.
1.5mm crochet hook

Garment weight
Size 10 weighs approx 370g

Main tension
28.5 sts and 44 rows to 10cm, measured over st st, using MC and appropriate contrasts double stranded throughout and after steam pressing (TD approx 6 = MT).
Tension must be matched exactly before starting garment.

Note
Knit side is used as right side. Measurements given are those of finished garment and should not be used to measure work on the machine.

Special note
Two ends of MC (and/or A, B and C) used together throughout. Wind off several balls of MC and thread one end from cone and one from ball, through the tension mast and into carriage feeder and treat as though they were the one yarn throughout.
You will need to remove the ribbing attachment from your machine to knit intarsia.
Check that main carr T6 approx is equivalent to T6 approx on the intarsia carr and that the gauge is as given for this pattern (you will need a tension swatch for both). Make the necessary alterations if not compatible.

Pattern note
You can either knit from Diag 1 and the written pattern or transfer the pattern to charter paper and work visually from the outline shown (see the *Style File* for alternative approaches to intarsia knitting).
Note: Only examples of stripe sequences given in Diag 1. See garment illustration and *Style File* for further variations.

Yeoman Yarns Brittany 100% 2ply cotton in Indiana shade 158 (MC) and Janeiro 50% viscose, 25% linen and 25% acrylic in Raffia shade 21 (A), Coral shade 4 (B) and Fig shade 17 (C)

These instructions are written for all standard gauge machines with intarsia carriage. Use of a full size charting device is optional

Back
Section A
Push 190[196:200] Ns to WP. Push alt Ns back to NWP. Using A, work a chain cast on over all Ns in WP. Push rem Ns to WP and using MT, K1 row. RC000. Using A, K4 rows. MC, K2 rows. A, K2 rows. C, K2 rows. B, K2 rows. C, K2 rows. Rep the last 14 rows once more. RC shows 28. WK.

Section B
Push 172[178:186] Ns to WP. With wrong side facing, pick up sts from below WY and hang thus:

First size: doubling up on every 9th N, 8 times and on every 10th N, 10 times. 172 sts.

Second size: doubling up on every 9th N twice and on every 10th N, 16 times. 178 sts.

Third size: doubling up on every 13th N 10 times and on every 14th N, 4 times. 186 sts.

Set RC to 000. Using the intarsia carr, MT and MC, K10 rows. Work spot patt centred over '0'. K12 rows RC shows 54. Work spot patt centred over L N62. K until RC shows 96 and WK.

Section C (Hips to waist)
Push 158[164:172] Ns to WP. With wrong side facing, pick up sts from below WY and hang thus:

First size: Doubling up on every 11th N, 14 times. Replace the 4 rem sts, 2 at either ends.

Second size: Doubling up on every 11th N, 4 times and every 12th N 10 times.

Third size: Doubling up on every 12th N, 9 times and every 13th N 6 times.

All sizes: K2 rows MC. RC000. Knit intarsia pattern foll instructions below but at the same time dec 1 st at each end of every 12 rows, 9[8:8] times in all. 140[148:156] sts. K until RC shows 108.

Intarsia patt: RC000. Work one full repeat of spot patt, centred over R N48. RC32. K12 rows MC. RC44. Work one full repeat of spot patt, centred over N '0'. RC76. K12 rows MC. RC88. Work first 20 rows of spot patt, centred over L N48. RC108.

Section D (Waist to Armhole shaping)
Place a marker at each edge (waistline). Knit intarsia patt foll instructions below at the same time inc 1 st at both ends of every 26[30:30] rows, 4[3:3] times in all, commencing when RC shows 110. 148[154:162] sts. K until RC shows 212.
Intarsia patt: RC 108. Complete the spot motif commenced in section C. RC120.
K12 rows. RC132. Work one full rep of spot patt, centred over R N32. RC164. K12 rows. RC176. Work one full rep of spot patt, centred over N '0'. RC208. K4 rows. RC212.

Section E (Armhole shaping)
Cont to work in intarsia patt, as below, and at the same time cast off 4 sts at beg of

next 2 rows. 140[146:154] sts. Cast off 3 sts beg next 2 rows. 134[140:148] sts. Dec 1 st at beg of next 4 rows. 130[136:144] sts. Dec 1 st at each end of next and every foll 4 rows, 8 times in all. 114[120:128] sts. RC shows 252. K until RC shows 296[300:304].
Intarsia patt: When RC shows 220 commence spot motif centred over L N32.

Section F (Shoulder shaping)
Using main carr and MC set carr for HP and always taking the yarn around the first inside N in HP:m.
Push 5[5:6] Ns at opp side to carr to HP on next 10[4:6] rows. Push 0[6:7] Ns at opp side to carr to HP on next 0[6:4] rows. Set carr so HP Ns will K and K1 row. WK over 25[28:32] sts at L and R in turn for shoulders. WK over rem 64 sts for back neck. Push 55 Ns to WP. Pick up back neck from below WY and hang on to Ns doubling up on every 6th N. K1 row and cast off.

Front
Work as given for back until RC shows 220 (Section E). WK (this method is used to ensure that the centre 'V' point is kept neat). Re-hang sts from L on equivalent Ns. Cont to shape armhole edge as for back and keep Intarsia patt as for back at the same time

Shape neck
K1 row. Dec 1 st ff at neck edge on next and every foll alt row 32 times in all. RC284. 25[28:32] sts rem. K until RC

shows 296[300:304]. CAR (CAL for R neck).
Section F (Shoulder shaping) Using main carr and MC set carr for HP.
Always taking the yarn around the first inside N in HP push 5[5:6] Ns at opp side to carr to HP on next and every foll alt row 5[2:3] times in all, K1 row. Push 0[6:7] Ns at opp side to carr to HP on next next and every foll alt row 0[3:2] times in all. Set carr so HP Ns will K and WK. CAL. Reset RC at 220 and work R side to correspond with L reversing all shaping.

To make up
Tidy all ends, taking care to do this neatly on the intarsia motifs. Block and steam press. Graft or link shoulder seams. Mattress stitch side seams.
Bottom hem
Using crochet hook and 2 strand MC, crochet finish the bottom hem by working a double and then a single chain stitch through each loop of the chain cast on.
Armhole edge
Work a treble stitch on every alt edge loop of the knitting except on the underarm cast off edge. Work a treble into each one of these loops. Work a further row of crochet by making a single crochet stitch into the edge loop of every stitch on the preceding row.
The 'V' neck is worked in the same manner as for the armhole. Give a final steam press.

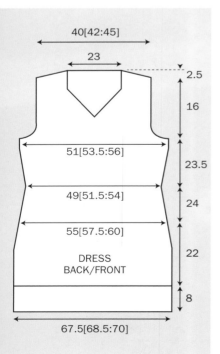

40[42:45]

23

2.5

16

51[53.5:56]

23.5

49[51.5:54]

24

55[57.5:60]

22

DRESS BACK/FRONT

8

67.5[68.5:70]

Diagram 1

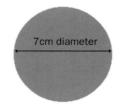

7cm diameter

Actual spot size for use with charting device

Spot Intarsia Designs 20sts x 32 rows

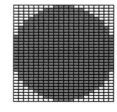 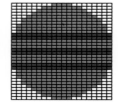 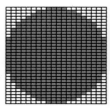

How to knit spots using intarsia or single-bed jacquard

Intarsia can be worked from a graph, or done using the charting device as a visual aid. The technique allows you to knit blocks of colour across a row, without floats of yarn crossing the back of the knitting. It is essentially a stocking stitch structure, and is relatively stretchy compared with single- or double-bed jacquard. Motif knitting jacquard-style is particularly effective on electronic knitting machines. Samples 5 & 6 show examples in which the first needle position has been altered on each subsequent placement of the motif, allowing the knitter to build up a widely spaced repeat pattern. As noted above, the handle of this fabric is more rigid than stocking stitch. Pfaff knitting techniques offer the knitter an automated version of single-bed intarsia, but this is limited to a maximum of four blocks of colour in any one row. Intarsia knitting can be combined with partial knitting on the Brother knitting machines. Sample 3 shows a shaped hem incorporated into an intarsia pattern. It is possible to push needles to holding position when using the current model of the Brother Intarsia Carriage.

Brother machines and intarsia carriages

A separate intarsia carriage is currently available for standard and chunky-gauge Brother machines. The current standard-gauge model is the KA-8210. Try Drummond's for new or reconditioned models. Their invaluable advice and help whilst preparing this article was much appreciated, particularly on the subject of compatibility of intarsia carriages with Brother Electronics and the Knitleader. Trippers are available with the KA-8210, and are used to operate the feeding levers of the row counter and the Knit Leader for most models of punchcard and electronic Brother machines. It is possible to use, for example, a full scale Knit Leader, the KA-8210 Intarsia carriage in conjunction with a Brother electronic KH970 on manual setting. It is possible, but rather time consuming, to improvise with an older style intarsia carriage that doesn't have the requisite trippers to connect with either your Knit Leader or the electronic row counter, by clicking one or other of the trippers by hand at the end of each row. Intarsia carriage sinkers are small plastic gizmos which help to give each bobbin of yarn an equal tension, and are supplied with the Brother KA-8210. Older models of intarsia carriage may not have been supplied with these devices.

Intarsia knitting working methods

My preferred method of knitting intarsia is to work from a full size visualisation of the design (including the pattern motifs) outlined on charter paper, simply because it is a much more versatile method and, to my mind, the quickest way of knitting, particularly where shaping is combined with intarsia patterning. This method gives you the freedom to interpret your polka dot pattern in any colour, weight and texture of yarn you like. If you prefer, you can work from a graph and/or a written pattern, depending upon the complexity of the intarsia pattern, but to knit the same size pattern in finer or coarser yarn you would need a different number of stitches and rows per 10cm. Each new variation would therefore require a new graph specific to just one tension.

Charter style intarsia knitting

To knit Sample 1 transfer the line drawing to charter paper. You might like to enlarge the image on the photocopier to suit individual requirements. If you are working with a full-scale charter, the pattern will be the same scale as the line drawing. Make a tension swatch in the chosen yarn and tension. Set the row mechanism and stitch rule correctly, and knit with the intarsia carriage as described below.

Intarsia graph 19sts x 34rows

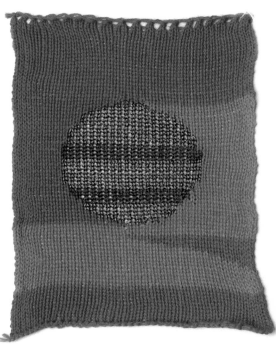

Sample 1

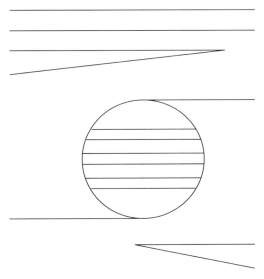

Line drawing for charter device

Wind off separate bobbins of yarn for each subsequent block of colour. Do not work directly from the full cones of yarn, particularly if you are plying together more than one end, as they will tangle easily. Knit from either a specially designed intarsia bobbin, or small bobbins of yarn made on the wool winder. Attach the sinkers to each individual bobbin. Cast on and knit several rows with the main knitting carriage. Place the bobbins of yarn on the floor in front of the machine in the

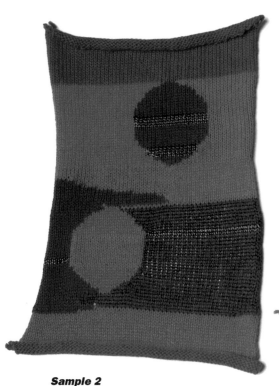

Sample 2

Sample 3

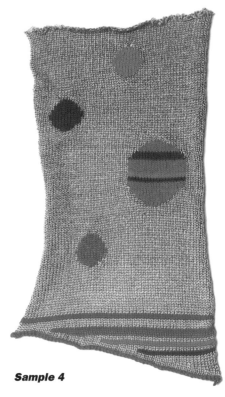

Sample 4

correct sequence of colours for the first row of the pattern. Set up for intarsia knitting, as described in your intarsia carriage manual, and commence knitting, using the line drawing on the charter paper as a visual guide as to the positioning of each block of colour across the entire row. To avoid holes in the knitting where one colour joins the next, remember to twist one yarn around the other when you are laying the yarn in across the needles before knitting the row. Samples 2 and 3 show a development of Sample 1. Try changing the background colour for foreground and vice versa, or the proportion of one colour against another. Sample 4 shows a variation in the size of the intarsia spots, and is finished with a partial knit border in matching stripes. The main body of the knitting is in 2 strand Janeiro, shade Raffia.

Pfaff electronic E6000 intarsia knitting techniques

Knitting techniques 245-248 enable you to knit a limited range of intarsia patterns automatically. You can knit up to four blocks of colour across a row, working from one pattern repeat only. This must be the same number of stitches as the knitting is wide. For example, if you choose a design with a 20 stitch pattern repeat and you have 120 stitches to knit, you will need to enlarge the stitch pattern by a factor of 6. To knit automatic intarsia, the colour changer is set up in such a way that colour 1 is in the first feeding eyelet on the left, colour 2 the second eyelet from the left, then so on for all four colours, remembering that the yarn designated

for the left part of the pattern is in the right hand feeding eyelet for knit-facing stocking stitch. You will find examples of this type of work beginning on page 116 in the Pfaff E6000 pattern book.

Jacquard knitting

Single motifs in two colour single-bed jacquard offer an alternative working method to intarsia: the main difference in the fabric structure being the floats which are present on the back of the work of the pattern motif. In this area, the knitting will be less stretchy than the surrounding areas of stocking stitch, a factor which might affect the hang of the garment, especially if you are knitting large-scale single motifs. It is important to choose your technique carefully in relationship to the end usage at the design stage. For example, a fluid, fitting shape such as the spotted dress works best in intarsia, whilst a jacquard technique would be more suitable for

Jacquard pattern 19sts x 34 rows

unstructured outwear, such as jackets and coats. Motifs knitted in double-bed jacquard will result in an evenly balanced fabric, but will have a more rigid handle than stocking stitch.

Finishing technique for single bed motifs

Single-bed motifs can be finished to avoid holes at the edges where the plain knitting meets the pattern motif. This is achieved by using a finishing yarn on the reverse of the work whilst the knitting progresses. Use a fine version of the main yarn, passing it from left to right across the back of the pattern motif under all the selected needles on each row. Then wrap the yarn around the last needle selected on the carriage side before knitting the row. For samples 5 and 6, I chose to embroider the edges of the spots to disguise the join between the pattern and the main body of the knitting, and to omit the finishing yarn.

Brother KH970

It is possible to program up to 9 different single motifs across the width of a piece of knitting. You can opt to position the individual patterns anywhere across the needle bed by selecting a first needle pattern position to either the left or the right of the centre '0'. You can even program in a selection of motifs which are not the same height. To knit designs similar to Samples 5 & 6 you will need to program-in the spot pattern, see the jacquard graph, and then the first needle position of the motif, for each different position of the pattern (refer to individual knitting machine manuals for more detailed instructions).

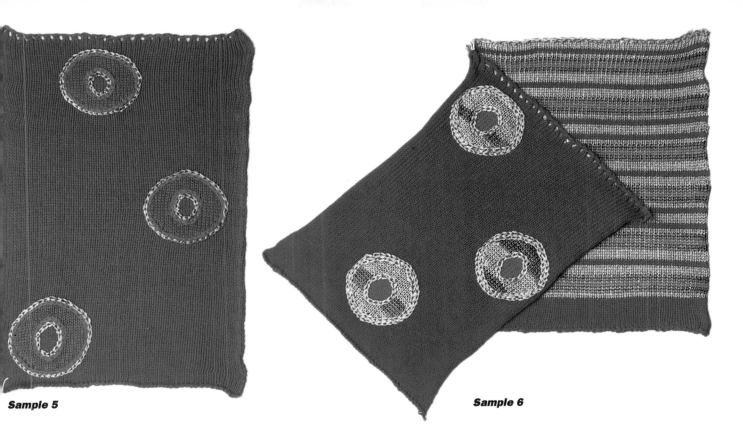

Sample 5

Sample 6

Yarns and tensions

The importance of tension swatches cannot be over emphasised. Compare tensions between the intarsia carriage and main carriage and adjust accordingly. The main difference is likely to result from variations in the tension of the hand-held yarn of the intarsia carriage, as compared with the yarn threaded up through the tension assembly. You will also need to ensure that all your chosen yarns knit up to the same tension. Knit a tension swatch in all the different qualities you intend to use, then compare the gauges. You can always ply-up thin yarns to match the gauge of a thicker yarn (and make interesting colour blends at the same time). The samples shown below are knitted in two-strands of Yeoman Yarns Brittany cotton in shades Sanguine, Purple, Rose and Lobelia or Janeiro shades Raffia, Fig and Myrtle; these produce similar tensions, although there is a slight discrepancy between the number of rows per 10cm. However, if you are careful, creative license can be used with a small row-count discrepancy such as this. For example, two-strand Janeiro knitted-up (for me) at 40 stitches to 14cm and 60 rows to 15.5cm, whereas 2-strand Brittany cotton, at the same tension, worked out as 40 stitches to 14cm and 60 rows to 13.7cm; a difference of approximately 5 rows over every 60 rows. If the pattern motifs are relatively small in relationship to the main colour (as in the *Dancing Queen* pattern), the differences in tension with regard to rows should make no difference to the hang of the fabric. Larger scale motifs in Janeiro set against

a cotton background, for example, might incur some distortion of the fabric. Sample, if in doubt, before starting a major project. It is most important, however, that there be no difference between the stitch count.

Designing large scale polka dot patterns as a pattern graph

To plot out a true circle, use proportional graph paper with an approximate ratio of 3:2; generally speaking, the height of a knit stitch is proportionally wider than it is high. You can use ordinary squared graph paper, but you should compensate for the differences between stitch and row ratio by elongating the height -Ð make each square on the grid three units high by two units wide. To find the correct ratio of rows to stitches, you will need to know the tension details of a 10cm square and divide the number of rows by the number of stitches. For example, 2-strand Brittany cotton at MT 6 knitted up at 28.5 sts and 44 rows to 10cm. The ratio of rows to stitches in this example is 1.5 to 1 or in whole numbers about 3:2. In the search for a perfect circle, a more rounded, less stepped motif will result when knitted in a fine gauge yarn than a similarly sized chunky gauge example comprising less rows and stitches per 10cm.

Planning the design

Make a full or half-scale paper pattern of the garment on dressmakers' drafting paper or strong, brown parcel paper. Plan the positioning of the polka dots by cutting out circles to the desired size in a contrasting colour (half-scale if you are working to this size). Move the polka

dots about until you are satisfied with the placement. Take care where you place the large scale polka dots. My first attempt worked visually as a flat composition, but it later emerged that one of the polka dots was positioned almost exactly on the bust point! For ease of intarsia knitting, plan a design so that you will be knitting only one polka dot at any one time.

Calculating the position of single motifs

If you are designing for jacquard motifs, or working from a graph for intarsia knitting, calculate the position of the motifs as follows. For example; the first spot motif is 12cm from the hem and 8cm in from the seam edge. Working from your tension square, calculate how many rows or stitches make 1cm. If, for instance, 1cm equals 3 stitches and 4.5 rows, then the first spot motif would be programmed-in at row 54, and 24 stitches from the seam edge. If the full width of the spot motif is equal to 19 stitches, you might want to make the first needle position 24 stitches plus half the circle stitches (say 11 stitches), which gives a first needle position of LHS or RHS 35.

LAYLA

TWINSET WITH A DIFFERENCE, CHOOSE YOUR
TRIMS FOR DRAMA OR SUBTLE EDGE DEFINITION

Yeoman Yarns
Polo 1ply 100% Merino wool in (A),
Brittany 2ply 100% cotton in shade
124 Lavender. All trimmings by
Kersen.com

**These instructions are
written for standard gauge
punchcard or electronic
machines with ribber and
plating feeders**

PATTERN INFORMATION

Sizes
To suit bust 81-86[91-96:101]cm
Jacket
Measurements are approximate due to the
elastic nature of tuck rib
Finished measurement 98[104:110]cm
Length 53[54:55]cm
Sleeve seam 41cm
Sweater
Finished measurement 92[98:104]cm
Length 48[49:50]
Sleeve seam 12.5cm

Figures in square brackets [ ] refer to larger
sizes; where there is only one set of figures,
this applies all sizes

Materials
2 x 250g cones of A
1 x 500g cone of B
2 x feather boas optional. 1 x feather boa if
you don't trim the cuffs.
10 buttons

Garment weight
For size 86-91cm
Cardigan approx 420g
Sweater approx 300g

Main tension
27 sts and 54 rows to 10cm measured over
tuck rib and counting Ns out of work as
though they were in work. Pin tension
swatch out, stretching sideways and
lengthways, lightly steam press before
measuring. (TD approx 4/4 = MT).
30 sts and 48 rows to 10cm measured over
st st after steam pressing (TD approx 6 = MT).
Tension must be matched exactly before
starting garment.

Note
Knit side is used as right side.
Measurements are those of finished garment
and should not be used to measure work on
machine.

Special note
Thread the plating feed for tuck rib pattern:
2 strand A in front feed and 1 strand B in
rear feed.
Thread the main bed plating feed for st st: 2
strand A in front feed and 1 strand B in rear
feed. Use end stitch pressers and claw
weights on tuck rib patt.
Ensure that the pattern knob is turned to KC
2 (Roman numeral 2) on tuck rib patt.
When dec/inc on tuck rib patt count the
spaces left by Ns in NWP as though they
were in WP.
The front button/buttonhole bands are
knitted as an integral part of the L and R
fronts excepting the edge trimming. See the
needle diagram.

Pattern note
Tuck rib pattern
N setting for tuck rib patt is in multiples of 6,
counting the spaces left by Ns in NWP as
though they were in WP — see needle diag.
Program stitch patt 45 from *Brother Stitch
World 3* or card 1 from basic set (birds eye
patt). Insert punch card or program
machine. Lock patt on first row and set carr
to select/memorise for patt and K1 row.
Release card and set MB carr to tuck and
RB carr to K.

Jacket
Back
With RB in position, set machine for a 1 x 1 rib. Push 65[69:73] Ns at L and 64[68:74] Ns at R of centre '0' on MB and corresponding Ns on RB to WP. 129[137:147] Ns. Arrange Ns for 1 x 1 rib. Using A + B cast on and K3 tubular rows. T2/2 K12 rows.

Push 1[1:0] extra N at L and 1[2:0] extra N at R to WP. 131[140:147] Ns in WP. Starting at R arrange 1[4:1] Ns at WP on MB (R edge st is seam allowance), re-arrange sts for tuck rib patt as patt note and N diag starting with 3 Ns in WP on MB. L edge st is seam allowance. CAR. Insert punch card and lock/program patt on first row. Set carr to select/memorise for patt and K1 row.

RC000. Release card and work in tuck rib (see patt note) throughout. K until RC shows 164.

Shape armhole
Cast off 7 sts at beg of next 2 rows. Cast off 4 sts at beg of next 2 rows. Cast off 2 sts at beg of next 4 rows. Dec 1 st at beg of next 8 rows. * K4 rows. Dec 1 st at each end *. Rep from * to * 4 times in all. 85[94:101] sts. K until RC shows 269[273:279].

Shape shoulders
Cast off 0[0:5] sts at beg of next 0[0:]8 rows in all. Cast off 0[4:4] sts on next 0[8:4] rows. Cast off 3[3:0] sts beg of next 12[4:0] rows in all. RC 283[288:293]. Transfer sts to MB and cast off, putting in markers to denote beg of neckline.

Left front
With RB in position, set machine for a 1 x 1 rib. Push 67[70:73] Ns at L and 7 Ns R of centre "0" and corresponding Ns on RB to WP. 74[77:80] Ns. Using A + B cast on and K3 tubular rows. T2/2 K12 rows. CAR. Re-arrange sts for tuck rib (see patt note) and make sure that side seams on front and back match. Insert punch card and lock/program patt on first row. Set carr to select/memorise for patt and K1 row.

RC000. Release card and work in tuck rib throughout. K164 rows. (K1 extra row for R front).

Shape armhole
Cast off 10 sts beg next row (armhole edge), K1 row.

Cast off 5 sts beg next row, K1 row. Cast off 2 sts beg of next and foll alt row, 2 times in all, K1 row. Dec 1 st beg of next row, K1 row. Dec 1 st beg of next and foll alt row 4 times in all. K until RC shows 247[251:257]. (K1 extra row for R front.) 50[53:56] sts.

Shape front neck
Cast off 10 sts at beg of next row, K1 row. Cast off 3 sts at beg of next row, K1 row. Cast off 2 sts at beg of next row, K1 row. Dec 1 st at neck edge on next and every foll alt row 7 times in all. 28[31:34] sts. Cont to dec 1 st on every alt row, 3 times in all and then dec 2 sts on every alt row 3 times in all. At the same time when RC shows 266[272:276] (K1 extra row for R front).

Shape shoulder
Cast off 4[4:5] sts at beg (shoulder edge) of next and every foll alt row 1[4:1] times in all, K1 row. Cast off 3[3:4] sts on next and every foll alt row 5[2:5] times in all.

Right front
Work as given for L front, noting difference in rows and reversing N arrangements to reverse shaping.

Sleeve
K a L and a R sleeve.
With RB in position, set machine for 1 x 1 rib. Push 31[34:37] Ns at L and 30[33:36] Ns at R of centre '0' on MB and corresponding Ns on RB to WP. 61[67:73] Ns. Using A+B (see special note), cast on and K3 tubular rows. T2/2 K12 rows. Inc 1 st at R. 62[68:74] sts. Re-arrange sts for tuck rib beg and end with 3 Ns in WP on L and R on MB, plus 1 extra N either end on MB for seam allowance. CAR. Insert punch card and lock/program patt on first row. Set carr to select/memorise Ns and K1 row.

RC000. Release card and work in tuck rib throughout. K1 row. Inc 1 st at each end of next and every foll 9 rows, 17 times in all. 96[102:108] sts. K until RC shows 200. (K1 extra row for second sleeve).

Shape top
Cast off 3 sts at beg (back sleeve head) of next row (and place contrast marker to denote back sleeve edge). Cast off 4 sts at beg (front sleeve head) on next row. Cast off 2 sts at beg of next 8 rows. 73[79:85] sts. Dec 1 st at beg of next 6 rows. Dec 1 st at both ends of next and every foll 3 rows 10[11:12] times in all. 41[45:49] sts. RC 245[248:251]. Dec 1 st at both ends of next and every foll alt row 18 times in all. Cast off rem 5[9:13] sts.

Work a second sleeve noting difference in rows to reverse shapings.

To make up
Neaten all ends. Block and steam press pieces to correct measurements. Mattress stitch shoulder seams. Set in sleeve heads, taking care to match centre of sleeve head with shoulder seam. Mattress stitch underarm and side seams. Give final press.

Trims
With wrong sides facing, pick up first 3 loops from edge of L front and using A + B, and T6, K6 rows. Miss one edge loop and pick up next 3 loops onto the 3 Ns. 2 sts on each N. K6 rows. Cont in this manner along L edge, back neck line and R front edge. Sew on buttons to correspond with loops on trim.

Needle diagram
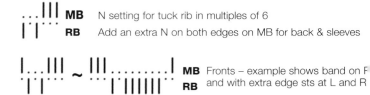

N setting for tuck rib in multiples of 6
Add an extra N on both edges on MB for back & sleeves

Fronts – example shows band on F and with extra edge sts at L and R

Stitch pattern for electronic or punchcard
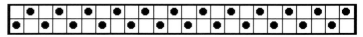

Card 1 from basic set or rep card until long enough to turn and join

Sweater
Back

With RB in position, set the machine for a 1 x 1 rib. Push 68[73:78] Ns to L and 69[74:79] Ns to R of centre '0' on MB and corresponding Ns on RB to WP. 137[147:157] Ns. Using A cast on and K3 tubular rows. T2/2 K12 rows. Transfer sts to MB. Inc 1 st at L. 138[148:158] sts. Insert plating feed on MB and thread up (see special notes).
RC000. Using MT K118 rows.

Shape armholes

Cast off 3 sts at beg of next 2 rows. 132[142:152] sts. Dec 1 st ff at each end of next and every foll alt row 49 [51:53] times in all. 34 [40:46] sts. K until RC shows 221[225:229]. At the same time when RC shows 210[214:218].

Shape neck

Note position in armhole dec sequence. CAR. Set carr for HP. Push all Ns to L and a further 4 Ns to R of centre '0' to HP. Always taking the yarn around the first inside N in HP, K2 rows. Push 4 Ns at opposite side to carr to HP on next and every foll alt row 1[4:1] times in all, K1 row. Push 3[0:0] Ns at opposite side to carr to HP on next and every foll alt row 3[0:0] times in all, K1 row. Push 0[0:5] Ns at opposite side to carr to HP on next and every foll alt row 0[0:3] times in all. All Ns in HP.
CAL. Reset RC to 210[214:218] and keeping armhole dec correct from noted position, work L side to correspond with R.
Set carr so HP Ns will K and K1 row over rem 34[40:46] sts. WK.

Front

Work as given for back until RC shows 118.

Shape armholes

Cast off 3 sts at beg of next 2 rows. 132[142:152] sts. Dec 1 st ff at each end of next and every foll alt row 43 [45:47] times in all. 46[52:58] sts. At the same time when RC shows 184[188:192].

Shape neck

Note position in armhole dec sequence. Set carr for HP. Push all Ns to L and a further 4 Ns to R of centre '0' to HP. Always taking the yarn around the first inside N in HP, K2 rows. Push 2 Ns at opposite side to carr to HP on next and every foll alt row 5[10:12] times.

Option 1
Feather boa and buttons

Option 2
Tassel, sequins and buttons

Option 3
Ribbon and buttons

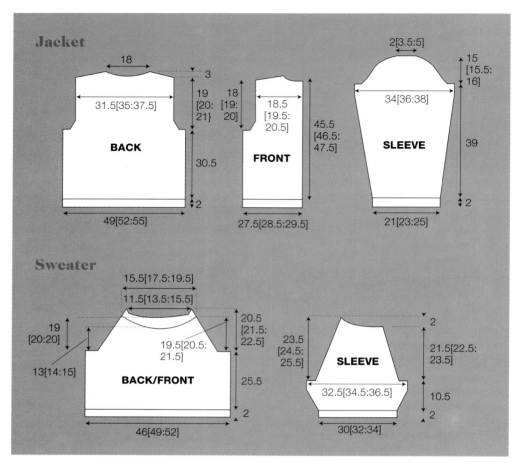

Jacket

BACK — 18, 3, 19 [20:21], 30.5, 31.5[35:37.5], 49[52:55], 2

FRONT — 18 [19:20], 18.5 [19.5:20.5], 45.5 [46.5:47.5], 27.5[28.5:29.5]

SLEEVE — 2[3.5:5], 15 [15.5:16], 34[36:38], 39, 21[23:25], 2

Sweater

BACK/FRONT — 15.5[17.5:19.5], 11.5[13.5:15.5], 19 [20:20], 20.5 [21.5:22.5], 19.5[20.5:21.5], 13[14:15], 25.5, 2, 46[49:52]

SLEEVE — 2, 23.5 [24.5:25.5], 21.5[22.5:23.5], 32.5[34.5:36.5], 10.5, 2, 30[32:34]

Push 1 N at opposite side to carr to HP on next and every foll alt row 9[2:1] times in all. All Ns are in HP. RC 212[216:220].
CAL. Reset RC to 184[188:192] and keeping armhole dec correct from noted position, work L side to correspond with R.
Set carr so HP Ns will K and K1 row over rem 46 [52:58] sts. WK.

Sleeve
K a L and a R sleeve, reversing all shapings.
With RB in position, set machine for 1 x 1 rib. Push 47 Ns at L and 48 Ns at R on MB and corresponding Ns on RB to WP. Using A, cast on and

K3 tubular rows. T2/2 K12 rows. Transfer sts to MB. Inc 1 st at L. 90[96:102] sts. Insert plating feed on and thread up (see special note).
RC000. Using MT K1 row. Inc 1 st at each end of next and every foll 12 rows 4 times in all. 98 [104:110] sts. K until RC shows 50.

Shape top
Cast off 3 sts at beg of next 2 rows. 92[98:104] sts. Dec 1 st ff at each end of next and every foll alt row 10[12:14] times in all, K2 rows. Dec 1 st ff at each end of next and every foll 3 rows 29 times. RC 159[163:167]. K until RC shows 163[167:171].

At the same time when the RC shows 147[157:167] (K1 extra row for second sleeve).

Shape front neck
Set carr for HP. Carr at armhole edge. Push 0[0:5] Ns at opposite side to carr (neck edge) to HP and always taking the yarn around the first inside N in HP, K2 rows 0[0:2] times in all. Push 4[4:4] Ns at neck edge to HP on next and every foll alt row 2 [4:2] times in all. Push 3[0:0] Ns at neck edge to HP on next and every foll alt row 2[0:0] times in all. 14[16:18] sts in HP. RC shows 157[167:177]. Set carr so HP Ns will K and K1 row. WK.

Interim make up
Neaten all ends. Block and press to measurements given.

Neckband
Push 108[124:140] Ns to WP. Using WY, cast on and K a few rows. Using A + B and MT K6 rows. T5. K6 rows. Using A only K2 rows. Change back to A + B. K6 rows. T6. K6 rows. Pick up sts from row above WY onto equivalent Ns. Manually pull one st through the other.

To attach neckband
Pick up sts from sleeves, back and front onto equivalent Ns. Manually pull one st through the other and cast off loosely.

To make up
Mattress stitch raglan sleeves to back and front, taking care to match front neckline with front of sleeve neckline and back neckline with back of sleeve. Block and press taking care not to stretch neckband. Mattress stitch under arm and side seams. Give a final press. Trim sleeve edges with fringe and sequins or braid and button as shown.

The independently-minded knitter can add personal touches with a wide range of trims – from the drama queen feather boa on the *Layla* twin set, to demure and feminine ribbon trims. You can, of course, make knitted, crocheted, beaded or embroidered trims from scratch, but for speed you might like to work with some of the many examples available off the shelf. These can be fun to use and come in all shapes and sizes – the result is limited only by your imagination.

Decoration options

An edge-to-edge cardigan with discreet loop trim fastenings and a knitted stocking stitch border can be decorated in any number of ways. The smoothness of stocking stitch is ideal for attaching ribbon trims or small buttons, beads or strips of sequins which contrast against the more textured tuck rib stitch. Consider decorating the edges of the sleeves, or around the neckline – even the shapings of the raglan could be embellished with tiny beads or buttons.

Removable trims offer optional extra decoration: little ribbon bows attached simply with a safety pin, perhaps, or even a stunning corsage made from the same feathers as the boa – you could really go to town on this by adding a length of silver sequins to dangle from it. The feathers can be used as lengths of trim, or cut down into smaller pieces.

Colour matching

When I began researching ready-made trims to decorate the *Layla* garments, I had trouble with colour matching. This is always a potential problem unless you dye your own yarns and trims, and my solution was to harmonise colours rather than attempt an exact match.

The feather boa, for example, is a pale, silvery grey, rather than an exact match to the pale, cool lilac wool, which was to be plied with lavender cotton. The latter is quite a cool shade with a blue bias, and many of the trims on offer had more of a warm, red bias to their colour make-up. The boa, though, is of roughly similar tone to the chosen yarns, and while different in hue, worked more successfully than trims of similar hue but biased towards the warmer end of the colour spectrum.

A useful trick would be to use the plating feed with the cotton coming to the foreground, as it has a warmer colour than the wool. Pink trims tone best with the yarn knitted in this way, while the cooler blue biased decoration works more successfully with the two colours reversed in the plating feed.

Alternatively, choose a trim with several different colours in the design, such as the embroidered Jacquard ribbon shown in sample 1. The pretty floral buttons pick up the colour in the ribbon to harmonise the design as a whole.

Attaching trims

Woven trims almost always have completely different properties to knitting, particularly in terms of their elasticity. It is important to make sure that both elements work with rather than against each other. If applying fabric braids to knit, lay the knitting out flat when pinning the braid into place, being careful not to pull it too tightly, to avoid puckering or distortion. I found that the flat, stocking-stitch band down the front of my cardigan was fairly easy to work onto as it had been knitted at a relatively tight tension, reducing the elasticity and giving a smooth surface on which to stitch. In some cases, though, an elasticated braid may be the best choice.

ALL THE TRIMMINGS

ADD-ON DECORATION FOR KNITWEAR HAS NEVER BEEN MORE FASHIONABLE

It is necessary to experiment with the best way of stitching one to the other, either by hand stitching – in which case back-stitch or slip-stitch are useful – or on the sewing machine. To use a machine successfully it must offer a stretch stitch. Experiment with decorative hand-embroidery stitches along the edge of ribbon trims; try blanket stitch, couching or fly stitch. Alternatively, couch down a string of sequins or tiny beads along the edge of the braid for added interest.

Stitch patterns with broad ribs should be decorated vertically along the ribs rather than horizontally across them, on the purl facing stitches with a continuous string of sequins or small beads. Couch the latter down with small stitches, spaced well apart. Additional decoration can be added as accents on either the purl or knit facing stitches.

Bear in mind the relative weight of the trim against the main body of knitting. Heavy, bulky trims can distort a finished item and adversely affect the hang

of the knitting. Take care where you place the decoration so it does not drag the garment out of shape and avoid too many heavy items close together, or the knitting will pucker and stretch.

Decorating necklines

When decorating around a fitted neckband with, for example, a non-stretch ribbon trim, make sure that you can still get the neck opening over the head. You may need to incorporate either a discreet placket opening vertically down the centre back, or a narrow button band running along the shoulder seam through into the neckband.

Wash care

If your trims won't stand laundering then you must be prepared to remove them. To my delight the suppliers of the feather boa say it is hand washable, just fluffing the feathers and using the cold setting of a hair dryer to gently blow them dry. If in doubt, test wash before deciding on usage.

Even if it is washable, check whether your ribbon or braid is pre-shrunk; if not, wash once before attaching it to the garment. You should also guard against any potential shrinkage of the main body of the garment, particularly if using ribbon trims stitched directly onto pure wool knitting where any shrinkage will make the ribbon cockle.

Sequins must be treated with special care, as heat can buckle or melt their surface. Once again, test wash if in doubt or be prepared to remove for washing.

For some trims that must be removed for washing, press studs might be the answer: even feathers could be sewn to some fine ribbon first, press studs then being sewn to the ribbon.

The samples

Knitted in tuck rib designs in a similar style to my cardigan stitch pattern, the samples shown explore different ways of decorating the same type of stitch patterns but with very different effects, depending upon the choice of trim and combination of yarns. All are knitted with two strands of Yeoman Polo in shade Lilac, combined with one strand of lavender Brittany cotton. The plating feeds have been used throughout. Tuck rib tension is approximately 4/4 and the stocking stitch is MT 6.

Sample 1

The trims are embroidered jacquard ribbon (ri 134). The buttons are small floral buttons in pastel shade with a pearl finish (bt 159).

Sample 2

The edge is trimmed with pastel viscose fringing (fr 039) which is further decorated with a length of aluminium silver strung sequins (se 001). The knitting is decorated with tiny real shell buttons in mother of pearl (bt 1130).

Sample 3

The satin ribbon in pale mauve is decorated with lightweight iridescent sequin flowers (ap 086).

Sample 4

Similar to sample 3 but trimmed with sparkly glass buttons.

Choose your trimmings to enhance the style of your existing knitwear as well as the *Layla* garments. Have fun altering the look and mood of a classic twinset, giving it a new personality

Suppliers

The trims used in this article were supplied by Kersen.com Codes in brackets () are for ordering. Order from the website www.kersen.com or call 0208 4400 833

Calypso

Diagonal stripes swirl around the skirt of this decidedly different summer dress

Yeoman Fettuccina 4ply 100% acrylic ribbon in shade 4 Pink (A). Citadella 100% Viscose ribbon in shade 7 (B). Cannele mercerised 100% cotton in 4ply, shades 153 Tango (C) and 39 Orchid (D).

These instructions are written for chunky gauge machines

Skirt back
Push 64[72:80] Ns to WP, taking note of the position of the Ns in relation to centre '0'. 50-0-14[50-0-22:50-0-30]. These Ns relate to the L of the knitting and are shaped initially using HP. The R is inc using ff shaping method unless otherwise indicated. Using WY, cast on and K a few rows. Using MT and

A K1 row.
RC000. Commence main stripe patt, shaping L and R edges thus: Shape R edge: Inc 1 st every alt row 12 times. RC24. Inc 1 st every 4 rows 21 times in all. RC108. Inc 1 st every 6 rows 9 times in all. RC162. Inc 1 st every alt row 9 times in all. RC180.
Set carr for HP. CAL. (Push 2 Ns to HP at R edge and K2 rows) 27 times in all. (Push 3 Ns to HP at R edge and K2 rows) 4 times in all. RC240.
At the same time shape L edge: Refer to the 64[72:80] sts cast on with WY. Set carr for HP. Push 62[70:78] Ns counting from L edge to HP, leaving 2 Ns only in WP. K2 rows. Cont to inc by 2 sts in the same manner, pushing 2 more Ns back into UWP on alt rows 30[30:22] times in all. RC60[60:44]. Inc 3 sts every alt row 0[4:12] times in all using HP. RC60[68:68] Inc 1 st every alt row 4[0:0] times in all using HP. RC68. Set carr so HP Ns will K. Dec 1 st ff, every alt row 12 times . RC92. Dec 1 st ff every 4 rows 21 times. RC176. Dec 1 st ff every alt row 21 times and K3 rows. RC221. Dec 1 st ff every 7 rows, 3 times in all. RC240. 56[64:72] sts rem. Using A, K1 row and WK.

Sizes
To suit bust 86-91[96-101:106-111]cm
Finished bust measurement 96[106:116]cm
Length 108cm (may drop slightly in wear. Store flat).
Figures in square brackets [ ] refer to larger sizes; where there is only one set of figures, this applies to all sizes.

Materials
150g in A
5[6:6] balls in B
125g in each of C and D
2.5mm/3mm crochet hook

Garment weight
96-101cm size approx 380g

Main Tension
15 sts and 27 rows to 10cm measured over st st (TD approx 4 = MT)

Note
Knit side is used as right side. Measurements given are those of finished garment and should not be used to measure work on the machine.

Special Note
Due to the nature of the diagonal/bias shape of the skirt sections, you will find it necessary at some point to strip off the knitting onto WY and re-hang the sts further along the N bed when there are no more empty Ns left on which to increase the work.

Pattern Note
Main stripe patt. K8 rows A, 4 rows B, 4 rows C or D, 2 rows B, 4 rows C or D and 4 rows B. Rep these 26 rows throughout, alternating C and D on alt repeats of the patt.

Skirt front
Follow skirt back patt reversing all instructions/shapings and N settings.

Back bodice
*With purl side facing, pick up 56[64:72] sts from top of back skirt. RC000. Inc 1 st at both ends of this and every foll alt row 8 times in all. K until RC shows 18. 72[80:88] sts.
Shape armhole
Cast off 3 sts at beg of next 4 rows. RC22. 60[68:76] sts.*
RC000. Cont in patt and dec 1 st ff at both ends of next and every foll 3 rows 18[19:20] times in all. K until RC shows 55[58:61]. 24[30:36] sts.
Shape shoulders
Set carr for HP. Push 3[4:5] Ns at opp end to carr to HP on next 2 rows. RC60. Push 4[5:6] Ns at opp end to carr to HP on next 2 rows. RC59[62:65]. Cast off 10[12:14] sts at centre. Push Ns at L to HP and WK over rem 7[9:11] sts at R for first side. CAL. Set carr so HP Ns will K and WK over rem 7[9:11] sts.

Front bodice
Work as given for back bodice from * to *.
RC000. At the armhole edge cont to knit in patt and dec 1 st ff at both ends on next and every foll 3 rows 2 times in all. K until RC shows 8. 56[64:72] sts. WK. Re-hang 28[32:36] sts at L. Cont to shape armhole edge as given for back. At the same time:
Shape neck
Shape L "V" neck: Dec 1 st on next and every foll 9[8:8] rows 5[6:7] times in all. K until RC shows 55[58:61]. 7[9:11] sts rem.
Shape shoulder
Set carr for HP. Push 3[4:5] Ns at opp end to carr to HP and K2 rows. Push a further 4[5:6] Ns at opp end to carr to HP and K2 rows. RC59[62:65]. WK over rem 7[9:11] sts.

Hem
With purl side facing, pick up sts from above WY cast on of back skirt, doubling up sts on every 12th N. 58[66:74] sts. Using MT, K6 rows B, 2 rows D and 6 rows B. Hook up sts from beg of hem. Manually pull one st through the other and cast off. Rep on front skirt.

To make up
Neaten all ends. Block and press pieces to correct measurements, making sure that stripes run parallel to one another. Join shoulder sts. Press gently on wrong side. Join side seams. (I used a stretch stitch using invisible thread on the sewing machine to give the neatest possible seam line.) Join front and back hems.

Armhole and neck edging
Using B, make a double crochet st into the armhole and neck edging. Give a final press.

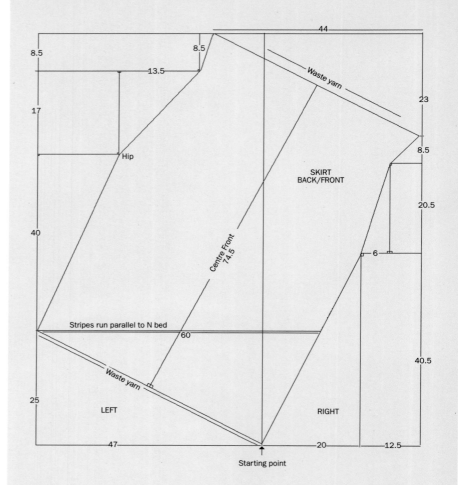

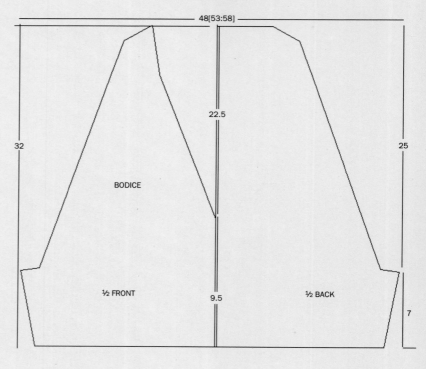

Style File

Knitting and designing with diagonal stripes

Stripes regularly feature in fashion designers' collections; horizontally, vertically or diagonally placed, and in eye-catching colours and fabrics.

Knitting techniques

Any number of techniques can be interpreted as a stripe pattern, simply by changing colours at regular or irregular intervals; the most obvious and easy to knit being horizontally knitted stripes in purl or knit facing stocking stitch. *Milan* and the accompanying *Style File* explored sideways knitted stripes. Diagonal stripes can be achieved by the use of partial-knitting, or by increasing and decreasing the side edges of the knitting and where the stitches and rows are designed so that they run at a pre-determined angle to the edges of the knitting (for example side seams). This is the main focus for *Calypso*, however other working methods can be used, for example intarsia, or single- or double-bed jacquard. Choose a working method which is sympathetic to the garment style and shape, considering carefully the handle and weight of each different type of stitch structure alongside choice of yarns and tension. Jacquard knitting, for example, tends to be less fluid and heavier in weight than stocking stitch in similar yarns and tension. It might also be advisable to review time available for knitting the finished item. A last minute beach dress in intarsia might not be a good idea!

Knitting notes

You may already know how to knit a bias strip, perhaps for use as a facing or trim using paired increases and decreases to shape the knitting. If you haven't tried this method of working it is quite simple

(see below). Work in either a single colour or in narrow stripes. Cast on (for example) 8 sts at the extreme left or right hand side of the needle bed. * Knit 2 rows. Inc 1 stitch at the left edge and decrease 1 stitch at the right * using fully-fashioned shaping techniques. Repeat from * to * as many times as required. At some point in the work, as you move across the needle bed, you will run out of empty needles on which to continue with the increasing. Simply strip off the work with waste yarn or the garter bar and re-hang at the opposite edge of the machine. Continue knitting as before. Use this method to knit diagonally striped trims for, say, the front edge of a plain knitted cardigan. Cast on more stitches than the sample suggested above, and you have a diagonally striped scarf or tie. The same principle can be applied to larger pieces, such as the skirt section of *Calypso*.

Designing with diagonal stripes

The stripes in my pattern are knitted parallel to the needle bed, but at an angle to the side seams. As I found to my woe, you need to plan the angle of the stripes in relationship to the tension and number of needles available at any one time.
Let me explain: The dress was initially designed on paper with steeper stripes. However, I hadn't taken into consideration the width of the longest (widest) stripe when converted into stitches, in conjunction with the number of needles available to me on the chunky gauge machine! In my original design, the longest stripe measured 85cm. At 1.5 sts per 1cm I would have needed 132 needles at the widest point. The Brother chunky gauge machine has only 110 needles, so a re-think was needed. Possible solutions to such a problem included making adjustments to the tension (if only a slight discrepancy), changing the yarns or stitch structure (tuck stitch will knit up wider than stocking stitch, but will give a completely different handle and look to stocking

stitch) or altering the angle of the stripes in relationship to the side seams. The latter was my chosen solution. A more radical answer might have been to knit the front and back skirt in two sections, with a centre front and back seam as well as a side seam, however with the open, shaped, chunky gauge fabric I designed, there were already enough ends to hide! The solution was to take a dressmaker's type of seam and use machine stitching in an invisible thread. Much to my surprise, this gave a much neater seam than hand sewing. This would not be a problem with a more solid fabric.

Initial explorations

To try some simple variations, cut out a series of identical rectangles from thin paper. Label the corners A, B, C and D. Now lay them out in front of you at different angles to each other, see Diagram 1, with point 'A' touching a common horizontal base line (a sheet of dressmakers' drafting paper or lined file paper will be perfect for this). Stick the rectangles in place and draw in stripes running parallel to the horizontal stripes of the file paper which equate with the orientation of the needle bed. As you can see, the angle of the stripes will be determined by the angle of the pattern piece in relationship to the horizontal/vertical lines of the file paper.

Design ideas

Moving on to the actual pattern piece for the skirt section of the dress, you can see that it is essentially rectangular in shape. Draw out or photocopy several versions of the garment outline in quarter-scale. Using the working method suggested above, sketch in the stripes, trying out different angles and width of stripes, see Diagram 2. At this stage I would work in black and white only. Once you are happy with the stripe pattern in visual terms, check that it will work in relationship to tension and availability of needles (see above) and make any alterations necessary. Remember also to

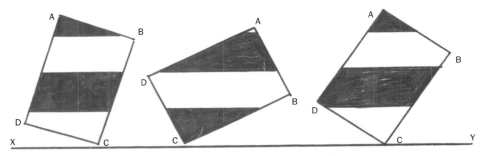

Stripes	Run parallel to needlebed (line X–Y)
Point 'C'	Touches baseline X–Y
To knit	Increase stitches working outwards from point 'C' (starting point)
	Decrease stitches to achieve slope D–A
	Increase stitches to achieve slope C–B
	Decrease stitches to achieve slope A–B

Diagram 1

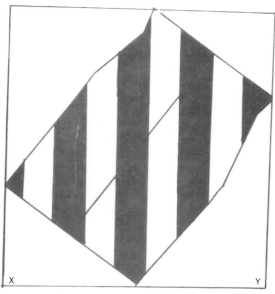

Diagram 2 Line X–Y is parallel to needlebed

Diagram 4 Diagram showing back/front skirt panel with side seam. Chevron style, diagonal stripes

Diagram 3

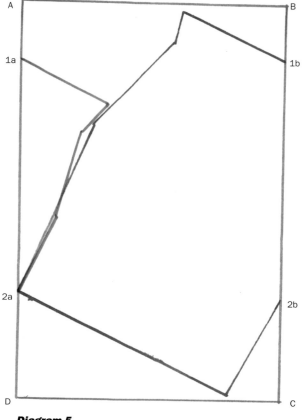

Diagram 5

Rectangle A, B, C, D represents charter paper

Purple outline – main skirt panel

Green outline – remainder of skirt panel. Match points 1a and 1b/2a and 2b

multiply all your measurements by 4 if working to quarter scale.

Finished visualisations
Re-photocopy your design ideas for the skirt. Cut them out and paste them onto a new sheet of paper orientated correctly against the bodice pattern. You should now be able to see roughly how the whole dress will look. Try the same stripe pattern for the skirt section, with different ideas for the bodice (see Diagram 3). This could be knitted in horizontal or vertical stripes, or in a single colour, perhaps in a contrasting

stitch structure. You might like to explore different colour combinations and juxtapositions of colours working in coloured pencils, felt-tips or strips of cut-out coloured papers before moving on to knitting the designs. Consider also how you want the stripes to meet on the side seam. For example, do you want a mirror image, reflection, or a continuation of the stripes in the same direction? (See Diagram 4.)

The knit charter and partial knitting
A note on transferring the outline pattern pieces to the charter paper. Dependant

upon the angle of the piece, you may find that the charter paper isn't wide enough to accommodate the full width. You will need to overlay the missing section, as shown in Diagram 5, making sure that the extension piece is correctly placed. It is probably easier to read if the latter is drawn in a contrasting colour.

Gem

Mix your patterns for this exciting Fair Isle collared cardigan

Yeoman Polo 1ply 100% Merino wool in shade 9 Carmen (A1). Poodle 75% acrylic, 25% nylon in shade 10 (A2). Grigna 2, 4ply 65% viscose, 35% acrylic gimp in shade 161 (B) and 141 (C). Pellonia 4ply 100% microfibre nylon in shade 3 (D).

These instructions are written for standard gauge electronic machines with ribber — punchcard alternative included

Back

Back pattern sequence. K9 rows of stripe patt. Program patt C on first row. Set carr to select/memorise for patt and K1 row. RC10. Set carr for Fair Isle and using MC in feeder 1/A and B in feeder 2/B, K20 rows. RC30. Set carr for st st and K9 rows of stripe patt. Program patt C on first row. Set carr to select/memorise for patt and K1 row. RC40. Set carr for Fair Isle and using C in feeder 1/A and MC in feeder 2/B, K100[104:108] rows. RC140 [144:148]. Set carr for st st and K9 rows of stripe patt. Program patt A. Set carr to select/memorise for patt and K1 row. RC150 [154:158]. Set carr for Fair Isle and using MC in feeder 1/A and B

in feeder 2/B, K32 rows. RC182[186:190]. Set carr for st st and K first 8 rows of stripe patt RC shows 190[194:198].

Back

Push 156[172:188] Ns to WP. Using WY cast on and using MT, K a few rows. Working in patt throughout, K100 rows.

Shape armholes

Keeping patt correct as set, cast off 5 sts at beg of next 4 rows. 136 sts. RC104. Cast off 3 sts at beg of next 4 rows. 124[140:156] sts. RC108. Cast off 2 sts at beg of next 2 rows. 120[136:152] sts. RC110. Dec 1 st at each end of next and every foll alt row 5 times in all. RC120. Dec 1 st each end of next and every foll 4 rows, twice in all. 106[122:138] sts. RC128. Cont in patt until RC shows 180[184:188].

Shape shoulders

Set carr for HP and always taking yarn around the first inside N in HP, push 6[7:8] Ns at opposite end to carr into HP on next 10 rows. RC 190[194:198].
Using MC, K1 row MC across 46[52:58] sts for back neck and WK.
CAL push 30[35:40] Ns nearest

carr to UWP and K1 row. WK.
CAR push 30[35:40] Ns nearest carr to UWP and K1 row. WK.

Right front pattern sequence

K first 7[9:11] rows of stripe patt. Program patt A. Set carr to select/memorise for patt and K1 row. RC8[10:12]. Set carr for Fair Isle using MC in feeder 1/A and B in feeder 2/B. K4 rep of patt A, each rep being 32 rows long. K2 rows of D between each rep. RC142[144:146] K first 7[9:11] rows of stripe patt. Program patt A. Set carr to select/memorise for patt and K1 row. RC150[154:156]. Set carr for Fair Isle using MC in feeder 1/A and B in feeder 2/B. K a further rep of patt A. RC182[186:188]. K first 8[8:10] rows of stripe patt. RC190[194:198]. Note: After each rep of patt A you will need to return to beg of the patt, alter the first N position and alternate between positive or negative patt variation on every other repeat. First N position is as folls:
Rep 1 is 26 sts to R. Rep 2 is 13 sts to R. Rep from * to * as required.

Right front

Push 78[86:94] Ns to WP. Using WY cast on and K a few rows. Working in patt throughout using MT, K100 rows.

Shape armhole

Cast off 8 sts beg of next row, K1 row. Cast off 7 sts beg next row, K1 row. RC104. Cast off 3 sts beg of next row, K1 row. RC106. Cast off 2 sts beg of next row, K1 row. RC108. Dec 1st beg of next and every foll alt row twice. RC112. Dec 1 st beg of next and every foll 4 rows 3 times in all. RC122. 53[61:69] sts. Cont in patt until RC shows 162[166:170].

Small size: Shape the neck edge using HP:
Set carr for HP. (Push 4 Ns at neck edge to HP, K2 rows) twice. RC166. Push 3 Ns at neck edge into HP and K2 rows. RC168. (Push 2 Ns into HP and K2 rows) 3 times. RC174. (Push 1 N into HP and K2 rows) 5 times in all. RC184 K until RC shows 190.

Medium size: Shape neck edge using HP:
Set carr to HP. Push 5 Ns at neck edge to HP. K2 rows. Rep twice. RC170. Push 4 Ns at neck edge to HP. K2 rows. RC172. Push 3 Ns at neck edge into HP and K2 rows. RC174. Push 2 Ns into HP and K2 rows. Rep the last

Sizes
To suit bust 86-91[96-101:106–111]cm
Finished measurement 97[107:117]cm
Length 53[54:55]cm
Sleeve Seam 39[40:41]cm
Figures in square brackets [ ] refer to larger sizes; where there is only one set of figures, this applies to all sizes

Materials
150[200:250]g in A1,
200[250:300]g in A2,
150[200:250]g in B,
125[175:225]g in C and 50g in D.
7 buttons

Garment weight
For size 86-91 cm approx 460g

Main tension
32 sts and 39 rows to 10cm measured over Fair Isle after blocking and pressing. (TD approx 6 = MT). Tension must be matched exactly before starting garment.

Note
Knit side is used as right side. Measurements are those of finished garment and should not be used to measure work on machine.

Special note
All yarns are used single strand excepting MC which is 1 strand A1 plus 1 strand A2 and excepting button and buttonhole band and welts which are 2 strand A1 plus 1 strand A2.

Pattern note
Punch cards or program patts before starting to knit.

Pattern and colour sequence
Stripe Patt: Stocking stitch. K2 rows each of MC, B, D, B and MC. 10 rows in total unless otherwise indicated.
Patt A: Large plaid pattern 26 sts x 28 rows Punchcard alternative 24 sts x 28 rows.
Patt B: Zig-zag pattern. 4 sts x 18 rows.
Patt C: Standard birds eye pattern. Double width and double height throughout. 2 sts x 2 rows.

set of instructions twice. RC178. Push 1N to HP and K2 rows. Rep the last set of instructions 5 times in all. RC188 K until RC shows 194.

Large size: Shape neck edge using HP:
Set carr for HP. Push 6 Ns at neck edge to HP. K2 rows. Push 5 Ns at neck edge to HP. K2 rows. RC 174. Push 4 Ns at neck edge to HP. K2 rows. RC176. Push 3 Ns at neck edge into HP and K2 rows. Rep the last set of instructions twice. RC180. Push 2 Ns into HP and K2 rows. Rep the last set of instructions twice. RC184. Push 1N into HP and K2 rows. Rep the last set of instructions 4 times in all. RC192 K until RC shows 198.

All sizes: at the same time when RC181.

Shape shoulder
Set carr for HP and always taking yarn around the first inside N in HP, push 6[7:8] Ns at opposite end to carr into HP on next and every foll alt row 4 times in all, K1 row. Set carr for st st and using MC K1 row WK. Push rem 23[26:29] Ns to UWP and K1 row MC across front neck edge and WK.

Left front pattern sequence
K first 7 rows of stripe patt. Program patt B. Set carr to select/memorise for patt and K1 row. RC8. Set carr for Fair Isle using MC in feeder 1/A and B in feeder 2/B and K18 rows (one full rep). RC26. K first 5 rows of stripe patt. Program patt B. Set carr to select/memorise for patt and K1 row. RC32. K 3 full rep, alt between positive or negative patt variation on every other rep using MC in feeder 1/A and alternating between B and C in feeder 2/B on alt rep. Cont to do this throughout L front until RC shows 86. K first 5 rows of stripe patt. Program patt B. Set carr to select/memorise for patt and K1 row. RC92. Set carr for Fair Isle and alt cols as already set, K one full rep. RC110. K first 5 rows of stripe patt. Program patt B. Set carr to select/memorise for patt and K1 row. RC116. Set carr for Fair Isle and alt cols as already set, K a further 4 rep of patt B. RC 188. K2[6:10] rows MC. RC190[194:198].

Left front
Work as given for R front but commencing CAL and reading for L and vice versa to reverse all instructions and shapings.

Pattern sequence left sleeve
K9 rows of stripe patt. Program patt C. Set carr to select/memorise for patt and K1 row. RC10. Set carr for Fair Isle using MC in feeder 1/A and C in feeder 2/B and K20 rows beg and ending with 2 rows C. RC30. On last of 2 rows of C, program patt A. Set carr to select/memorise for patt and K1 row. Set carr for Fair Isle using MC in feeder 1/A and B in feeder 2/B and K32 rows. RC62. Set carr for st st and using C, K1 row. Program patt C. Set carr to select/memorise for patt and K1 row. RC64. Set carr for Fair Isle using MC in feeder 1/A and C in feeder 2/B and cont in patt C until end sleeve.

Pattern sequence left sleeve

K9 rows of stripe patt. Program patt C. Set carr to select/memorise for patt and K1 row. RC10. Set carr for Fair Isle using MC in feeder 1/A and B in feeder 2/B and K20 rows beg and ending with 2 rows B. RC30. On last of 2 rows of B, program patt B. Set carr to select/memorise for patt and K1 row. Set carr for Fair Isle using MC in feeder 1/A and C in feeder 2/B and K52 rows beg and ending with 2 rows MC. On last of 2 rows of MC, program patt C. Set carr to select/memorise for patt and K1 row. RC82. Set carr for Fair Isle using MC in feeder 1/A and B in feeder 2/B and K in patt until end sleeve.

Sleeve

Push 76[84:92] Ns to WP. Using WY cast on and K a few rows. Start and work in patt as appropriate for each sleeve and K4 rows. Inc 1 st at each end of next and every 5 rows 20 times in all. RC100. 116[124:132] sts. Cont in patt until RC shows 130[134:138].

Shape top

Cast off 5 sts beg of next 2 rows. Cast off 3 sts beg next 4 rows. RC136[140:144]. 94[102:110] sts. Cast off 2 sts beg of next 8 rows. 78[86:94] sts. RC144[148:152]. Dec 1 st at each end of this and every foll alt row 17 times. 44[52:60] sts. Cast off 2 sts beg of next 8 rows. RC186[190:194]. Cast off 5 sts beg of next 4 rows. RC190[194:198].

Small size: Cast off rem 8 sts.
Medium size: Cast off 4 sts beg of next 2 rows. RC196. Cast off rem 8 sts.
Large size: Cast off 4 sts beg next 4 rows. RC202. Cast off rem 8 sts.

Cuff

Push 60[66:72] Ns to WP. With wrong side of sleeve facing pick up sts from row above WY and hang on to Ns placing 2 sts on every 3rd N 12[6:8] times and on every 4th N 6[12:12] times. Using MT, K16 rows MC, 2 rows B, 2 rows D. MT+4. Using MT, K2 rows B and 16 rows MC. Pick up sts from beg of cuff and hang evenly along the row. Cast off.

Interim make up

Neaten all ends. Block and press to correct measurements. Join shoulder seams.

Back welt

With RB in position set machine for FNR. Push 138[154:170] Ns on MB and corresponding Ns on RB to WP. Arrange Ns for cast on position of 2 up 1 down rib. Using A (3 strand see notes) cast on and K3 tubular rows at T1/1. Rack RB half a position to align Ns correctly for RB and K24 rows T4/4.

Transfer sts to MB. With wrong side of work facing pick up sts from just above WY, doubling up every 7[8:9]th N 18 times. Manually pull one st through the other and cast off.

Front welts

Work 2 alike, as given for half back welt.

Button band

Push 11 Ns on MB and corresponding Ns on RB to WP. Arrange Ns as shown in Diag 1. Rack one position to L and cast on. K3 rows tubular. Rack one position to R. K approx 180 rows T4/4 putting in tie markers every 30 rows. Leave to relax for a few hours before attaching to garment. Unravel any extra rows and bind off. Note the number of rows knitted and use this as a guide to planning the buttonhole band.

Buttonhole band

Work as given for button band but make a vertical buttonhole at evenly spaced intervals. The diameter of the button will determine the number of rows per buttonhole. We used 6 rows.

To make up

Set in sleeves, taking care to match centre of sleeve head with shoulder seam. Block and press. Link underarm and side seams using mattress stitch. Neaten bands and sew to garment fronts. Sew on buttons to correspond with buttonholes.

Collar

Push 106[118:130] Ns to WP. Using WY, cast on and K a few rows. Using MT, K18

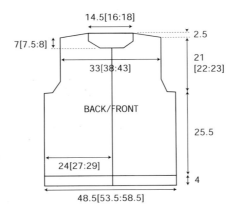

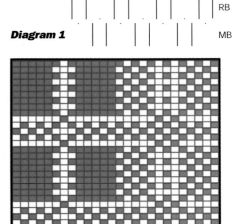

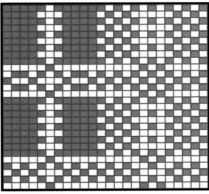

Patt A Electronics 26sts x 28rows

Patt A version for punchcard machines 24sts x 28rows

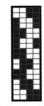

Patt B Electronics 4sts x 18rows

Punchcard machines Rep x 6 across card and x 3 up card

Patt C 2sts x 2rows

Punchcard machines Use double height and width Punchcard machines use Card 1

rows MC, 2 rows B, 2 rows D. Using MT + 4 K2 rows B. Using MT, K18 rows MC. At the same time inc 1 st at each end of alt rows 10 times in all. Dec 1 st at each end of alt rows after fold rows to match front of collar. Pick up sts from beg of collar onto Ns in WP. Pull 1 st through the other. 1 st per N.

Attach collar

With right side if garment facing, pick up sts from neckline thus: 5 sts from front rib band, 23[26:29] sts from WY at front neck and a further 5 sts from rem of front edge, 40[46:52] sts from back neckline doubling up sts where necessary. Rem of sts to be picked up as before. Cast off loosely. Neaten ends of collar. Join front collar to back collar. Give a final press.

Washcare

This garment is made from a mix of natural and man made fibres and should be hand washed with great care at 30˚c with a warm rinse. Do not rub or hand wring. Dry flat.

Style File

Pieces of pattern

Pattern and colour are making a strong comeback in all areas of fashion and design generally. With this in mind, we focus on one of the recent trends in knitwear that gives traditional patterns such as plaids, tartans and Argyll's a contemporary twist by the use of contrasting yarn textures in patterned knitting, and the juxtaposition of different scales and types of patterns in the same piece of work.

Jacquard and intarsia knitting techniques are important working methods, as is embroidery, appliqué and the addition of tiny beads, sequins and glittery yarn to highlight certain aspects of the design. *Gem* combines three different geometric patterns patchwork-style to in a mix of smooth and textured yarns; but first, a look at colour trends across the broad fashion spectrum.

Colour

Cheerful winter brights, with red as an important element, feature strongly at the moment.

These range through rich reds, Bordeaux, plums, purples, deep lilacs and cerise. This is my favourite colour story and the one on which the *Gem* pattern is based. Perhaps the most classic colour scheme for autumn/winter takes in camel, tobacco — deep rich browns — and the colours of warmed and warming drinks such as cognacs, whiskey, malts, and coffee. 'Gem' would work well knitted up in soft, luxurious yarns from this colour story, perhaps mixed with a fine, gold yarn for an elegant, retro chic look. Blues to work with denim, such as Indigo, blue-greens, olives, yellow ochre, lilac, peacock and darker shades of blue are also popular, as is black and white. The latter always makes a strong statement and is well suited to the geometric look. Update the latter with gold, or add red from the first colour group and knit in yarns of contrasting weights or textures for a really contemporary update of traditional patternings. Finally, you do not need to be a complete slave to fashion trends and predictions. Devise your own versions of the seasons colour schemes by picking and mixing colours from two different groups, for example, introducing a deep indigo blue or olive green into the red colour story highlighted by subtle touches of gold lurex. Or take one of the main colours such as camel and work your own palette around this shade.

Yarns

In broad terms, textured knitting is about to make a comeback either through choice of yarns, treatment of the knitted fabric (brushed/felted) or stitch structure. Here we focus on how we can change the look of traditional jacquard stitch patterns into something more modern through the use of contrasting textured yarns, alongside interesting placements of one pattern against the other.

Jacquards knitted in a mix of hairy and shiny yarns, or a combination of rough and smooth fibres, look totally different to the same design knitted in lambswool throughout. Brushed, felted, and furry yarns tend to blur the edges of normally hard-edge geometrics, and lend themselves to the soft, comfortable look that is another key element of this season.

Look at feathery, spongy yarns such as Yeoman's Pellonia, Chenille or Castro for soft, plush surfaces, alongside boucle such as Yeoman Poodle. Mohair and modern blends are all possible choices, particularly if knitted against, for instance, a smooth soft lambswool plied with a fine glittery sewing thread, or a lightweight tweedy yarn. Empress Mills sells a good range of sewing and embroidery threads. Experiment with oversized jacquards, knitted with loosely twisted yarns on the chunky-gauge machine. Experiment with gold chainette thread paired with a lightweight, bulky rustic tweed yarn for heavier weight jacquards with a twist!

Rovings that are too nubbly to go through the main tension assembly could be woven in to create tartans and checks on a grand scale, possibly against a finer backing yarn. Try Texere yarns for interesting weaving yarns, as well as their selection of yarns aimed at hand

Figure 1

Figure 2

and machine knitters. Another novel way of interpreting traditional tartan patterns might be to combine space-dyed yarns, such as silks and viscose, with a microfibre tweedy look yarn or Forsell's Touch of Silk.

Pattern

Obvious sources of inspiration include traditional woven patterns such as Scottish tartans, Argyll's, Prince of Wales and Burberry window pane style checks, Donegal tweeds, houndstooth and herringbone weaves. Vary the basic idea by altering the scale and orientation of these patterns, combining big and small sizes and shapes in the same design. Turn plaid patterns into patterned stripes that work diagonally across another type of pattern, such as a small-scale tweed. Focus on the idea of contrasts between the new and the old, mixing and matching traditional patterns in random, patchwork layouts, rather a strict formal grid.

Knitting notes

Utilise the electronic patterning program on the Pfaff 6000E to superimpose one pattern over the top of another, such that slices or stripes of contrasting pattern cut across the main pattern. Program the first needle position so that stripes or blocks of pattern are placed off-centre. Try altering the height, width and direction of any given pattern. You may also be able to program more than one pattern across the width of the needle bed depending upon make and/or model of machine. This is possible on the Brother KH 970. Use partial knitting to create wedge shapes of contrasting patterns. This is not difficult to do on most machines, as

long as you remember to realign needles into the correct positions for the pattern when returning needles from holding position back into working position. Combine thick and thin gauges in the same outfit, for example, knit the cuffs and welts on chunky gauge and the remainder of the piece on fine gauge. Include light hearted elements, such as bobbles, tassels, fun-fur collars on plaid cardigans. Combine crochet lacy ruffles with formal herringbone patterns, or perhaps a tartan cardigan with appliqué hearts decorated in big beads or sequins. Mix areas of jacquard knitting with a single-colour stocking stitch or textured stitch patterns, for example, a modern styled sweater with back, short sleeves, welts and border of neckline in black with heavily patterned front panels in reds, mauves, cerise and white.

Design sheets

The design sheets shown in Figs 1 - 4 offer starting points to set off your own creativity, and specifically explore ways of incorporating several patterns together in the same design. It is important that you consider the overall composition of the design if you are working from scratch. It is good practice to make a series of quick sketches before embarking on the finished piece. Think about how you will balance out areas of bold patterning with smaller, more discreet patterns, or where you will end one pattern in relationship to another but also in relationship to the framework of the garment shape; if the patterns on the front and back, or the left and right fronts are offset one from another, make sure that there is enough difference between them that the effect looks deliberate, not just a case of poor making up!

Consideration must also be given to balancing the tensions of each pattern. It is particularly important to do this if the patchwork pieces are oddly shaped and seemingly randomly placed, to ensure a perfect hang of the finished item. The most simple solution is to use the same combination of yarns throughout. Self-coloured areas could be knitted in jacquard rather than in stocking stitch to ensure even weight and handle of knitting. To do this, thread up the same colour in feed A and feed B and knit to the standard birdseye design. You could of course opt for a rough and smooth version of the same colour, threading the former through feed A and the latter into B.

Over to you

Why not change the published design by choosing your own yarns or colour combinations or by altering the scale of the patterns. This kind of fabric will also suit luxurious, tactile throws and cushions, but don't forget that if you choose to work with different yarns or gauge then you will of course need to make a new tension swatch and rework the number of rows and stitches given to suit individual tensions. I would love to see the results! If you don't want to design completely from scratch, simply choose another colour palette from the same yarns that I have used in the original design, substituting like for like so that the tension is unaltered.

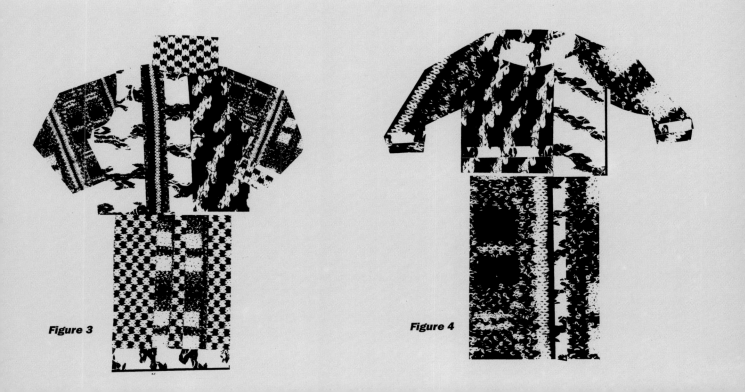

Figure 3

Figure 4

Linear

Minimalist stripe detail on a sideways knitted top for maximum effect with minimum effort

Yeoman Sari 55% cotton, 20% linen, 25% acrylic in Hessian shade 1 (MC) and Janeiro 50% viscose, 25% linen and 25% acrylic in Flint shade 23 (C)

These instructions are written for standard gauge machines

Armhole trims
Knit 2 alike and 2 reversing all shapings.
Push 50[52:54:56:58:60:62] sts to WP and cast on with WY. CAL.
RC000. Change to MC and MT, and K4 rows. Set carr to HP.

Shape sleeve trim
Push 1 N at opp end to carr into HP and K1 row. Push 3 Ns into HP and K1 row. Rep last 2 rows 5[3:1:0:0:0:0] times in all. Push 1 N at opp end to carr into HP and K1 row. Push 4 Ns into HP and K1 row. Rep last 2 rows 6[8:10:10:8:6:4] times in all.

Sizes
To suit bust
87[92:97:102:107:112:117]cm
Finished measurement
92[97:102:107:112:117:122]cm
Length
55.5[56:56.5:57.5:58:59:59.5]cm
Figures in square brackets[] refer to larger sizes; where there is only one set of figures, this applies to all sizes.

Materials
1[1:1:1:1:2] x 500g cones in MC
Approx 50g in C
12cm lightweight zip

Garment weight
92cm size weighs approx 350g

Main tension
28 sts and 40 rows to 10cm, measured over st st using 2 ends together throughout after steaming (TD approx 8 = MT).
Tension must be matched exactly before starting garment.

Note
Knit side is used as right side.
Measurements given are those of finished garment and should not be used to measure work on the machine.

Special note
This garment is knitted sideways and grafted together on the side seams and collar.
Wind off several balls of MC and an extra ball of C. Feed one end from cone and one from ball (for C) or 1 end from each of 2 balls (C) and feed through respective tension mast and into feeder. Each set of strands treated as though it were the one yarn throughout.
Sari is used 2 strand throughout at MT and Janiero is used 2 strand at MT-2 approx. Make a separate tension swatch for each quality of yarn and remember to switch tensions for the stripe feature.

Knitting notes
The fold back collar is knitted using partial knit technique as an integral part of the front/back. Remember to wind last N in HP before knitting the next row to avoid a hole in the knitting. The same applies to the armhole trims.
Prepare 6 pieces of waste yarn knitting, 2 each of 30 sts, 50[52:54:56:58:60:62]sts and 90 sts wide in a contrast colour to MC. Use a 3 pronged transfer tool for fully fashioned shapings on shoulder line thus. To inc move 3 edge sts 1 position outwards and pick up the heel of the next st onto empty N. To dec move the 4th st from the outside edge to the 3rd N from outside edge and then move all 3 sts in by 1 N.

Push 1 N at opp end to carr into HP and K1 row. Push 5 Ns into HP and K1 row. Rep last 2 rows 0[0:0:1:3:5:7] times in all. All Ns should now be in HP. RC shows 026. Now push Ns back into WP on every row to match, reversing the instructions outlined above. RC052. Pick up sts from first row onto corresponding Ns, K1 row and WK.

Back

Push 90 Ns to WP making sure that you have enough empty Ns left for armhole trim and an additional 30 Ns for collar. The shoulder/collar edge is at L facing the knitter. Pick up prepared WY knitting. Push a further 50[52:54:56:58:60:62] Ns at L to WP for armhole opening. Pick up prepared WY knitting. 140[142:144:146:148:150:152] sts. RC000. Using MC and MT, inc 1 st every 3 rows on shoulder edge 18[14:10:6:2:0:0] times in all. Inc 1 st every 4 rows 0[4:8:12:16:16:12] times in all. Inc 1 st every 5 rows 0[0:0:0:0:2:6] times in all. RC shows 54[58:62:66:70:74:78]. 158[160:162:164:166:168:170] sts.

Collar

Break off MC. Pick up 30 sts of WY knitting onto collar edge. 188[190:192:194:196:198:200] sts. RC000. Using MC and MT, K10[11:12:13:14:15:16] rows.

Shape collar

Set carr for HP. Take CAL in free move. 15 Ns in WP at L. K rem sts with nylon

cord, taking Ns down to NWP. Cont to K on L Ns only. K2 rows. * Push 5 more Ns into HP. K2 rows *. Rep from * to * twice in all. RC16 [17:18:19:20:21:22]. All Ns now in HP. Break off yarn and transfer carr to R of N bed (bottom hem edge of knitting). Lock RC. Push 20 Ns at L into HP and K2 rows. * Push 5 more Ns into HP and K2 rows *. Rep from * to * twice in all. Release RC and make the same shapings again when RC shows 20[21:22:23:24:25:26] and when RC shows 30[31:32:33:34:35:36] and at RC44[45:46:47:48:49:50] and on the foll 10 rows twice more. Final shaping is complete when RC shows 70[71:72:73:74:75:76]. Cancel HP and K until RC shows 80[82:84:86:88:90:92]. Break off MC. Set carr for HP and push all Ns to HP except 30 sts at L (collar). WK collar sts. Reset RC000. Using MC, dec 1 st every 3 rows on the shoulder edge 18[14:10:6:2:0:0] times in all. Dec 1 st every 4 rows 0[4:8:12:16:16:12] times in all. Dec 1 st every 5 rows 0[0:0:0:0:2:6] times in all. RC54[58:62:66:70:74:78]. 140[142:144:146:148:150:152] sts rem. Strip off onto separate WY thus: 50[52:54:56:58:60:62] sts at shoulder edge and 90 sts armhole to bottom hem.

Front

Work as given for back until collar shaping. (**Designer note:** This is the hard bit where all your concentration will be

needed!) There are 3 tasks happening simultaneously.

1 Shape the 30 sts for the collar as for back.

2 At the same time you will need to dec sts and then inc sts for the front neckline thus. Always do this 30 sts in from the outside edge of the knitting by either moving sts in one full position to decrease or out one full position to increase. If Ns are in HP remember to return them to this position after shaping has been carried out.
Dec 1 st on every row 6 times RC6. Dec 1 st every alt row 3 times in all RC10. Knit without shaping until RC shows 18. Dec 1 st on this and every row 3 times in all. RC20. K without shaping until RC shows 28 . Dec 1 st on this and every foll row 3 times in all. RC30. K until RC shows 30[31:32:33:34:35:36]. Reverse these neckline instructions, inc 1 st instead of dec starting when RC shows 50[51:52:53:54:55:56]. This is at the point where you have changed back to MC and MT and you have backed the RC as described below.

3 And at the same time remember to knit the stripe. Change to C and MT-2 when RC shows 30[31:32:33:34:35:36]. K 24 rows in C. Using MC and MT and reset RC to 50[51:52:53:54:55:56] to match back pattern. (This is because you will have needed to K an extra 4 rows in Janiero to match the tension of the Sari yarn.)

Blocking and pressing

Neaten all ends. Carefully block and press with a damp cloth taking care not to stretch outer edge of collar.

To attach armhole trims

Pick up armhole edge 50[52:54:56:58:60:62] sts from main body section onto equivalent Ns with right side facing knitter. Pick up armhole trim sts just above the WY, onto corresponding Ns, making sure that the long edge of the triangular shape is at armhole edge and short edge of triangular section is at neck edge. Pull sts one through the other and cast off. Remove WY. Attach all 4 trims in the same way.

To make up

Mattress stitch shoulder seams together except for zip edges. Shoulder seam includes short edge of triangular trim. Graft underarm seams and collar seam on non-opening side. Fold collar in half and graft sts together on zip edge. Carefully stitch collar to neckline on the inside. Baste zip seam. Block and press. Insert zip from top of collar and into shoulder seam. Make a 1cm turning for bottom hem. Stitch neatly into place. Give a final block and press.

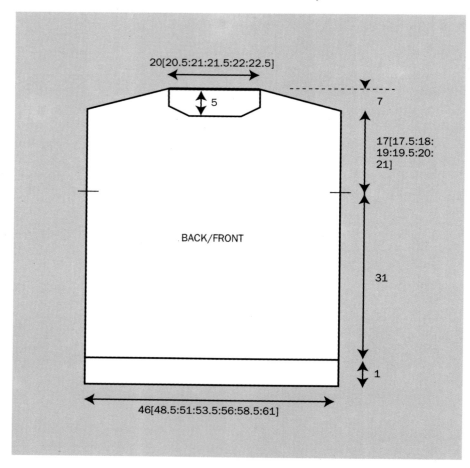

20[20.5:21:21.5:22:22.5]

5

7

17[17.5:18:19:19.5:20:21]

BACK/FRONT

31

1

46[48.5:51:53.5:56:58.5:61]

Dizzy

Yeoman Yarns Polo 100% Merino wool in Melange (MC) and Elsa 30% kid Mohair, 30% nylon and 40% acrylic in Teal (C)

Sizes
To suit bust 97[102:107:112:117]cm
Finished (hip) measurement 123[128:133:138:143]cm
Length 75cm
Sleeve seam 41cm
Figures in square brackets [] refer to larger sizes; where there is only one set of figures, this applies to all sizes.

Materials
1[2:2:2:3] x 250g cones in MC
Approx 150[200:225:250:300]g in C
Lightweight open end zipper

Garment weight
97cm size approx 380g

Main tension
33 sts and 34 rows to 10cm, using MC two ends together throughout and measured over Fair Isle patt after steam pressing (TD approx 6 = MT).
Tension must be matched exactly before starting garment.

Note
Knit side is used as right side. Measurements given are those of finished garment and should not be used to measure work on the machine.

Special note
MC is used 2 strand throughout except for hems, collar and cuffs where it is used 3 strand. Wind off several balls and thread one end from ball(s) and one end from cone into same tension mast and into feeder and treat as though they were the one yarn throughout.

Pattern note
Brother electronics: Use patt 38 from Stitchworld 1 (the yellow cover) or patt 39 from Stitchworld 3.
Other electronics/punchcard machines: Punch card/program patt before starting to knit.
Note that each panel commences with 2 rows MC (pattern set up) thus:
Using MC and MT, K1 row. Insert punchcard and lock/program patt on first row. Set carr to select/memorise for patt and K1 row.
Set carr for Fair Isle and use MC in feeder 1/A and C in feeder 2/B throughout.

These instructions are written for standard gauge electronic or punchcard machines

Centre back panel
Push 84[88:92:96:100] Ns to WP. Using WY, cast on and K a few rows ending CAR. Using MC work patt set up (see patt note). RC000. Start and work in patt throughout. K100 rows. Place a marker at each edge. K until RC shows 110. Inc 1 st at each end of next and every foll 10 rows 3 times in all. 90[94:98:102:106] sts. K until RC shows 136. Inc 1 st each end of next and every foll 6 rows 4 times in all. 98[102:106:110:114] sts. K until RC shows 158. Inc 1 st each end of next and every foll 4 rows 4 times in all. 106[110:114:118:122] sts. K until RC shows 172. Inc 1 st each end of next and every foll alt row 10 times in all. 126[130:134:138:142] sts. K until RC shows 190. Cast on 3 sts beg next 2 rows. Cast on 2 sts beg next 2 rows. Inc 1 st beg of next 2 rows. 138[142:146:150:154] sts. RC shows 198. Place a marker at each edge. K until RC shows 245[249:251:255:257].

Shape shoulders
Set carr for HP and always taking yarn

Electronic pattern 8sts x 8rows

around the first inside N in HP push 6[7:8:9:10] Ns into HP at opp end to carr on next 2 rows.

Shape neck
CAL. Note patt row.

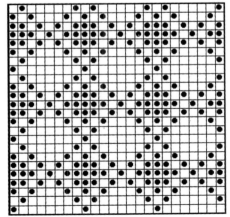

Punchcard pattern 24sts x 24rows

Push all Ns to R and 5[6:7:8:9] sts to L of centre '0' into HP. K1 row (to R). Cont to work on L side only: Push 12 Ns at L (shoulder edge) into HP on next row. Push 5 Ns at R (neck edge) into HP on next row. Cont in this manner pushing into HP in sequence, 10 Ns shoulder edge, 3 Ns neck edge, 9 Ns shoulder edge, 4 Ns neck edge, 9 Ns shoulder edge, 3 Ns neck edge and 3 Ns shoulder edge - all Ns are in HP. CAL. Set patt for noted row. Set carr to select/memorise without K and take to R. Leave all Ns to L and 5[6:7:8:9] Ns to L of centre '0' into HP. Complete as given for L side reversing all shapings by reading R for L and vice versa.
Set carr for st st and so HP Ns will K and using MC K1 row (across all sts). Push all but 49[50:51:52:53] Ns nearest carr to HP and WK. Push 40[42:44:46:48] Ns at centre of N bed to UWP and WK. WK over rem 49[50:51:52:53] Ns.

Right hand centre front panel
With placket extension. Push 72[74:76:78:80] Ns to WP. Note that the placket extension is 30 sts on all sizes. Work as given for back but only shaping at R edge (L for L centre front panel) until RC shows 190 (K1 extra row for L centre front). 91[93:95:97:99] sts. Cast on 3 sts at beg of next row, K1 row. Cast on 2 sts at beg of next row, K1 row. Inc 1 st at beg of next row. 97[99:101:103:105] sts. Place a marker at R edge when RC shows 198. K until RC shows 227[231:233:237:239]. (K1 extra row for L centre front).

Shape neck
Cast off 15 sts at beg of next and foll alt row, K1 row. *Cast off 5[6:7:8:9] sts at beg of next row, K1 row. Cast off 4 sts at beg of next row, K1 row. Cast off 3 sts at beg of next row, K1 row. Dec 1 st at neck edge on next and every foll alt row 6 times. At the same time when RC shows 245[249:251:255:257]. (K1 extra row for L centre front).

Shape shoulders
Set carr for HP and always taking the yarn around the first inside N in HP, push 6[7:8:9:10] Ns at shoulder edge into HP on next row, K1 row. Push 12 Ns at shoulder edge into HP on next row, K1 row. Push 10 Ns at shoulder edge into HP on next row, K1 row. Push 9 Ns at shoulder edge into HP on next and foll alt row, K1 row. Set carr for st st and so HP Ns will K and K1 row. WK over rem 49[50:51:52:53] sts.

Left hand centre front panel
With 5 stitch seam allowance at centre front. Push 48[50:52:54:56] Ns to WP. Work as given for R centre front panel reversing shapings by reading L for R and vice versa until RC shows 228[232:234:238:240]. 73[75:77:79:81] sts.

Shape neck
Cast off 6 sts at beg of next row, K1 row. Complete as given for R centre front panel from * to end - reversing shaping by reading L for R and vice versa and noting difference in rows.

Side back and side front panels
Knit 2 side panels alike and then a further 2 side panels alike reversing all shapings. Push 65[67:69:71:73] Ns to WP Using WY, cast on and K a few rows ending CAR.

Princess line Fair Isle zipped jacket for knitters with some experience of complex shaping

Using MC work patt set up (see patt note). RC000. Start and work in patt throughout. K10 rows. Dec 1 st at beg of next and every foll 15 rows 7 times in all 58[60:62:64:66] sts. Place a marker at each edge when RC shows 100. Cont to dec 1 st at armhole edge every 15 rows 4 times in all. At the same time dec 1 st on inner edge when RC shows 108, 118, 128, 136, 144, 150, 154 and 158. 46[48:50:52:54] sts. K until RC shows 162.

Shape armhole
Cast off 4[4:5:5:5] sts at the beg of next and foll alt row. Cast off 3[3:3:3:4] sts at the beg of next and foll alt row. Cast off 2 sts at the beg of next and foll alt row 5 times in all. At the same time dec 1 st on inner edge when RC shows 162 and on every foll 3 rows 6 times in all. K until RC shows 180. Dec 1 st at each end of next row, K1 row. Cont to dec 1 st at armhole edge every alt row 4[5:4:5:4] times in all. At the same time dec 1 st every row 9 times in all on inner edge. K until RC shows 190. Cast off rem 1[2:3:4:5] sts.

Sleeve
Knit a L and a R sleeve reversing all shapings for the second sleeve.

Cuffs
Push 86[89:92:95:96] Ns to WP. Using WY, cast on and K a few rows ending CAR. RC000. Using MC (3 strands see special note) and MT K 28 rows. MT+2 K2 rows. MT, K28 rows. Pick up sts from below WY and hang evenly along the row. Change to 2 strand MC. K2 rows for patt set up (see patt note). RC000. Start and work in patt throughout. K4 rows. Inc 1 st at each edge of next and every foll 5 rows 24[22:18:14:10] times in all, K0[3:3:3:3] rows. Inc 1 st at each end of next and every foll 4 rows 0[3:8:13:18] times in all. 134[139:144:149:154] sts. K until RC shows 122. Cast off for sleeve head, noting that shapings for back and front sleeve edge are different.

Back sleeve edge only
RC122. Cast off 4 sts at beg of next row, K1 row. Cast off 3 sts at beg next and every foll alt row 4 times in all. Cast off 2 sts at beg of row beg of next and every foll alt row 4 times in all at the same time shape front sleeve edge thus.

Front sleeve edge only
RC122. K1 row. RC123. Cast off 5 sts at the beg of next and foll alt row, K1 row. Cast off 4 sts at beg of next row, K1 row. Cast off 3 sts at beg of next row, K1 row. Cast off 2 sts beg of next and every foll alt row 3 times in all K1 row. K until RC shows 140.

Back and front sleeve edges
RC140 86[91:96:101:106] sts Dec 1 st at each end of next and every foll alt row 15[16:17:18:19] times in all and every row 4 times in all. RC174[176:178:180:182]. 48[51:54:57:60] sts.

Shape top
Cast off 2 sts at the beg of next 4 rows. 40[43:46:49:52] sts. Cast off 3[3:4:4:5] sts at the beg of next 6 rows. 22[25:22:25:22] sts. Cast off 6 sts at the beg of next two rows. Cast off rem 10[13:10:13:10] sts.

Interim make up
Neaten all ends. Block and steam press pieces to correct measurements. Join back side panels to centre back panel using the marker ties as guides. Do the same for the L and R fronts. Press seams.

Back hem
Push 195[204:212:220:228] Ns to WP. With wrong sides facing pick up sts from main back sections onto corresponding Ns, doubling up on every 16th N. Using MC (3 strand) and MT, K 28 rows MT+2, K2 rows. MT K28 rows. Turn hem by picking up sts from first row of main back sections onto equivalent Ns. Manually draw one st through the other and cast off.

Right front hem
Push 115[119:122:126:130] Ns to WP. With wrong side facing and omitting first 15 sts at centre front edge, pick up sts from below WY on front and hang onto machine, dec 7[7:8:8:8] sts evenly along the row. Work as given for back, leaving rem 15 sts on WY at centre front which you should cast off once hem has been completed.

Left front hem
Push 102[105:109:113:116] Ns to WP. With wrong side facing and omitting first 5 sts at centre front edge, pick up sts from below WY on front and hang onto machine, dec 6[7:7:7:8] sts evenly along the row. Work as given for back, leaving rem 5 sts on WY at centre front which you should cast off once hem has been completed.

To make up
Turn a small hem on L front equivalent to the 5 extra sts. Very carefully tack into place taking great care not to stretch the centre front edge of jacket. Do the same thing on the R folding (15 sts) placket in half. Press very carefully on the wrong side. Carefully stitch to bottom hem. Join shoulder seams. Carefully press.

Collar
Push 106[113:113:121:121] Ns to WP. With wrong side of work facing pick up sts from neck edge (inclusive of front placket opening) and hang evenly on to Ns. Using MC (3 strand) and MT, K 28 rows. MT+2, K2 rows. MT K28 rows. Turn hem by picking up sts from first row of main back sections onto equivalent Ns. Manually draw one st through the other and cast off. To neaten neckline seam, with front facing carefully mattress stitch around the seam. Close L and R edges.

Inserting the zipper
Hand stitch zipper in place from the front, using the Fair Isle patt as a guide to keep the seam line straight. The R hand side placket should overlap the L hand side slightly.

To complete make up
Neaten edges of hems. Set in sleeves ensuring that R sleeve head fits R armhole and vice versa. Press seam. Mattress stitch underarm and side seams. Give a final press.

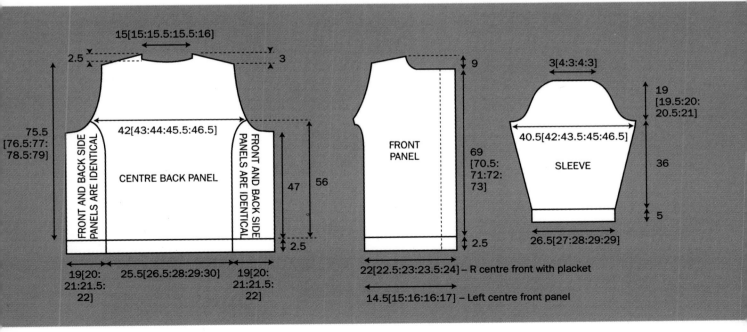

VENUS

A YOKED LONG LINE TOP WITH SLASHED
SLEEVES IN PURE SILK FOR THOSE 'I'M WORTH
IT' MOMENTS!

Texere Yarns

Super Spun Pure Silk 16/2nm
(2ply) in natural (MC)

**These instructions are written
for standard gauge machines**

Back and Front

Work 2 pieces alike.

Section A

Push 192 Ns to WP. Using WY cast
on and K a few rows ending CAR.
RC000. Using MT and MC, K84
rows and WK.

Section B

Push 180 Ns to WP. With wrong
side facing replace sts, doubling up
on every 15th N, 12 times in all.
RC000. Using MT and MC, K84
rows and WK.

Section C

Push 160 Ns to WP. With wrong
side facing replace sts, doubling up
on every 8th N, 20 times in all.
RC000. Using MT and MC,
K56 rows.

Shape armhole

Cast off 6 sts at beg of next 2
rows. 148 sts.
RC000. Dec 1 st at armhole edge
every alt row 21 times. RC42 at
the same time when RC shows 14.

Shape neckline

Set carr for HP. Push all sts to L
and a further 12 sts to R of centre
'0' into HP. K2 rows. Cont to push
the foll numbers of sts into HP on
every alt row thus:
3 sts into HP, 13 times. 54 - 0 - 54
sts in HP.
CAL. Push Ns to L of N12 L to UWP
and complete to correspond with
first side.
Set carr so HP Ns will K and using
MC and MT K1 row across all sts
and WK.

PATTERN INFORMATION

Sizes

Free size: The garment is meant to be
loose fitting in the body, for dress sizes 10-
16, with a yoked elasticated neckline which
can be adjusted to fit individual
measurements. The spun silk yarn moulds
beautifully to the body without excess bulk.
Finished bust measurement 104cm
Length (side seam) 52cm
Sleeve seam 42cm
Figures in square brackets [ ] refer to larger
sizes; where there is only one set of
figures, this applies to all sizes.

Materials

3 x 100g cones of MC
Small amount of knitting elastic

Garment weight

Approx 300g

Main tension

Allow for shrinkage during first wash. After
washing, blocking and pressing over st st
40 sts = 13cm (14.7 prior to washing) and
60 rows = 12.8cm (13.7 prior to washing)
TD approximately 5 = MT
Tension must be matched exactly before
starting garment.

Note

Knit side is used as right side.
Measurements are those of finished
garment and should not be used to
measure work on machine.

Hems

Work 2 alike.
Push 180 Ns to WP. Replace sts from first row above WY on back or front, onto equivalent Ns, doubling up on every 15th N, 12 times in all.
RC000. Using MC and MT, K20 rows. MT + 2, K2 rows. MT K20 rows. Pick up sts from first row worked in MC and hang evenly along the row and cast off loosely.

Upper sleeve

Knitted sideways using HP. Work pieces alike.
Push 140 Ns to WP. Using WY cast on and K a few rows ending CAR. Using MC and MT K5 rows.

Shape slash detail
Push all Ns into HP excepting the first 8 Ns at L. Set carr for HP. K30 rows and break off yarn. Push these 8 Ns into HP. *Push the next 20 Ns into UWP. K30 rows on these 20 Ns. Push into HP*. Rep from * to * until 12 sts rem. Push these 12 Ns into UWP and K30 rows, at the same time dec 1 st every 7th row 4 times in all on the outside edge. 8 sts rem. Set carr so HP Ns will K and K24 rows. Work the slit section again so that it is a mirror image of the first section and WK.
Neatly sew in the loose ends of each slit section.

Under sleeve

Work 2 pieces alike.
Refer to Diag 1 for order of knitting commencing knitting from below armhole shaping through to above cuff.

Section C
Push 46 Ns to WP. Cast on and K several rows in WY.
RC000. Using MT and MC, K84 rows and WK.

Section B
Push 40 Ns to WP. With wrong side facing, pick up sts from below WY on section C and hang evenly on to Ns doubling up on every 6th N, 6 times in all.
RC000. Using MC and MT, K56 rows and WK.

Section A
Push 34 Ns to WP. With wrong side facing, pick up sts from below WY on section B and hang evenly on to Ns doubling up on every 5th N, 6 times in all.
RC000. Using MC and MT, K20 rows and WK.

Section D
K firstly a L and then a R underarm section thus:
Pick up all sts to L and 6 sts to R of centre '0'. Cast off these 12 sts to form L and R underarm shaping.
* RC000. Working on rem 17 sts, K4 rows. Dec 1 st ff at armhole edge every 4th row 6 times. K2 rows. Dec 1 st ff at armhole edge every 3rd row 9 times. RC shows 51. K1 row. Cast off rem 2 sts.*
Rep from * to * picking up sts to R.

Cuffs

Push 68 Ns to WP. Using WY cast on and K a few rows.
RC000. Using MC and MT, K40 rows. MT+2 K2 rows. MT K40 rows. Pick up sts from first row worked in MC and hang evenly along the row. With right sides facing, pick up loop/sts from cuff end of sleeve

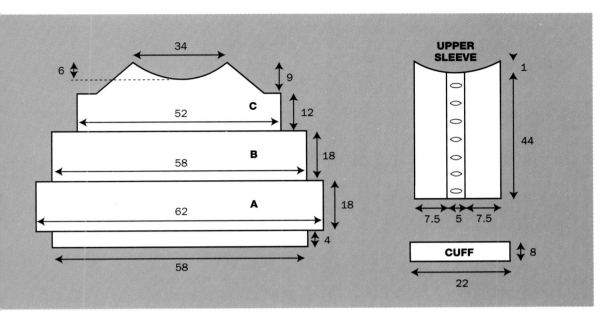

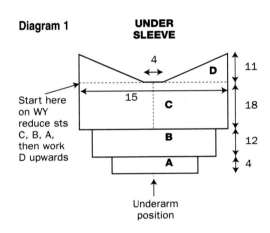

nto equivalent Ns. Pull one loop/st
rough the other and cast off.

Back and front yoke
Work 2 pieces alike.
Push 168 Ns to WP. With wrong
side facing, pick up 108 sts from
below WY on back and 30 sts each
side for half sleeve head. Using
MC and MT, K20 rows and WK.
Push 140 Ns to WP. With wrong
side facing, pick up sts from below
WY doubling up on every 5th N.
Using MC and MT, K10 rows and
WK.
Push 120 Ns to WP. With wrong
side facing, pick up sts from below
WY doubling up every 6th N. Place
a marker at each edge. Using MC
and MT, K12 rows. Using knitting
elastic and MT+2, K2 rows. Using
MC and MT K12 rows. Turn a hem
by picking up loops from marked
row below and hang evenly along
the row. Cast off loosely.

Rope trim
The trim shown was made using a
cord twister. For details of
alternative trims that do not require
special equipment see *Style File*.
Further details of the cord twister
also appear in *Style File*.
To make a four strand cord, using
the cord twister: Wind off 24 single
lengths each 210cm long for each
of the 4 cords. Twist each individual
cord 30 times and then continuing
to twist in the same direction, let
go of the catch and twist all 4 cords
around one another for a further 30
times. Knot off the ends.

To make up
Neaten all ends. Block and press
pieces to correct measurements.
Assemble the sleeves: Push 140 Ns
to WP. With right sides facing, pick
up sts from upper sleeve onto
equivalent Ns and loops from the
under-sleeve section. Pull one loop
through the other. K1 row and cast
off. Rep this operation 4 times in all
on sleeve seams.
Join raglan then yoke and side
seams using mattress st, leaving
casing open on top neck edge if you
intend to insert optional elastic.
Insert elastic into neck trim and join
remaining seam. Attach rope trim.

Diagram 1

Here we explore different ways of making plaited and twisted cords for use as decorative trims, or to develop into a custom made belt. The equipment is simple and you can do it with any yarn; here I've explored white and cream, matt and shiny for the popular theme of classical draped, Grecian robes.

Equipment for cord making

Twisted cords can be made by hand. Attach a number of lengths of yarn to a door handle and twist them together under tension. Once you have twisted the threads sufficiently, walk the cord back on itself, keeping your finger at the centre point, then allow the threads to spiral around each other, tying a knot at both ends to secure the twists. Try attaching a pencil or hand drill at the other end to assist in the twisting process.

You can also twist two separate cords together, working on first one and then the other element, repeating the number of twists put into each separate cord as required, then crossing them one over the other.

On a more sophisticated level, there are various devices on the market to assist in this process. The most versatile is a manually operated cord twister, which lets you twist up to four separate lengths of yarn (each of which can be made up of several ends of threads) independently of each other, and then twisting them around each other to complete the cord by releasing a switch on the device.

I brought a couple of simpler cord twisters back with me from Australia. They work on a similar principle to the one described above, but without the mechanism to automatically spiral all four yarns around one another. You need to complete the cord manually, in the manner described above (door handle method).

Of course, if you have access to a spinning wheel you can ply yarns together to make thick cords, or you can make crochet or finger-knitted cords to work with.

Picture 1 illustrates a range of twisted cords in a variety of materials, some of which have been wrapped with another yarn once the braid has been completed.

You could incorporate elastic into the twisted cords or, for interesting decorative effects, try threading up beads, tap washers, or natural forms such as

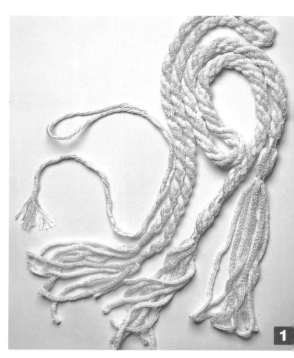

shells, threaded prior to twisting. See picture 2 for a twisted cord which incorporates silver coloured tap washers.

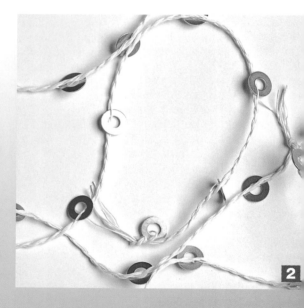

TWIST AGAIN

PLAIT OR TWIST YOUR KNITTED CORDS FOR DECORATION OR BELT MAKING

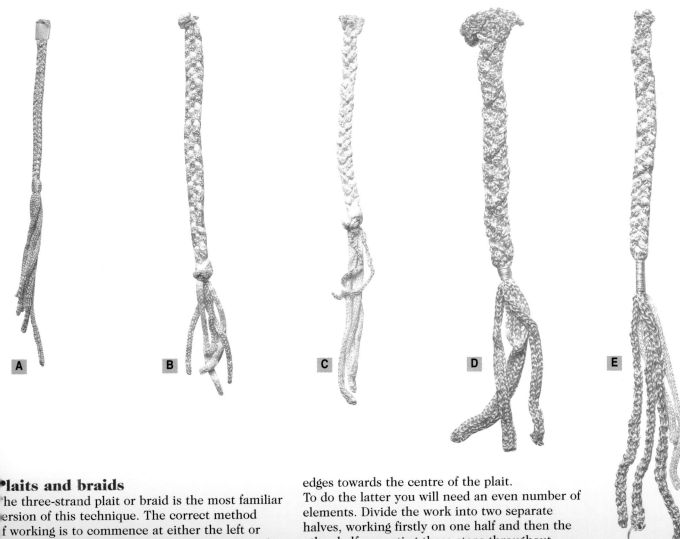

A   B   C   D   E

Plaits and braids

The three-strand plait or braid is the most familiar version of this technique. The correct method of working is to commence at either the left or right edge with the outside element being brought over and under the remaining two strands. Continue working in this manner, always from the same side.

You will need to keep the work under tension as you work, either as described below for the belt, attaching it to the knitting machine, or trapping the ends in a drawer. Alternative solutions are to either pin, clamp or tape (use masking tape) the separate ends to a suitable board.

It is possible to plait with many more elements, using a simple finger weaving technique, where all the elements are used as both warp and weft in the same manner as described for the three strand plait. Warp becomes weft and turns back into warp again as the work progresses. Try a few examples where you work from one side only as described for the three strand braid but with a greater number of elements. In this type of braid it doesn't matter whether you have an even or odd number of threads.

Once you are confident, try some more complex braids: for example, start plaiting from the centre point and move out towards the left and right edges, or conversely move inwards from both edges towards the centre of the plait.

To do the latter you will need an even number of elements. Divide the work into two separate halves, working firstly on one half and then the other half, repeating these steps throughout.

Five strand plaits

Here we look at ways of working with five ends constructed from plain knitted strips. You could of course choose to work with more elements and alter the weave structure once you become familiar with the basic working method.

These plaits lie perfectly flat and are a good choice for belts and edgings and you could use them instead of the twisted cord on the pattern *Venus*. The examples A to E show a collection of five strand braids in different materials and dimensions. The yarns were chosen for their textural differences, for example, matt, sheen, smooth, corded and for their subtle variations in shades of cream and white.

Braid A

A five strand plait knitted in Texere spun silk 16/2 nm at MT 5.

Knit five separate lengths, each 5 stitches wide and 150 rows deep. Strip off with waste yarn. Re-hang them from knitting machine and plait, keeping the work under tension.

Each strand is used in turn from the left hand edge across to the right, and is worked in a basic plain weave structure — under one strand, over one strand.

Braid B
This example is made with three strands knitted in Texere Bright Cord Viscose, which is creamy in colour and two strands in a bright white, slub cotton, knitted at MT10.

Braid C
Here the strand width varies; with the three wide strands made in Empress Mills 7/16's cotton over 7 stitches at MT 10. Two narrow strands are knitted in Texere Fine Bright Viscose Cord over 3 stitches, MT 10. Plait the viscose cord quite tightly so that it almost disappears into the soft cotton.

Braid D
A chunky-gauge version, constructed from two lengths of viscose ribbon knitted over 3 stitches; two lengths of 2 strand thick, bright Texere Viscose Cord worked over 5 stitches and one length on 7 stitches. This sample would work really well as a belt as it is quite firm and stable.

Braid E
Chunky and standard gauge knitting combine here: Two strands of Empress Mills 7/16's cotton knitted on the standard gauge over 7 stitches at MT 10 for 150 row. Three strands of Texere thick Bright Viscose Cord knitted on the chunky gauge over 3 stitches at MT8 for 100 rows.

Belts and girdles

You might like to make a belt using the plaiting technique to complement the *Venus* pattern, taking your inspiration from the girdles which were used to gather the waist of the classical Greek chiton or Roman toga. The chiton was a simple, draped garment made from two lengths of uncut fabric which were sewn at the sides and held at the neckline with a clasp.

3

Twelve element plait

Picture 3 shows a sample suitable for developing into a belt. This has been plaited using 12 elements to make a wider piece of work than the initial samples shown above. To make a similar piece, work as follows: Choose three different types of yarn in white or cream, and of contrasting texture. For example crisp white cotton, a white and cream mix and a cream textured viscose.
Knit four lengths in 1 strand white cotton with 1 strand in Texere Boucle bright Viscose over 5 stitches at MT10. Do the same in 1 strand white cotton plied with 1 strand white slub cotton and again in thick cord in bright viscose.
Thread your strands onto a piece of thin dowel. Sit on the floor and hold the dowel with your feet and then work towards your body. As an alternative working method, attach the separate lengths of knitting to a wide belt buckle before starting to plait. Plait for the desired length and make a fringe with the remaining lengths of yarn. You can, of course, vary the order in which you arrange the different elements, or work with pairs of elements to create a more chunky plait.

If this article has whetted your appetite to learn more about braiding, you might be interested to read about Kumihimo braiding (a Japanese silk braiding technique) or cord making using a Lucet. Check them out on the web along with sites dedicated to other methods of working, such as ply-split braiding. *The Techniques of Ply-Split Braiding* by Peter Collingwood ISBN 1 85725 1334 is an excellent book which explores this method of making braids where one cord is pulled through many to create angled and curved pieces with coloured ridges, interesting textures and patterns.

Further information

Passementerie cord twister £38.50 plus £3 p&p from Anna Crutchley, 8 Canterbury St, Cambridge, CB4 3QF 01223 327 685. Specialist items for tassel and braid making also available.

Classic Knitting

Updated classic knitwear

Yeoman Polo 100% Merino Wool - Extra Fine 1ply in shade Mercury (20). Texere silk yarns for the embroidery

These Instructions are written for standard gauge machines

Back
Push 83[89:95] Ns to L and R of centre '0' to WP. 166[178:190] Ns. Using WY, cast on and K several rows. RC000. Using MC and MT, K 170 rows*.

Shape armhole
Cast off 7 sts at beg of next 2

Sizes
To suit bust 81-86[86-91:96-101]cm
Finished measurement 92[98:104]cm
Length 57[58:59]cm
Sleeve Seam 48cm
Figures in square brackets [ ] refer to larger sizes; where there is only one set of figures this applies to all sizes.

Materials
1[2:2] x 250g cones MC
64 round, silver-grey beads approx. 6-7 mm in diameter.
Embroidery threads in creamy white Super spun Silk (2/4.5 wc) and 4ply fancy bleached Tussah silk in ecru.
15 Small buttons approx 1cm diameter.

Garment weight
Second size: 265g with beads and buttons.
(Note: Using 1 x 250g cone for this size gives no leeway for tension swatches.)

Main tension
36 sts and 56 rows to 10cm measured over st st, after light steaming (tension dial approx 3 = MT).
Tension must be matched exactly before starting garment.

Note
Knit side is used as R side. Measurements given are those of finished garment and should not be used to measure work on the machine.

Special note
Fully fitted sleeves have been used in this cardigan. This means that not only does the back and front of the sleeves head have slightly different shaping instructions, but that the armhole depth (number of rows) for the back and the front shaping also differ. These differences are correct and you should find that the garment fits together beautifully!

rows. Cast off 4 sts at beg of next 2 rows. Cast off 3 sts at beg of next 2 rows. Cast off 2 sts at beg of next 4 rows. 130[142:154] sts. Dec 1 st at each end of next and every foll alt row 9 times in all. 112[124:136] sts. K until RC shows 282[288:294].

Shape shoulders
Set carr for HP. Push 3[3:4] Ns at opposite end to carr to HP on next 12[8:4] rows. RC 290[296:302]. Push 4[5:5] Ns to HP at opposite end to carr on next 4[8:12] rows. RC298[304:310]. Break off yarn. Cancel HP. K1 row across all Ns. Strip off with separate lengths of WY, 26[32:38] sts each for L and R shoulder and 60 sts for neck.

Bottom hem
Push 150[160:171] Ns to WP. Ns. Pick up sts from above WY dec evenly by putting 2 sts onto every 10th N. Using MT K15 rows, MT+2 K2 rows, MT K15 rows. Pick up loops from first row worked above WY and hang evenly along the row (to make hem). Cast off.

Right front
Push 83[89:95] Ns to WP. Work as given for back to *. (K1 extra row for L front).

Shape armhole
Cast off 8 sts at beg of next row, K1 row. Cast off 6 sts at beg of next row, K1 row. Cast off 3 sts at beg of next row, K1 row. Cast off 2 sts at beg of next and foll alt row, K1 row. 62[68:74] sts. Dec 1 st at armhole edge on next and every foll alt row 6 times in all, 56[62:68] sts. K until RC shows 249[255:261] (K1 extra row for L front).

Shape neck
Set carr for HP. Always taking the yarn around the first inside N in HP push 5 Ns at neck edge to HP on next row, K1 row. Push 4 Ns at neck edge to HP on next row, K1 row. RC253[259:265]. Push 2 Ns at neck edge to HP on next and every foll alt row 4 times in all. RC 261[267:273]. Push 1 N at neck edge to HP on next and every foll alt row 13 times in all. At the same time, when RC shows 265[271:277] (K1 extra row for L front).

Shape shoulder
Push 3[3:4] Ns at opposite end to carr to HP on next and every foll alt row 6[4:2] times in all. RC290[296:302]. Push 4[5:5] Ns at opposite end to carr to HP on next and every foll alt row 2[4:6] times in all. RC298[304:310]. Push 30 neck sts to UWP and WK.
Set carr so HP Ns will K and WK over rem 26[32:38] sts (for shoulder).

Bottom hem
Push 75[80:86] Ns to WP. Complete as given for bottom hem of back.

Left front
Work as given for R front, noting difference in rows to reverse shaping.

Sleeves
Knit a L and a R sleeve reversing all shapings for second sleeve. Note that the shaping are different for back and front sleeve head.
Push 38(42:46) Ns to L and R of centre '0' to WP. 76(84:92) Ns. Using WY, cast on and K several rows.
RC000. Using MC and MT, K6 rows. Inc 1 st at both ends of next and every foll 6th row 24 times. 124[132:140] sts RC shows

.44. K until RC shows 238
K1 extra row for second
sleeve).

Shape top

Cast off 5 sts front sleeve
head on next row. Cast off 4
sts back sleeve head on next
row. Cont in this manner. Cast
off 4[4:5] sts at beg next row.
Cast off 3 sts at beg next row
and cast off 2 sts at beg next
row) twice. RC245. Cast off 3
sts at beg of next row. Cast off
[2:3] sts at beg of next row.
RC247. Dec 1 st at beg of
next 64[68:72] rows.
2[36:40] sts rem. RC shows
11[315:319]. Set carr for HP.
Always taking the yarn around
the first inside N in HP push 2
s on front armhole edge to
HP on next row. Push 1 N on
ack armhole edge to HP on
ext row. Push 1[2:3] Ns at
pposite end to carr to HP on
ext 5 rows. RC318[322:326].
ush 5 Ns at opposite end to
arr to HP on next 2 rows.
ush 6[5:4] Ns at opposite
nd to carriage to HP on next
ow. RC321[325:329].
17[19:21] sts for back
eeve head to L of centre 0
nd 15[17:19] sts for front
leeve head to R of centre 0).
ut in WY marker on N next
o centre '0'. Push Ns at
pposite side to carr to
WP and K1 row. Set carr so
P Ns will K and K1 row.
ast off.
lace contrast marker at back
leeve head to facilitate the
aking up process.

Cuff

Push 69[76:83] Ns to WP.
Complete as given for back
bottom hem.
Work second sleeve alike,
noting difference in rows to
reverse shapings and reading
L for R and vice versa.

Interim make up

Neaten all ends. Block and
press pieces to correct
measurements, taking care
not to stretch hems.

Shoulder seams

Push 26[32:38] Ns to WP.
With right side facing replace
sts of left back shoulder evenly
on to Ns, remove WY and push
sts behind latches. With wrong
side facing, replace left front
shoulder onto same Ns,
ensuring these sts rem in N
hook. Remove WY. Pull one st
through the other manually
and cast off, taking care not
to cast off too tightly. Do the
same for the right back
shoulder seam.

Collar

Push 120 Ns to WP. With
wrong sides facing pick up 30
sts from L front neck, 60 sts
from back neck and 30 sts
from R front neck and hang
evenly on to Ns. Leave the
WY in place. Using MT, K15
rows, MT+2 K2 rows, MT K15
rows. Pick up loops from first,
row worked above WY and re-
hang evenly along the row to
make hem. Remove WY and
cast off.

Button band

Push 128[132:136] Ns to WP.
With wrong side of front facing
pick up front edge loops and
hang evenly on to Ns. Using
MC and MT, K15 rows. MT+2
K2 rows, MT K15 rows. RC32.
Pick up loops from first row of
band and hang evenly along
the row to make hem. Cast off.

Buttonhole band

Work as given for button band
but work transfer eyelets for
small buttonholes on the 4th
and 8th N from both the L and
R edges and a further 11
evenly spaced eyelets
between. Make eyelets on the
7th and 24th rows.

Blocking and pressing

Carefully block front bands and
shoulder seams, taking care
not to stretch the edges of
front bands.

Embroidery and beading

Transfer the design for the
embroidery onto L and R
fronts, using one of the
methods described in the
Style File.

To make up

On completion of the
embroidery, block and press.
Set in sleeves, taking care to
match back (front) sleeve head
with back (front) armhole.
Backstitch armhole seam.
Block and press. Mattress
stitch side seams and
underarm seams. Stitch on
buttons. Give a final press.

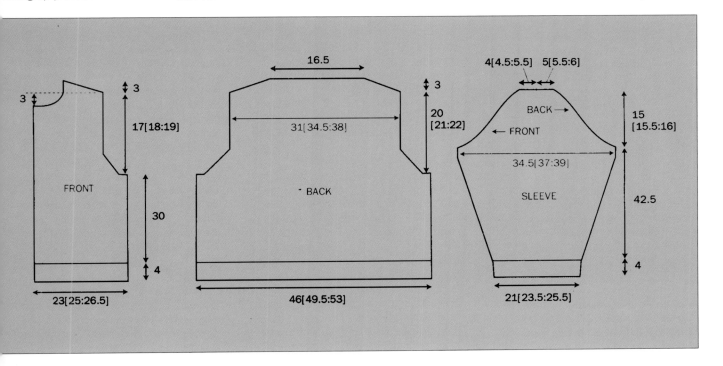

Beading and embroidery

Here we look back to the 1950s with beaded and embroidered cardigans. Knitted in shades of cream, pale blues and pinks or black, the original so-called 'sweater girl' cardigans typically used a soft, fine gauge yarn, and were frequently lined. Styles tended to be close fitting, with classic set-in sleeves.

The beading and embroidery were worked either in a range of close tones and colours; for example pale pinks and white on a cream background, pale blues and white on pale blue background, or made use of a stronger contrasting design of copper embroidery mixed with white and pearl beads on a cream or black background.

The main bead patterns, based on swirling floral or leaf imagery, would balance out small-scale geometric border designs placed beside the button/buttonhole bands and above the welts. Here we develop a more contemporary appearance; stylish knitwear, still with design references from the 1950s in both style and decoration, but the latter having a more abstract look. If you are considering making the beaded cardigan in *Classic Knitting*, the working method, outlined below, should prove useful, particularly the section on transferring the embroidery design to the fabric.

Yeoman Polo in Mercury, Cream 50/50 wool & silk, Super Spun Silk, Fancy Bleached Tussah Silk, Sun silk, Viscose.

Embroidery stitches, threads and beads

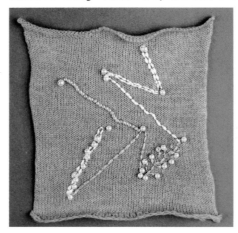

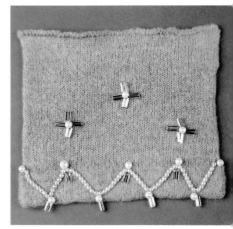

The four samples shown here explore the use of simple hand-embroidery techniques to emphasise the linear qualities of the pattern motifs. Suitable stitches might include couching, backstitch, straight stitch and running stitch. Couching is a very useful stitching technique for this type of work, as it allows you to sew down a thick thread, cord or bundle of threads with a finer thread.

You simply lay the thread to be couched along the line of the design, (transferred to the knitting using one of the methods outlined below). Thread up the needle with a second finer thread, bring the needle up through the knitting next to the thread to be couched, pass over the main thread, and take the needle down through the knitting at the opposite side. Repeat this operation at regular intervals. In the examples shown I used a fine strand of wool or viscose rayon to stitch over silk and strings of beads. I worked without using an embroidery

hoop, since I found it easier to keep an even tension this way. Don't stretch the knitting, but also be sure not to pull the couching thread too tight, especially when embroidering with silks or cottons on a wool base.

Knit the base fabric on a reasonably tight tension so it retains its shape once the decoration has been applied. All my sample swatches were knitted at MT3 in two strands of 1ply Polo (100% Merino wool), shade Mercury (20) from Yeoman, with the exception of the felted samples which were knitted at MT4.

Try Texere Yarns of Bradford for undyed silk yarns for couching threads such as the Pure Super Spun Silk or the filament Tussah Silk. The sheen and the sheer luxurious handle of these yarns add something special to your work and contrast beautifully with the texture of, for example, a soft Botany wool. A less expensive alternative would be a 100% Viscose twisted floss yarn, which is also very lustrous.

Design ideas for bead embroidery

If you intend to design from scratch, you need to develop suitable pattern motifs before experimenting with layout and pattern repeats. You should also decide on the basic garment style you want to work with and make an outline drawing of the shape, just as you would if you were working on the knit charter. Regard your cardigan shape as a blank canvas. To try out different design ideas, cut out or draw several scaled down versions of the cardigan shape. Choose a motif, then try placing it variously as an all-over pattern, border design or single motif. Vary the spacings between individual pattern elements: closely packed or widely spaced. Consider altering the orientation of the pattern units: upside down, reflections, different angles. Do you want a formal repeat pattern based on a geometrical framework or a more free-flowing or abstract pattern?

Alternative design method

You will need either the actual garment pieces or a full-scale paper pattern of the cardigan. Trace off or photocopy multiple copies of the pattern unit(s) in question, then place them by eye onto the garment shape until you feel that the pattern motifs work in harmony with the garment shape, Fig 4. You are then ready to transfer the images to the knitting by one of the methods suggested below. Do bear in mind that beads will add weight to your sweater, so should be evenly spaced to avoid distorting the garment shape.

More design ideas

A good inspirational source for this type of work could be the spiky linear shapes with a modern, pared-down look seen in post-war textile designs. Look at the abstract shapes based on plant forms and structures from the 1950s, for example the work of such designers as Lucienne Day and the work of artists such as Joan Miro and Paul Klee. Those of you with less experience of designing from scratch might like to try the following method for pattern design. Simple linear patterns that resemble explosions, or branching and spiral motifs can be generated by joining up regularly spaced dots within a hexagonal or square shape, Figs 5 and 6. Start at the centre dot and connect the dots so that they all link up, but in such a way that any two dots connect along one pathway only (except of course for the centre dot). Patterns developed in this

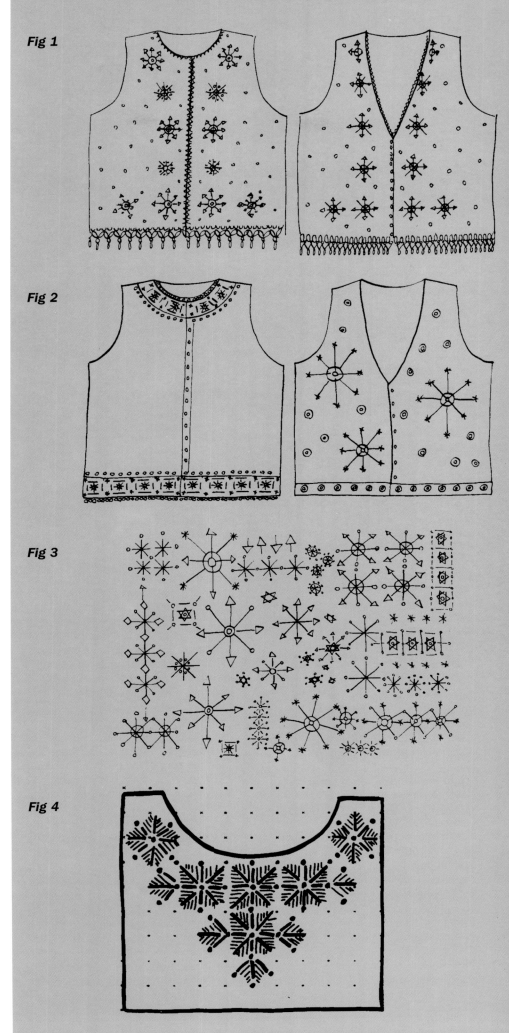

Fig 1

Fig 2

Fig 3

Fig 4

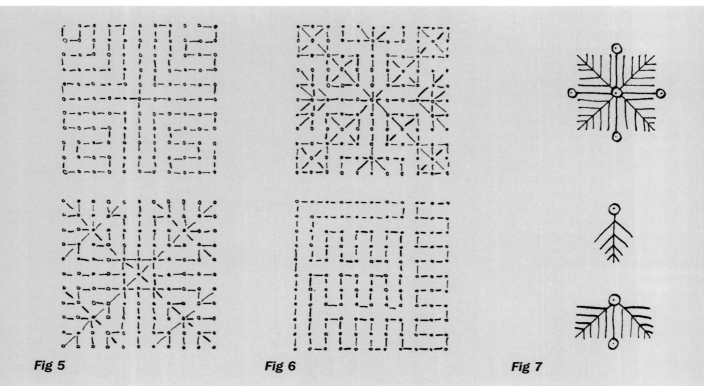

Fig 5

Fig 6

Fig 7

manner can be formal and symmetrical or a more meandering spiral, depending upon how the dots are joined.

Work on graph paper, dressmakers' dot-and-cross paper or on the computer screen, if you have suitable design software. Imagine the dots as beads and the lines as thread, and then as abstract tree shapes, cell structures, stars or simply elegant patterns just waiting to be transferred onto your designer cardigan. Fig 7 shows three versions of the pattern used in the *Classic Knitting* beaded cardigan.

Transferring your design to the knitted fabric

There are many ways of transferring imagery to knit, depending upon the complexity of the pattern to be transferred, the colour of the background fabric and availability of equipment.

1 To transfer relatively simple patterns onto knitting, you can use dressmakers' tracing carbon, available in white and yellow. Draw or trace off the motif to be transferred onto thin white paper. Place the tracing carbon coloured-side up on a flat surface. Pin or tape the pattern motif to the reverse side of the knitting.

Then, place the knitting with right side facing the coloured side of the tracing paper. Use a tracing wheel to trace over the outline of the pattern. This works best with lightly felted knits or relatively stable knitting. You will get a stronger outline of the design if you lay the right

side of the knitting over the coloured side of the tracing carbon, before tracing off the design. To do this you will need to draw the design onto the back of the tracing carbon freehand as a guide for the tracing wheel.

2 The next method needs access to a light box or a large, light window and is the method I used to transfer the design for the beaded cardigan. This method is best suited to light coloured knitting. The marker pen will not show up on dark fabrics and it is impossible to see through them to trace off the image. First draw the design up to full scale on a white sheet of paper with bold black lines (use a black marker pen). You will need to draw in the outline of the garment as well. Using masking tape, stick the design right side uppermost to the window or light table, then tape down the front of the cardigan in the same way, making sure that it is correctly aligned with the garment shape. Using a vanishing marking pen (for example Newey Craft Vanishing Marker Pen) trace off a portion of the design, remembering that the bright pink marks, in this case, fade within 72 hours.
Note: Always test vanishing marker pens on a sample before use on a garment.

3 Alternatively, you could trace the design off onto tissue paper. Pin the tissue paper to the knitting, face sides uppermost. Using small, neat stitches tack along the main lines of the design. Remove the tissue paper by scratching

under each stitch before proceeding with the embroidery. You should be able to lift it off in one go. Do not rip the tissue off or you might damage the knitting.

4 Finally, here is a method I haven't tried on knitting called pouncing, which is the traditional method of transferring an image on paper to another surface. It might just work! To do this, draw an outline of the pattern onto greaseproof paper. Prick along the design lines with a metal point. Lay the pricked surface onto the knitting; the latter pinned out onto your blocking mat. Make a roll of fabric. Dip into French chalk and then dab the roll onto the pounced image to transfer the design. Traditionally, the dots were joined with a very fine brush in water colour when working on fabric, but you just might be able to see what you are doing using the dots as a guide.

Recycle and sparkle!

If you are in a hurry for something special to wear, why not try recycling existing knitwear into up-to-the-minute fashion items by adding some suitable embroidery. You might like to try lightly felting them first if they are either Botany or lambswool, particularly if you intend to remove the ribbed welt and replace it with a beaded trim, as shown at Fig 2. Check out your local charity shops for good-quality classic knitwear in fine industrial-weight wools and for strings of beads and old jewellery, which can be broken down and recycled for decoration.

Salome

Two tone plating and tuck ribs with integral shaping in this seductive sweater

Yeoman Polo Melange 1ply 100% Merino wool in Palamino M2 (MC), and Manila 2ply 86% viscose, 5% nylon and 9% polyester in Old Gold 12 (C)

These instructions are written for standard gauge punchcard or electronic machines with ribber

Sleeves
Work 2 alike.
With RB in position and set for FNR, push 58[64:70] Ns on MB and corresponding Ns on RP to WP. Pitch H arrange Ns for FNR. Using WY cast on and K approx 30 rows ending CAR.
Using MC T0/0, cast on. T2/2, K3 tubular rows.
RC000. T3/3 K1 row. Insert punchcard and lock/program patt on first row. Set MB carr to

Sizes
To suit bust 87[97:107]cm.
All measurements are approx due to the elasticity of the rib structures used.
Finished measurement just below underarm shaping 94[104:114]cm.
Length 60cm.
Sleeve Seam 45cm.

Figures in square brackets [ ] refer to larger sizes; where there is only one set of figures, this applies to all sizes

Materials
350[375:425]g in MC and 200[250:325]g in C.

Garment weight
For size 97cm approx 525g.

Main tension
Allow tension swatches to relax overnight for the most accurate measurements. Pin onto blocking board, lightly steam press and measure whilst pinned out. All measurements are approx due to the elasticity of the rib.
FNR tuck: 20 sts and 66 rows to 10cm T3/3.
6 x 6 (P) tuck rib: 27 sts and 57 rows to 10cm T5/5.
3 x 3 (P) tuck rib: 27 sts and 56 rows to 10cm T5/5.
Tension must be matched exactly before starting garment.

Note
Tuck side is used as right side.
Measurements are those of finished

select/memorise for patt and K1 row. Release card and set MB carr for tuck (RB carr K) and K86 rows. Set both carr to K and K1 row. RC89. Change lever 'P'.

Section 2
RC000. Transfer sts between MB and RB to form 6 x 6 rib beg and end with 2 extra Ns on MB. Insert punchcard and lock/program patt on first row. Set MB carr to select/memorise for patt and K1 row. Release card and set MB carr for tuck (RB carr K) and K62 rows. Set both carr to K and K1 row. RC shows 65*.

Section 3
RC000. Transfer sts between MB and RB to form 3 x 3 rib beg and end with 2 extra Ns on MB. Insert punchcard and lock/program patt on first row. Set MB carr to

garment and should not be used to measure work on machine.

Special notes
Two ends of Polo yarn used together as MC throughout. Wind off several balls before starting to knit. Thread one end from cone and one end from ball through the same tension mast and into carriage feeder, treating as though they were the same yarn throughout.
MC threaded into rear of plating feed and 1 strand C in front feed.
Work both sleeves first so that they can be hooked up in to the machine once the front/back reaches the yoke section.
When setting up for rib patterns the number of Ns given refers to MB both in WP and NWP.
To ensure tuck rib knits off cleanly, cast on combs should be left on back and front until yoke shaping is completed and used in conjunction with the appropriate number of weights. You can also use single bed claw weights on the sleeve sections when knitting the yoke.
Waste yarn cast on is advised for tuck ribs.
Fully fashion shaping is used on raglan sections. Transfer the 4th st from the end to the 3rd N from the end. This group of sts is then moved inwards one full position.
Inc, dec or cast off sts on MB and transfer RB sts to suit.

Pattern note
Punch card is Card 1 birds-eye from basic set.

select/memorise for patt and K1 row. Release card and set MB carr for tuck (RB carr K). Inc 1 st at each end of next and every foll 7 rows 15 times in all. 88[94:100] sts. K until RC shows 112.

Shape raglan
Cast off 6 sts at beg of next 2 rows. Dec 1 st at each end of next and every foll 4 rows 12 times in all. K until RC shows 162.

Shape top
Set both carr for HP. Push all Ns to L and 5[6:7] Ns to R of centre to HP. Note position in patt. Always taking the yarn around the first inside N in HP, K2 rows. Push 5[6:7] Ns to HP at opposite end to carr on next and every foll alt row 3 times in all, at the same time in all cont to shape armhole edge when RC shows 166. Push rem 6[5:4] Ns into HP.
Break yarn. CAR. Manually return all Ns to L of 5[6:7] L of centre to WP. Reset punchcard to noted row. Set both carr to slip/part/empty and take to L to select/memorise for patt. Reset RC to 162 and working in patt, work L side to correspond with R.
Set both carr to K and so HP Ns will K and K1 row. 52[58:64] sts. Transfer RB sts to MB and using T5, K1 row. WK front and back sleeve sts onto separate lengths of WY (i.e. sts to L of centre on one piece and sts to R on the other).

Back
With RB in position set machine for FNR rib. Push 140[152:164] Ns on MB and corresponding Ns on RB to WP. Arrange Ns for FNR. Work as given for sleeve to *.
Transfer RB sts to MB and using T5, K1 row and WK.

Section 3
Push 128[140:152] Ns to WP. Pick up sts from below WY and hang on to Ns, putting 2 sts on every 10[11:12]th N until 12 dec made. With RB in position transfer sts for 3 x 3 rib beg and end with one extra N at each end. Insert punchcard and lock/program patt on first row.
RC000. Set MB carr to select/memorise for patt and K1 row. Release card and set MB carr for tuck (RB carr K). K66 rows.

Shape Armhole
RC000. Cast off 6 sts at beg of next 2 rows. 116[128:140] sts. Dec 1 st at each end of next and every foll alt row 10 times in all, K2 rows. Dec 1 st at

Birdseye pattern
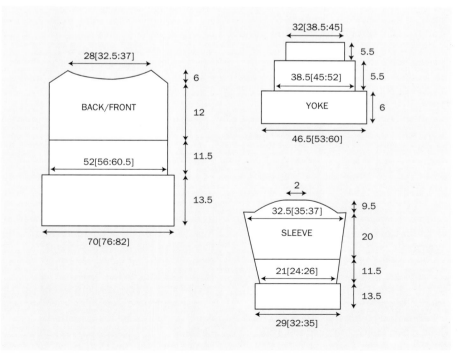

each end of next and every foll 3 rows 10 times in all. RC52. At the same time, when RC shows 12.

Shape yoke
Note patt row. Set both carr for HP. CAR. Push all Ns to L of centre '0' to HP. K2 rows. Always taking the yarn around the first inside N in HP push 0[3:4] Ns at opposite side to carr to HP on next and every foll alt row 0[5:5] times in all, K0[1:1] row. Push 2 Ns at opposite side to carr to HP on next and every foll alt row 18[13:15] times in all, K1[1:0] rows. Push 1 N at opposite side to carr to HP on next and every foll alt row 2[2:0] times in all, K1[1:0] rows. Push rem Ns to HP. Break yarn. CAR. Manually return all Ns to L of centre to WP. Reset punchcard to noted row. Set both carr to slip/part/empty and take to L to select/memorise for patt. Reset RC to 12 and working in patt, work L side to correspond with R.
Set carr so HP Ns will K and K1 row. 76[88:100] sts. Transfer RB sts to MB. T5, K1 row. Leave on machine and follow back yoke directions as below.

Front
Work as given for back excepting N arrangement in section 2. Start and end 6 x 6 rib with 1 N at each end - i.e. 1 N in WP, 6 Ns in NWP, 6 Ns in WP etc. along MB, with RB sts to correspond (in NWP opposite WP and vice versa).

Yokes
Work 2 sections alike for back and front yoke except for arrangement of Ns for 6 x 6 (P) rib. Check that you have a perfect match of rib structure between front and back yokes.
With back 76[88:100] sts already on MB, push 26[29:32] Ns at L and R into WP. Pick up 26[29:32] sts from L back sleeve and 26[29:32] sts from R back sleeve to L and R of back respectively. 126[144:162] sts. Hang claw weights on sleeve sections. With RB in position transfer sts for form 6 x 6 rib beg and end with 2 extra Ns on MB as for section 2, back. Insert punchcard and lock/program patt on first row. RC000. T5/5. Set MB carr to select/memorise for patt and K1 row. Release card and set MB carr for tuck

(RB carr K). K 34 rows. RC36. Set both carr to K and K1 row. Transfer sts to MB and K1 row. WK.

Section 2
K2 sections alike for back and front yoke.
Push 104[122:140] Ns to WP on MB. Replace sts from back yoke section 1 onto equivalent Ns, doubling up sts every 4th N, 6[0:0] times and every 5th N 16[10:0] times and every 6th N, 0[12:14] times and every 7th N, 0[0:8] times in all. With RB in position and pitch 'P', transfer sts to form a 6 x 6 rib, beg and end with 2 extra Ns on MB. RC000. T5/5. Set MB carr to select/memorise for patt and K1 row. Release card and set MB carr for tuck (RB carr K). K28 rows. RC30. Set both carr to K and K1 row . Set both carr to K and K1 row. Transfer sts to MB and K1 row. WK.

Section 3
Back yoke only. *Push 86[104:122] Ns to WP. Replace sts from back yoke section 1 onto Ns, doubling up sts every 4th N, 6[0:0] times, every 5th N, 12[4:0] times, every 6th N, 0[14:6] times and every 7th N, 0[0:16] times in all. With RB in position and pitch P, transfer sts for a 6 x 6 rib, beg and end with 2 extra Ns on MB.
RC000. T5/5. Set MB carr to select/memorise for patt and K1 row. Release card and set MB carr for tuck (RB carr K). *K28 rows. RC30. Set both carr to K and K1 row . Set both carr to K and K1 row. Transfer sts to MB and K1 row. WK.
Front yoke only. Work as given for back yoke from * to *. K10 rows. RC12. Set both carr to HP. CAR. Push all sts to L

and a further 8[10:12] sts to R of centre '0' into HP. K2 rows. RC14. Always taking the yarn around the first inside N in HP, push groups of 5[6:7] sts into HP at opp end to carr and K2 rows, 7 times in all. RC28. Reset RC to 12 and rep shapings on L of front yoke.
Set both carr so HP Ns will K and K1 row. Transfer sts to MB and K1 row. WK.

Interim make up
Block and steam press as for tension swatches. Mattress stitch yoke and raglan sections together. Gently steam press seams.

Neckbands
Work 2 alike.
Push 65[83:99] Ns to WP on MB. With back of front yoke facing knitter pick up sts onto equivalent Ns, doubling up every 3rd N, 19[0:0] times, every 4th N, 2[1:4] times, every 5th N, 0[20:17] times in all. Do not strip off WY as this will give you a guide for hooking up neckline stitches before casting off neckband. Attach claw weights along the full length of the knitting onto the WY to ensure that sts K off cleanly and to stop the WY tangling with the knitting carriages. With RB in position, pitch 'P' transfer sts to form a 3 x 3 rib. Set both carr to K, T3/3. K60 rows. Transfer sts to MB. Pick up sts just above WY onto equivalent Ns and cast off loosely.
(You could K1 row on the MB before and after knitting 3 x 3 rib at T5. It would be easier to pick up the neckband sts but would look slightly different to the sample garment.)

To make up
Mattress stitch rem underarm, bodice and neckband seams. Give a final gentle steam press.

Style File

Shaped knitting

One of the most fascinating aspects of knitted textiles is the ability to combine shape, form, texture and pattern. It is a way of working which gives the experienced knitter a real challenge to use their technical know how and craft skills in a creative way, while fully exploiting the potential of hand framed double bed knitting.

My yoke sweater *Salome* shows how a combination of double bed, tuck rib pattern worked on varying needle settings can influence the final shape of a garment.

Possible methods to shape and form knitting

Shape in knit can be created variously through tension changes, fully fashioned increasing and decreasing, cut and sew, juxtaposition of different weights of fabric, partial knitting techniques, knitting thick and thin yarns in the same piece, combining single and double bed knitting techniques, altering the number of needles in and out of working position on one or both beds, and using different types of stitch structures within the same piece of work!

More esoteric techniques can include heavily steam pressing selective areas of the knitting to kill the elasticity of a particular section of the knitting, partially felting/shrinking wool swatches, felting swatches which include areas which won't felt (knitted in cotton or glitter yarns for example), applying weights or inserting piping cord, metal rods or wooden canes to stretch out certain areas of the fabric kite-style, applying starch, or knitting in Grillon!

The list is endless once you start experimenting but here we'll focus on double bed knitting techniques, with the emphasis on the juxtaposition of contrasting stitch structures and needle arrangements.

Initial explorations

It's a good idea to build up a reference collection of individual samples of different stitch structures for this sort of work, but do use a standard format throughout. I tend to do all my samples 60 rows x 40 stitches. As I use my Knit Leader a lot, this means another job is avoided if and when I decide to use the samples as basis for a garment. Initially, try various needle arrangements with the same stitch pattern; for example, all plain knitting, tuck or slip. Once you feel confident working between beds, introduce an area of slip knitting into a group of tuck ribs (see sample) or try altering the tensions.

Choice of yarns and colours

Single colours in paler shades emphasise the stitch structure; a good example being the traditional Aran sweater. Darker colours, or contrasting colours used, for example, in a stripe pattern will overwhelm the subtle textures to be found in rib structures. Contrasting yarn-qualities in like colours can be effective in adding interest to double bed work, more so if you have access to a plating feed. With this you can combine two types of yarn, for example matt and sheen, where one yarn emphasizes the purl face of the knitting and the other the knit stitches, see *Salome* for this effect.

Suggested combinations of yarn are fine wool and lame, viscose and cotton, spun silk and matt cotton. Alternatively, you could make a gradual transition working, for example, between three different colours of wool such as pale golds, camel and off white, but with each colour the same tone and the second yarn the same throughout.

Samples

All samples shown below were knitted on Brother machine with ribbing attachment and plating feed (this device allows you to split two different yarns into yarn feed A and B, so that one colour comes to the fore on the knit facing stitch and the other on the purl facing stitch). Machines that do not have this device give a more random mix of yarns, sometimes resulting in what could appear to be badly knitted stripes. Try plying the yarns together before you start knitting so that only one composite end of yarn runs through each yarn brake; or use a yarn winder which twists as it winds. This loosely plies yarns together much like the spinning process, and will give a good, even cover when knitting with multiple ends.

Sample 1

Sample 1

Full needle set up throughout knitted over 60 stitches and at T3/3 showing a comparison between bands of selective tuck and slip ribs (Birds Eye Pattern). As with single bed knitting tuck stitch knits up wider than slip stitch.

Sample 2

In this example, greater contrast in widths is achieved by changing the

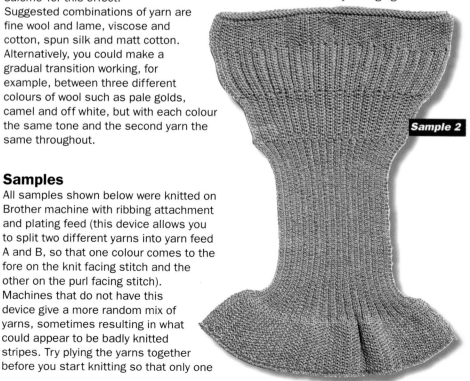

Sample 2

needle arrangement as well as working between selective tuck and slip ribs. This sample suggests a sleeve with a fluted cuff, fitted mid section and a wider underarm section. The sequence is as follows:

Sample 3

Band 1. Knit 60 rows tuck rib on a 2 up 1 down setting, pitch lever set to half pitch. Tension 3/3. Band 2. Knit 90 rows slip rib on same needle setting as before, tension 3/3. Band 3. Push all needles on the main bed back into working position. Knit 30 rows slip rib. Band 4. Knit 30 rows tuck rib. Band 5. Push all needles on the rib bed into working position. Knit 20 rows of tuck rib. Move all ribber stitches to the main bed and knit a few rows plain before casting off.

Sample 3

Here, the gradual reduction in width is due to changes in the needle setting and stitch structure. The sample was knitted over 60 stitches throughout and was developed from the previous swatch and suggests a ribbed yoke. The final section may need a reduced number of stitches for a snug fit at the neck, also some shaping to curve the front neckline. The sample details are as follows:
Band 1 is full needle tuck rib. Band 2 is tuck rib where every 3rd needle on the ribber is put into NWP. Band 3 is 2 up 1 down needle setting knitted as a tuck rib. Band 4 is knitted on the same needle setting as 3 but as slip rib. Band 5 is 12 rows plain knit rib, needle arrangement as before.

Sample 4

This is the prototype for the *Salome* sweater, and clearly shows the differences in width between differing stitch structures. You could steam press these ribs and,

depending upon the yarn, flatten selected sections to give additional shaping possibilities, particularly if you are using synthetics. For this example a light steam press was applied. The wool has a natural resilience which helps retain the elasticity of the rib, but which is slightly inhibited by the Manila yarn (which lacks the same degree of elasticity).

Four steps to smooth double bed knitting

1 Double-bed waste yarn cast on. Set up for a 1 x 1 full pitch setting or full needle rib for half pitch settings. Cast on with waste yarn. Knit about 20 rows of waste knitting and an optional one row of ravel cord. Thread up with main colour. Cast on and knit 3 rows tubular. Knit rib, making any necessary adjustments to the needle setting, tensions and stitch structure.

Sample 4

Referring to the full pitch setting, you can set up for a 1 x 1 or 2 x 2 rib when you cast on with waste yarn. Anything over a 3 x 3 full pitch rib should be cast on as for 1 x 1, then adjusted after cast-on in the main colour. Half pitch ribs can be dealt with in much the same way. In anything other than a full needle rib or a 2 up 1 down rib, needles will need to put into either WP or NWP after the main cast on. You can make a single bed cast on if the rib is a full pitch setting. This is a good technique for broad rib structures, and where the design requires a straight fall hem rather than a gathered in welt. Cast on with waste yarn and knit at least 20 rows. With main yarn and the latch tool make a crochet cast on over the waste yarn and knit an optional 1 row. Now transfer the stitches between the ribber and the main bed for your preferred needle arrangement.

2 Transferring stitches between beds when knitting on the half pitch setting. It is easier to transfer stitches between beds if you move the pitch lever to full pitch to transfer stitches, remembering to return it to half pitch on completion.

3 KH970 Brother machines — a cautionary tale! With regard to the KC1 and KC2 settings on the change knob. When you are working with an automatically selected rib pattern such as tuck or slip, and you have a rib structure with needles in and out of working position on the main bed, it is vitally important to choose the KC 2 setting where the end needles are selected to D or B position according to the pattern data. The KC 1 setting brings end needles to D position irrespective of pattern data. This applies to each new group of needles in WP across the needlebed, not just needles at the LHS and RHS edges!

4 To reduce stitches evenly across the row, the working method is the same as single bed yoke-style knitting. It is easier to perform this operation if you work with full pitch rib structures. First transfer all ribber stitches to the main bed, and knit one row plain. Strip off with waste yarn. Replace stitches onto the appropriate number of needles on the main bed, then transfer stitches from the main bed to the ribber. Leave the ribber cast-on comb in position throughout if you are using a Brother or Silver Reed machine, so that you can re-hang the weights. If this is not possible, hang single-bed claw weights across the width of the knitting and use your hand to pull the knitting down between the beds for an even tension.

Milan

Sideways knitting means big sizes are easy, while coloured stripes add pizazz to a chunky knit

Sizes
To suit medium[large]
Finished measurement from back shoulder to shoulder 44[49]cm
Length 60cm
Sleeve seam 34cm
Figures in square brackets [ ] refer to larger sizes; where there is only one set of figures, this applies to all sizes.

Materials
1 x 450g cone in A
4 x 50g balls in B
1 cone in each of C and D
2.5mm crochet hook

Garment weight
Large size approx 475g

Main tension
16 sts and 26 rows to 10cm, measured over st st after light steaming (TD approx 4 = MT). Tension must be matched exactly before starting garment.

Note
Knit side is used as right side excepting welts and cuffs which are purl facing.
Measurements given are those of finished garment and should not be used to measure work on the machine.

Special note
The main body of the garment is knitted sideways in one piece starting with the right front, then the back, and finally the left front. The sleeves are knitted vertically and grafted to the armholes. The fronts are shaped using the partial knitting technique. Shoulder shaping and back neckline are shaped using FF techniques. To increase move 3

edge sts one position to the outer edge and hook up loop of thread from preceding stitch. To decrease move the fourth stitch from the edge to the third needle from the edge and move all three stitches in one full position.
The ties are knitted tubular style if you have access to a chunky ribber, otherwise knit as for single bed and mattress stitch seams to form tube. Commence the tubular knitting on WY to give a neater edge.

Sizing and the stripe pattern
This shape will accommodate most average measurements. If you wish to alter the sizes you will need to rework the arrangements of the stripes in relationship to side edges, centre back and at the graft point at the armhole. Note in this version in order for the stripes to continue around the body in the correct sequence, and for the stripe pattern on the back to be symmetrical, the instructions have been designed so that the left and right sleeves begin and end at different points in the stripe sequence. More or less rows on the main body of the garment will mean that you may need to rework the stripe sequence.

Pattern note
Stripe pattern
K8 rows A, 2 rows B, 2 rows C (or D on every other alt rep of the pattern) and 2 rows B. These 14 rows form the main stripe pattern.

Waste yarn
Before starting to knit make two separate pieces of WY knitting in a contrast colour and 30 sts wide for armhole edge cast ons.

Yeoman Yarns Fettuccin 4ply 100% Bright acrylic ribbon in Pink (A), Citadella 100% viscose in Cream shade 7 (B), Cannele 4ply corded 100% cotton in Tango shad 153 (C) and Orchid shade 39 (D)

These instructions are written fo chunky gauge machines with or without ribber

Right front
Push 88 Ns to WP. Using WY, cast on and K several rows ending CAR Using A and MT K1 row. CAL (Welt edge).
RC000. Start and work in stripe patt throughout (see patt note). S carr for HP. Push all Ns into HP excepting 4 nearest carr, K2 rows (Push a further 4 Ns into WP and K2 rows) 5 times in all. RC8. 16 s rem in WP.
Push 1 N back into UWP on every alt row 17[20] times in all. RC 42[48]. 33[36] sts rem in WP. Pus 2 Ns back into UWP on every alt row 11[14] times in all. Push 3 Ns to UWP on alt rows 3[0] times in a RC 70[76]. 64 sts rem in WP. Pus 3 Ns back into UWP on every alt row 4 times in all. RC 78[84]. 76 sts rem in WP. Push 4 Ns back int UWP on every alt row 3 times in a RC 84[90]. 88 sts rem in WP.

Shape front shoulder and side seam
Cont to work in stripe patt dec 1 s at shoulder edge every alt row 7[0 times in all. Dec 1 st at shoulder edge every 3 rows, 5[12] times in all. K until RC shows 114[128] 76

sts. At the same time shape lower side seam as follows commencing when CAL (welt edge) and RC shows 106[120]. Push all Ns into HP excepting 16 sts at L. K2 rows.

NOTE: To incorporate the tie opening into the knitting, knit back and forth by hand on the 5 Ns on the R of this group of 16 Ns, in a separate end of yarn. K the rem 11 Ns as normal. Push a further 4 Ns to HP and K2 rows. Rep until all Ns are in HP. RC 128 and at the same time return RC to 106[120]. Push 16 Ns at L (welt edge) into HP. CAR. K2 rows. (Push 7 Ns to HP at L and K2 rows) twice in all. (Push 8 Ns to HP and K2 rows) twice. Remember to cont to shape the shoulder. RC 114[128]. 76 sts rem.

Armhole edge

Push 46 Ns into HP at L. 30 sts rem. WK these 30sts (for front armhole). 46 sts. Pick up WY knitting onto these 30 empty Ns for back armhole. 76 sts.

Shape back shoulder and side seam

RC 000. Cont to work in stripe patt inc 1 st every alt row 7[0] times in all. Inc 1 st at shoulder edge on next and every foll 3 rows, 5[12] times in all on the shoulder edge. 88 sts. K until RC shows 31[38] at the same time shape side seam to mirror image front side seam shaping. Push all Ns to HP excepting 16 sts at L. K2 rows. Push 4 Ns into HP and K2 rows. Rep until all Ns are in HP. RC8 and at the same time.

Return RC to 000. Push 16 Ns at L (welt edge) into HP. CAR. K2 rows. (Push 7 Ns into HP at L and K2 rows) twice. Push 8 Ns into HP and K2 rows) twice. Remember to cont to shape the shoulder. RC8.

Shape back neck

RC31[38]. Dec 1 st at neck edge on this and every foll alt row 6 times in all. 82 sts. RC43[50]. K until RC shows 79[86]. Inc 1 st at neck edge on this and every foll alt row 6 times in all. 88 sts. RC 91[98].

Shape back shoulder and side seam

Cont to work in stripe patt dec 1 st every alt row 7[0] times in all. Dec 1 st at shoulder edge every 3 rows, 5[12] times in all on the shoulder edge. At the same time shape side seam as follows commencing when CAL and RC shows 114[128]. Push all Ns into HP excepting 16 sts at L. K2 rows. Push 4 Ns into HP and K2 rows. Rep until all Ns are in HP. RC136 and at the same time Return RC to 128. Push 16 Ns at L (welt edge) into HP. CAR. K2 rows. (Push 7 Ns into HP at L and K2 rows) twice. (Push 8 Ns into HP and K2 rows) twice. Remember to cont to shape the shoulder. RC122[136]. 76 sts.

Armhole edge

Push 46 Ns into HP at L. 30 sts. WK these 30 sts for back armhole. 46 sts. Pick up WY knitting onto these 30 empty Ns for front armhole. 76 sts.

Left front

Work the L front as for R front reversing all shapings and partial knit instructions. 88 sts rem. K1 row in A to return all Ns to WP before WK.

Interim making up

Block and press pieces to correct measurements. Neaten all ends. Mattress stitch shoulder seams and press.

Front bands

With wrong side facing pick up 88 sts from R front and 12 sts from half back neck. Using A and MT, K8 rows. MT+ 2 K2 rows, MT K8 rows. Turn hem by picking up sts from first row worked in A and hang evenly along the row and cast off.

Work left hand side and half back neckline to match.

Trims

Knit 3 alike. Push 94[100] Ns to WP. Using WY cast on and K several rows. Using A and MT+2, K10 rows. MT+4 K2 rows. MT+2, K10 rows and WK. Push 74[80] Ns to WP. Pick up sts above WY doubling up on every 5th N. Using A and MT, K10 rows and WK. Do the same at the other end of the knitting.

To complete trim push 80 Ns into WP. With K side of trim facing, pick up sts from one edge onto equivalent Ns. Do the same for the other edge. 2 sts per N. Pull one st through the other. Leave trim sts on machine.

To attach main body of knitting to trim, pick up edge loops from back (or front) onto equivalent Ns with knit side of main body facing purl side of trim. Pull one loop through the other and cast off. Complete each trim thus. With front of work facing knitter, pick up 100 sts from the turn point of the trim onto equivalent Ns and MT+4, K1 row and cast off.

Join back trim to front trim and neaten front edges.

Using a 2.5mm crochet hook, crochet through each cast off loop using B.

Sleeve

Knit a L and a R sleeve paying particular attention to the stripe sequence. Make trims as for main body of garment excepting that the wider section is 60 sts and the narrower section 50 sts. Double over as before and pull one stitch through the other to form single row of sts. WK and replace onto 44 Ns, doubling up every 7th N, 6 times in all. K 70 rows in patt*** (see note below), inc 1 st both edges on this and every foll 8 rows 8 times in all. 60 sts. WK.

*****Large size only:** Commence patt with 3 rows A and then follow sequence as before making sure that one sleeve starts the rep sequence with B, C and B and the other with B, D and B.

Ties

Knit 2 pieces alike.
With ribber in position and machine set for FNR, push 5 Ns on MB and corresponding Ns on RB to WP (following the N rule for tubular knitting - see manual if in doubt). Using WY, cast on and K several rows. Using A and T1/1, cast on (over WY). T4/4 K200 rounds. Alternatively use single bed and st st and K400 rows at MT.

To make up

Block and press sleeves to correct measurements. Graft sleeve head to armhole stitch for stitch, unravelling the WY as you go. Press carefully. Mattress stitch underarm seams. Join centre back neck seam and ties as appropriate. Neaten opening for tie by stitching through loops of actual knitting. Pull out contrast thread. Attach ties on the underneath of the front bands. Give a final press.

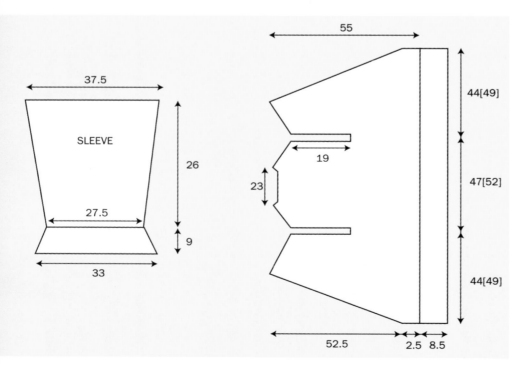

Ice Dreams

Yeoman Polo 100% Merino wool in Sea Foam, shade P11 (MC) and Janeiro 50% Viscose, 25% Linen and 25% Acrylic in Silver shade 10 (C)

These instructions are written for standard gauge punchcard or electronic machines

Sweater

Centre back of yoke

Push 82[88:94:100] Ns to WP. Using WY, cast on and K a few rows. RC000. Using MC and MT K42 rows. Place a marker at each edge. K until RC shows 62. Inc 1 st at each end of next row and then when RC shows 76, 88, 98, 106, 112, 118, 124, 128, 134, 138, 142, 146, and 150. K4 rows. RC 154. Inc 0[1:1:1] sts at each end of next row. K0[2:4:4] rows. RC 154[156:158:158]. Inc 0[0:0:1] sts at each end next row. K0[0:1:3] rows. RC 154[156:159:161]. 110[118:124:132] sts rem. Place a marker at each edge (to denote beg of sleeve dec) *K2 rows. Dec 1 st at each end of next row*. Rep from * to * 3[2:1:0] times. RC 160[160:161:161]. K1[1:0:0] row. RC 161 all sizes. 104[114:122:132] sts.

Back armhole and yoke shaping

Dec 1 st at each end of next and every foll alt row 17[16:12:11] times in all. Dec 1 st at each end of next and every 3 rows 2[4:8:10] times in all. RC 201[205:209:213]. At the same time shape the yoke using HP when RC shows 189. Set carr to HP. Strip off onto WY all sts to L (or R) of centre 0. Work on rem sts only. At the neck edge and then on every alt row push 12 Ns into HP once and K2 rows, 5 Ns once and K2 rows, 4 Ns 4 times and K2 rows, 2 Ns 0[2:4:6] times and K2 rows. 66[74:82:90] sts rem for yoke neckline. WK.
Knit a second side to match reversing all shapings.

Centre front panel

Work as given for centre back panel until RC shows 161.

Shape armhole and front of yoke

To shape armhole edge work as given for back until RC shows 189[193:197:201] at the same time shape back yoke using HP as foll when the RC shows 189. Set carr to HP. Strip off onto WY all sts to L (or R) of centre 0. Work on rem sts only. At the neck edge and then on every alt row push 10 sts into HP once and K2 rows. Push 4 sts into HP and K2 rows 3 times. Push 3 sts into HP and K2 rows 0[1:2:3] times. Push 2 sts into HP and K2 rows 7 times. Push 1 N into HP and K2 rows 3[4:5:6] times. 39[43:47:51] sts rem for front yoke neckline. RC shows 189[193:197:201]. WK.

Side panels

Work 2 alike. Push 88[92:96:100] Ns to WP. Using WY, cast on and K a few rows. RC 000. Using MC and MT K42 rows. WK. Push 72[76:80:84] Ns into WP. Re-hang sts doubling up every 4th N, 8[4:0:0] times and every 5th N, 8[12:16:12] times and every 6th N, 0[0:0:4] times. K until RC shows 62. Dec 1 st at the end of the next row and when RC shows 76, 88, 98, 106, 112, 118, 124. Cast off centre 18 sts with a separate end of MC. Strip off rem 19 [21:23:25] sts on LHS and RHS on separate pieces of WY. Re-hang 19 (21:23:25] sts. Cont to dec 1 st on inner edge when RC shows 128, 134, 138, 142, 146 and 150. K4 rows. RC 154. Dec 0 [1:1:1] sts at inner edge on next row. K0[2:4:4] rows. RC 154[156: 158:158]. Dec 0[0:0:1] sts at inner edge next row. K0[0:1:3] rows. RC 154[156:159:161] at the same time

Shape armhole edge

Dec 1 st every alt row 5[4:6:5] times. Dec 1 st every 3 rows 6[8:8:10] times. 2 sts rem. Cast off. RC 154[156:159:161].

Welts
Back and front panel

Work 2 alike. Push 78[84:90:94] Ns to WP. With wrong side facing, pick up sts from below WY from centre back and hang on to Ns dec 4[4:4:6] sts evenly along the row. Using MC and MT-1, K18 rows. Using C and MT, K2 rows. Using MC and MT-1, K18 rows. Turn a hem by picking up loops from first row of welt and hang evenly along the row. Cast off loosely.

Sizes
To suit bust 92[97:102:107]cm
Top
Finished measurement taken prior to under arm cast off is 97.5[102.5:107.5:112.5]cm
Length 48cm
Sleeve seam 25.5cm
Skirt
To suit hip sizes 87[92:97:102]cm
Actual hip measurement is 92[97:102:107]cm
Length including trim and excluding waistband is 67.5cm
Figures in square brackets[] refer to larger sizes; where there is only one set of figures, this applies to all sizes.

Materials
2[3:3:3]x 250g cones in MC
1 x 500g cone in C
Length of elastic for skirt waistband

Garment weight
92cm size weighs approx
Top 300g
Skirt 300g

Main tension
31 sts and 44 rows to 10cm, measured over st st using 3 strand Merino or 2 strand Janeiro after steam pressing (TD approx 6 = MT).
33 sts and 40 rows to 10cm, measured over birds-eye Fair Isle patt using 2 strand MC and 2 strand C and using fine needle bar, after steam pressing (TD approx 4 = MT for skirt).
Tension must be matched exactly before starting garment.

Note
Knit side is used as right side.
Measurements given are those of finished garment and should not be used to measure work on the machine.

Special note
Yeoman Polo 1ply used 3 strand for the sweater and 2 strand for skirt (excluding trims which are 3 strand).
Yeoman Janiero used 2 strand throughout.

Pattern note
Punch card or mark mylar sheet for birds-eye patt - noting this is generally card 1 for punchcards and is no 45 for Brother KH970 machines.

Side panels

Work 2 alike. Push 84[88:92:94] Ns to WP. With wrong side facing pick up sts from below WY on side panel and hang on to Ns dec 4[4:4:6] sts evenly along the row. Complete as given for back and front panels.

Sleeves

Knit a L and a R sleeve reversing all shapings on sleeve head.
Push 80[84:88:92] Ns to WP. Using WY, cast on and K a few rows.
RC000. Using MC and MT K96 rows, inc 1 st at each end of next and every foll 6 rows, 16 times in all.
112[116:120:124] sts. K until RC shows 104.

Shape top

Cast off 6 sts at beg of next two rows. 100 [104:108: 112] sts. Dec 1 st at each end of next and every foll alt row 15[11:7:3] times in all. Dec 1 st at each end of next and every foll 3 rows 10[14:14:22] times in all. 50[54:58:62] sts. K until RC shows 174[178:182:186].

Shape sleeve head

Set carr to HP. Cont to dec 1 st on back armhole thus. Dec 1 st every alt row once and every 3 rows 4 times in all. At the same time Push Ns into HP on front armhole every alt row as folls:
12 Ns 0[1 :0:1] times, 11 Ns 1[0:1:0] times, 7 Ns, 1[1:5:6] times in all, 5 Ns, 3[6:0:0] times in all, 4 Ns, 3[0:1:1] times in all and 3 Ns, 0[0:1:1] times in all. 45[49:53:57] sts rem. Cancel HP. K1 row. WK.

Blocking and pressing

Neaten ends. Block out to measurements given. Steam press.

Interim make up

Join L and R front side panels to centre front panel and L and R back side panels to centre back panel. Join underarm raglan seams. Press seams with wrong sides facing.

Yoke

With wrong sides facing pick up 23[24:26:28] sts from front half of sleeve head, 78[86:94:102] from front yoke, 23[24:26:28] sts from front half of sleeve head. 124[134:146 :158] sts.

A flattering deep yoke makes this a very feminine suit with panels that are easily scaled up for larger figures

Using MC and MT, K2 rows. Using C, K18[18:20:20] rows. WK.
With wrong sides facing pick up 22[25:27:29] sts from back half of sleeve head, 66[74:82:90] sts from back yoke, 22[25:27:29] sts from back half of sleeve head. 110[124:136:148] sts. Using MC and MT, K2 rows. Using C, K18[18:20:20] rows. WK.
With wrong sides facing pick up front yoke sts doubling up every 5th N. Using MC and MT, K2 rows. Using C, K18[18:20:20] rows. WK.
With wrong sides facing pick up back yoke sts doubling up every 5th N. Using MC and MT, K2 rows. Using C, K18[18:20:20] rows. WK.

Neckband
With wrong sides facing pick up front yoke sts doubling up sts every 10th N. Using MC and MT, K5 rows. MT-1 K5 rows. Using C and MT+1 K2 rows. Using MC and MT-1, K5 rows. MT, K5 rows. Pick up yoke sts to make hem. Cast off.
With wrong sides facing pick up back yoke sts and work as given for front neckband.

Sleeve trims
Push 72[76:80:83] Ns to WP. With wrong sides facing pick up sleeve sts, doubling up sts every 10th N. Using C and MT K20 rows. To make hem, using MC and MT-1, K10 rows, using C and MT+1, K2

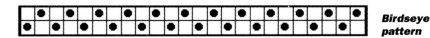

Birdseye pattern

rows, using MC and MT-1, K10 rows. Pick up first row MC and hang evenly along the row to make hem. Cast off.

To make up
Neaten rem ends. Join sleeve, front and back shoulder seams and front and back neck bands using mattress stitch. Give a final press wrong side facing.

Skirt

Centre front and centre back panels
Push 82[88:94:100] Ns to WP. Using WY, cast on and K a few rows. RC000. Using MC and MT K1 row. Insert punchcard/program patt on first row. Set carr to select/memorise for patt and K1 row. Set carr for Fair Isle (see patt note)* and K258 rows, inserting edge markers when RC shows 186 to denote hip line. WK.

Side panels
Work 2 alike. Push 72[76:80:84] Ns to WP. Work as given for centre front panel to * and K186 rows. Note patt row and WK.
Pick up 36[38:40:42] sts from below WY onto equivalent Ns with 1 extra st at centre (side seam). Dec 1 st on outer edge on next and every foll 7 rows, 10

times in all. K2 rows. WK.
Replace rem 36[38:40:42] sts and rep operation.

To make up
Neaten all ends. Block and steam press pieces to correct measurements. Mattress stitch side seams. Press.

Waistband
Work back and front alike. With wrong sides facing pick up front skirt sts. Using 3 strands MC and MT K12 rows. Using C and MT+1, K2 rows. Using MC and MT, K12 rows. Pick up last row of skirt sts to make hem. Cast off.
Rep on back skirt sts.

Trims
Make separate hems for centre back and centre front panels and both side panels in 3 strands MC and doubling up sts every 15 Ns. Using MC and MT, K12 rows using C and T7 K2 rows and using MC and MT-1, K12 rows. Pick up first row of skirt sts onto equivalent Ns and cast off.

Final make up
Insert length of elastic to complete waistband and neaten seam.

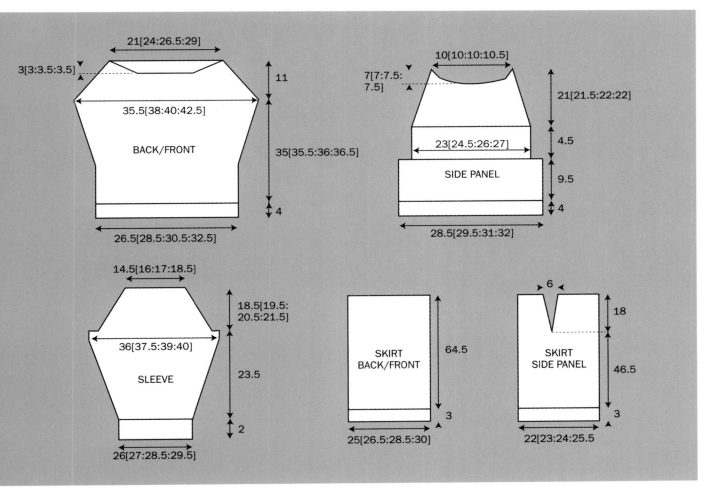

Red Hot Mama

Sizes
To suit bust 86-91[91-96]cm
Finished measurement
98[104]cm
Length of top (to longest
point) 73cm
Length of skirt (to longest
point exc. waistband) 64cm
Figures in square brackets
[ ] refer to larger sizes;
where there is only one set
of figures, this applies to
all sizes.

Materials
1 x 500g cone in MC
1 x 50g ball in each of A
and B
Length of elastic to fit
waist measurement
48 brass washers or similar
1.5mm crochet hook

Garment weight
91-96cm size weighs:
Top approx 150g
Skirt approx 175g

Main tension
32 sts and 45 rows to
10cm, measured over st st,
after steam pressing (TD
approx 3 = MT).
Tension must be matched
exactly before starting
garment.

Ff = fully fashioned dart for
this pattern, see *Style File*

Note
Knit side is used as right
side.
Measurements given are
those of finished garment
and should not be used to
measure work on the
machine.

Special note
Please refer to the *Style
File* for a more detailed
explanation of fully
fashioned shaping
techniques and placed
eyelets.

Yeoman Yarns Janeiro
50% viscose, 25% linen and
25% acrylic in Poppy shade 22
(MC) and Yeoman Citadella
100% viscose in Poppy shade
12 (A) and Fushia shade 1 (B)

**These instructions are written
for standard gauge machines**

Asymmetrical hemline with vertical slashes for tunic and skirt
Work 2 pieces alike and 2
pieces reversing all shapings.
Push 190[200] Ns to WP.
Using WY, cast on and K
several rows.
RC000. Using A, make a chain
cast on over the WY on alt Ns
only. Push rem Ns into WP.
Using MT and A K2 rows. K2
rows MC. * 'e' wrap alt Ns
with A. K1 row MC. 'e' wrap alt
Ns in B. K1 row MC. K2 rows
MC*. RC8. Repeat from * to
*. RC12. WK.

Slits
Re-hang the first 10 sts from
the L onto equivalent Ns.
Using MC and MT, K10 rows.
WK.
Rep this operation on every
foll group of 10 sts. 19[20]
strips x 10 sts in total.
Re-hang all sts on equivalent
Ns. 190[200] sts.
RC000. Using MC and MT, K2
rows. Rep from * to * twice in
all. RC8. WK. Turn knitting.
Re-hang sts on equivalent Ns.
RC000. CAL. Using MC and
MT, K2 rows. Set carr for HP
and always taking the yarn
around the first inside N in HP,
push 7[8] Ns at opposite side
to carr into HP on next and
every foll alt row, 10[25] times
in all, K1[0] row. Push 7[0] Ns
at opposite side to carr to HP
on next and every foll alt row
15[0] times in all. RC50. Set
carr so HP Ns will K and K2
rows. RC52. WK.

An asymmetrically styled skirt and top with slit borders and fully fashioned eyelet style shaping is worked mainly in stocking stitch

Tunic

Back
Section A
Make a shaped and slitted border section as given above.
Section B hip to waist
Turn knitting. Push 156 [166] Ns to WP. Replace sts thus. Double up on every 4th N, 14[4] times and on every 5th N, 20[30] times.
RC000. Using Ff shaping dec 1 st on L and R every 8 rows, 9 times in all. Shaping should take place to L and R of Ns 30 - 0 - 30 at all times. RC 78. 138[148] sts.
Section C waist to armhole
RC000. Using Ff shaping inc 1 st on L and R every 6 rows, 9 times in all shaping should take place to L and R of Ns 30 - 0 - 30 at all times. RC 54. K until RC shows 60. 156[166] sts rem.
Section D raglan shaping
Cast off 7 sts begin of next 2 rows. 142[152] sts rem. RC000.
To make the fully fashioned eyelet style shaping, set the adjustable transfer tool for 5 prongs. You will also need a single eyed transfer tool. Dec 1 st both sides every 3 rows until RC shows 106 using the fully fashioned method with eyelets. (For each set of decreases there will be a corresponding eyelet.) 72[82] sts rem. WK. Replace knitting onto equivalent Ns thus. Re-hang 6 sts at both L and R and double up on approx every 5th N on the rem 60[70] sts. K2 rows. Strip off 6 sts at L and R with separate lengths of WY. Cast off rem sts for back neckline.

Front
As for back but reversing all shapings until commencement of section D.
Section D raglan shaping
Work as for back raglan shaping until RC shows 54. 106[116] sts.
Section E shape neck
Cast off 14 sts at centre front. Set carr for HP and push all Ns at R to HP. WK over rem sts at L. CAR. RC54 cont to K R side thus: Keeping armhole shaping correct as set (and as given for back) throughout and making eyelets on neck edge every 3 rows to correspond with same on armhole edge, dec 1 st at neck edge on every foll alt rows 7[22] times in all, K1 row. Dec 1 st at neck edge on next and every foll 3 rows 12[2] times in all. 10 sts. K until RC shows 104. Without making eyelets, dec 1 st at each edge on every alt row until RC shows 108. WK over rem 6 sts. CAL Push 46[51] Ns to WP. With wrong side facing, pick up sts from below WY of L front and hang evenly on to Ns. Reset RC at 54 and work L side to correspond with R.

To make up
Block pieces to correct measurements and steam press. Link shoulder seams. Mattress stitch side seams. Work a row of double crochet around hemline edges using yarns A then B. Attach washers or beads on every alt segment on the slitted border and decorate front neckline with same. Give a final steam press to seams.

Skirt

Back
Section A
Slitted and shaped border section as for top.
Section
Push 156[166] Ns to WP. Turn knitting and replace 2 sts on every 4th N, 14[4] times and on every 5th N, 20[30] times.
RC000. Using MC and MT, K128 rows. WK.
(Lengthen or shorten here, referring to tension details if you want to make alterations.)
Section C
Push 144[154] Ns to WP. With wrong side facing, pick up from below WY and replace 1 st on to each of first 11[5] Ns, 2 sts on next and every foll 12th N, 12 times in all 1 st on each rem N to end.
RC000. Using MC and MT, K44 rows and WK.
Section D
Push 136[146] Ns to WP. With wrong side facing pick up sts from below WY and hang on to Ns putting 1 st on each of first 16[17] Ns and 2 sts on next and every foll 17[18] Ns 8 times, then 1 st on each N to end.
RC000. Using MC and MT K36 rows.
Section E
Using 1 x 1 ruler edge, push alt Ns to HP. Set carr for slip/part/empty and K1 row. Set carr for st st and K15 rows. Using MT+2, K1 row. Using MT, K15 rows. Turn a hem by picking up sts from slip row below (which will have alt threads along it serving as a marker) and hang evenly along the row. Cast off.

Front
Work as given for back but reversing all shapings.

To make up
Block pieces to correct measurements and steam press. Mattress stitch side seams and front side of casing. Work a row of double crochet around hemline edges using yarns A then B. Attach washers on every alt segment on the slitted border. Insert elastic. Mattress stitch remainder of casing seam. Give a final steam press to seams.

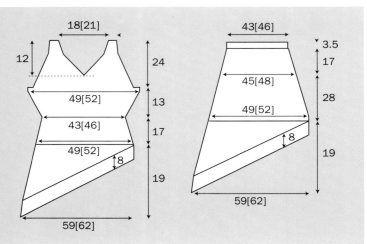

Style File

Fully fashioned shaping with decorative decreasing and edge detail

The focus is on lightweight, softly clinging knitwear that combines simple stocking stitch knitting with discreet fully fashioned shapings and slashed borders designed to reveal contrasting coloured underlayers. Decorate with ribbon crochet, metallic threads, buttons and beads of your choosing. The samples and design ideas suggested below should be seen as a starting point for your own interpretations of this summer's look. If you already have a standard raglan block on your knit charter, you can develop custom styles quickly and easily from these.

Colours
Hot deserts, Chilli peppers, Indian spices, Chinese temples and the rainbow brilliance of South American and Mexican textiles are all good sources of inspiration for colour. Try sampling with some really vivid contrasts for the underlayer; for example, purply magenta or Jade green under hot reds, with gold and copper threads. Or, you could work everything around close colours in subtly different textures, weights and hues; for example all the reds through from orangey reds to blue-reds.

Styling
Slip skirts, handkerchief-style halter tops, asymmetrical hemlines, one layered over the other, are all suitable candidates for cool, shapely knits. Slits in the knitting reveal the next layer down. A must-have design feature! Wear over swimwear or soft, floaty Indian cottons, plain or printed voiles, embroidered viscose or silks to complement your summer wardrobe. Complete the look with ethnic-inspired necklaces, bracelets or earrings, or decorate the knitting in the same manner with, for example, brass tap washers obtainable from your local hardware store, or unusual buttons and beads.

Knitting Techniques
Fully fashioned shaping techniques are a must for sophisticated and stylish knitwear where garment shape, form and stitch patterns are integrated. It can be more time consuming than the standard methods, but to my mind it's worth the extra effort to give your knitting that extra added value, and to show off your craft skills. Look at some of the beautiful 2 and 3ply hand knits from the 1930's period. I often draw on these as a source of inspiration for shapely machine knitting. Here we look at a development of the double bed, fully fashioned shaping methods covered in the *Style File* on pages 12-14, but this time using single bed knitting techniques. Raglan shaping and long vertical darts get the treatment. Other techniques used below include vertical and horizontal, patchwork-style knitting and waste yarn techniques or partial knitting for slits and shape. The purl and knit face of stocking stitch is sometimes combined in the same swatch to exploit the way that light reflects differently from each side of the same fabric.

The samples
Knitted on the Brother Electronic KH970 on manual setting, all the samples shown below are single bed work and are knitted in 1 strand of Yeoman Yarns Janiero, shade Poppy at MT3, unless otherwise stated. Janiero was chosen because of its good draping qualities.

Sample 1
Eyelets and raglan shaping combine the decorative and the functional for the single bed knitting machine. You will need an adjustable multi-pronged transfer tool and a one eyed transfer tool. You can decide for yourselves on the positioning of the eyelets in relationship to the outer edge of the raglan. In this example the eyelet is always positioned over needle 7, counting from the outer edge (see needle diagram where X = WP and O = NWP). The right hand side of the swatch is a mirror image of the left hand side. Reverse all shapings so that the decreases are paired as shown in the first example below.

Work in the following order. Firstly make the eyelet by moving the stitch on the needle marked 7 to needle 8 with the one eyed transfer tool. Push the empty needle back down into working position. Next transfer the stitch from needle 6 onto needle 5. Push this empty needle back down into working position. Then using the multi-pronged tool move stitches 1-5 simultaneously one needle inwards. Push the end needle on the outer most edge to non working position. Knit as many rows as required between shapings and repeat the operation.

```
X X X X X X X etc  X X X X X X X X
1 2 3 4 5 6 7 8        8 7 6 5 4 3 2 1

X X X X X O O X
1 2 3 4 5 6 7 8

X X X X X O X
1 2 3 4 5 7 8

X X X X X X X
1 2 3 4 5 7 8   (8 sts become 7)
```

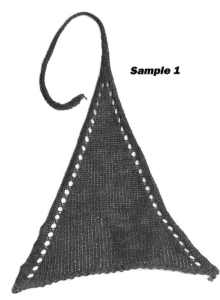

Sample 1

Sample 2

Sample 3

To complete the top section of this example work as follows once 13 sts remain.

```
X X X X X X X X X X X X
1 2 3 4 5 6   6 5 4 3 2 1
```

Transfer the stitch on needles 6 to needles 5 and shift stitches 1-5 one position inwards from both the left and the right hand sides (11 stitches remain).

```
X X X X X X X X X X
1 2 3 4 5   5 4 3 2 1
```

Transfer the stitch on needles 5 to needles 4 and shift stitches 1-4 one position inwards from both the left and the right hand sides (9 stitches remain).

```
X X X X X X X X
1 2 3 4   4 3 2 1
```

Transfer the stitch on needles 4 to needles 3 and shift stitches 1-3 one position inwards from both the left and the right hand sides (7 stitches remain).

```
X X X X X X
1 2 3   3 2 1
```

Transfer the stitch on needles 3 to needles 2 and shift stitches 1-2 one position inwards from both the left and the right hand sides (5 stitches remain). If you want to incorporate a built in shoulder strap continue knitting on these 5 stitches. Set the carriage to knit in one direction and slip in the other direction.
Note: If your shaping dictates that an

irregular number of rows are knitted between shapings, then you will need to carefully plan the positioning of the eyelets. They may not always take place on the same row as the shaping, see front neckline shaping of *Dancing Queen*.

Samples 2 & 3
Here, various methods of shaping are combined with purl facing slitted borders. Shaping techniques include decreasing a number of stitches evenly across the width of a row as you would in a yoke-style sweater, long vertical darts where the shaping takes place away from the outer most edges and partial knitted wedge shapes.

Knitting the slits
This is a favourite technique of mine, described in some detail in my first book for Batsford, *Pattern on the Knitting Machine*. To knit an example of a slitted border, cast on with waste yarn and knit several rows. Make a chain cast-on over alternate needles with either ribbon yarn or 3ply Cannele cotton (also by Yeoman). Knit 2 rows over all stitches. Thread up main yarn. Make a decorative border knitting 2 rows plain followed by 2 rows of handwrapping. Do the latter over alternate needles only. Finish this section on 2 rows plain knitting. Strip off on waste yarn and work as directed below. You can of course use holding position to achieve the same results although you will need to be careful not to catch the loose ends of yarn at the beginning and end of each strip in the underside of the sinker plate. The waste

yarn method gives you the option of every alternate strip knit-facing and every other alternate strip purl-facing. This is my preferred method of working. To make the slits using the waste yarn method, simply re-hang the first 10 stitches (for example) from either the left or right outer most edge. Knit 10 rows (for example) and strip off on waste yarn. Move on to the next 10 stitches and repeat the operation until all stitches have been knitted in this manner. Once you have knitted all stitches in this manner, re-hang all stitches back onto their equivalent needles. Knit several more rows of plain knit alternating with hand wrapping.

Sample 2
* Make a slitted border as described above. Strip off on waste yarn. Turn the knitting and re-hang the stitches as before. Knit 2 rows main colour. Set carriage to holding position. Push 5 needles (for example) into HP at opposite end to the carriage. Knit 2 rows. Repeat this operation until all needles are in HP. Knit 2 rows. * Strip off with waste yarn. Turn the knitting. Repeat from * to * once more. Continue to knit straight as required.

Sample 3
Cast on 70 stitches. Knit one repeat of the slitted border section, followed by a knit-facing wedge shaped section. Strip off with waste yarn. Re-hang stitches onto 50 needles, decreasing evenly across the whole row. Use the so-called Magic Formula to work this out. In this case you will need to double up stitches

Sample 4

Sample 5

on every 3rd needle 10 times and every 2nd needle 10 times. Knit 20 rows. This is the point where the vertical darts commence.

Vertical darts

To make a paired decrease using the fully fashioned method you will need to establish the positioning of the vertical dart. In this example, the decrease is always situated above needles 15 to the left and the right of the centre '0' on the needle bed. Here you will see two lines of vertical shapings parallel to each other with the outermost edge-stitches falling at an angle to the central straight panel (think of how a princess-style dress pattern works). To do this, you will need the multi-pronged and one eyed transfer tools. The working method is similar to that described in Sample 1. Counting from the left outermost edge

Janeiro Poppy, Citadella Fushia and Poppy, Brittany Sanguine, Cannele Raspberry, Texere stock similar gold braid

(1, 2 and so on) move the stitch on needle 14 back to needle 13, then shift all the remaining stitches one needle position inwards. This will fill in the empty 14th needle. Push empty needle 1 back into NWP. You have decreased 1 stitch. Repeat this operation on the right hand side. You have now decreased 2 stitches. Knit as many rows as required until the next shaping. In Sample 4, there are 4 rows between each set of decreases.

Decoration

To decorate, attach ready made gold braid (try Texere Yarns for similar), washers and gold floral motifs.

Sample 4

Make a shaped sample using the fully fashioned raglan technique as described in Sample 1, but omitting the eyelets. Cast on 60 stitches shaping every 4th row 20 times on one edge only. 4 sts remain. Add slitted borders by picking up the Raglan edge back onto the machine. The main section is knit-facing and the border purl-facing. To introduce an element of contrast, make the slitted borders in a contrasting yarn and/or colour.

Sample 5

A heavier weight swatch knitted in 2 strands of Janiero combining straight and shaped slits. Cast on 60 stitches. Knit approximately 10 rows. Hand wrap 1 row with Cannele cotton. Divide stitches into 3 equal sections (20 stitches in this example). Knit the centre strip straight for 20 rows. Decrease the left and right

edge strips by 1 stitch every 4th row, 5 times in total on their outer edges. Replace remaining 40 stitches onto equivalent needles. Continue to work in the same manner to complete the swatch. Decorate with buttons or similar.

Developing design ideas

Once you have completed a small group of samples, it helps to pin them onto a dress stand to assess how they hang in relationship to the body shape (especially when the emphasis is on shape and form). I quite often find that new ideas suggest themselves to me at this stage. The knitting takes on a completely different life when viewed in three dimensions. Sometimes intriguing results occur just because I've pinned swatches almost at random on the stand (maybe to store them while I'm working on something else). I will make quick sketches to refer to later, and end up re-arranging the swatches to see (for example) if the swatch that originally was destined as a skirt panel might work as part of a sleeve if turned on its side. I generally find that my best ideas develop over a few days.

REEF

SIDEWAYS KNITTING, CHEVRON STRIPES AND A WHOLE
LOT OF ATTITUDE!

Yeoman Yarns
Brittany 2ply 100% cotton in
shade 135, Spring Green (A).
Janeiro 3ply 50% viscose, 25%
linen, 25% acrylic in shade 30,
Tahiti (B). Citadella 4ply ribbon
100% polyamide in shade 7,
Cream (C)

**These instructions are written for
standard gauge machines with
ribber and plating feed**

Cropped top
Main body section
Work 2 pieces alike.
Push 60 Ns to WP. Using WY cast on
and K a few rows ending CAR. Using

PATTERN INFORMATION

Sizes
To suit bust small[medium:large]
Finished measurement across top, from
under arm to under arm seam over st st
52[60:68]cm
Crop top length to top of rib 21cm
Skirt seam 48[51:54]cm
Waist 92[102:112]cm — choose a
size larger to wear the skirt on hips
as shown.

Figures in square brackets [ ] refer to larger
sizes; where there is only one set of figures,
this applies to all sizes.

Materials
1 cone in each of A and B
1 x 50g ball in C
Waist length of elastic

Garment weight
For small size
Top approx 220g
Skirt approx 240g

Main tension
28 sts and 36 rows to 10cm measured over
patt* after light steaming. TD approximately
8 = MT
Tension must be matched exactly before
starting garment.

Note
Knit side is used as right side.
Measurements are those of finished garment
and should not be used to measure work on
machine.

Pattern note
Partial knit chevrons
* Using A and MT, K6 rows. Set carr for HP.
Push 3 Ns at opp end to carr into HP and
K1 row. Rep last row until all Ns are in HP.
Set carr so HP Ns will K and using B, K1
row. Transfer alt sts to adj Ns, leaving empty
Ns in NWP. C, K2 rows. Push Ns in NWP to
UWP. B, K1 row. CAR and set for HP. ** Push
all Ns to into HP except the 3 Ns nearest
carr. K back and forth on these 3 Ns. Push
the next 3 Ns into UWP and K2 rows. Cont
in this manner until you reach the centre 'O'
**. Break off yarn. Push all Ns to HP and
place CAL. Rep from ** to **. Set carr so
HP Ns will K.* Using B, K6 rows. Rep from *
to * but reversing the colour sequence, ie.
swopping A for B throughout. This sequence
is a complete patt rep.

Special note
The chevron pattern is knitted using the
partial knit setting. The cropped top is
sideways knitted.
*A and B are used 2 strand throughout and
C as a single end excepting the plated ribs
which are knitted in 1 strand each A plus
B. B is in rear of the plating feed and a to
the front.

MT and A, K6 rows. K 5[5.5:6] rep of the chevron patt (see patt note). A, K6 rows and WK.

Interim make up
Measure 26[30:34]cm from top armhole edge inwards for shoulder seam on both L and R. Join shoulder seam. Press seam.
Work cuff before continuing.
Measure 15cm from bottom armhole edge inwards for underarm seam. Join underarm seam. Press seam.

Cuffs
Work 2 alike.
With RB in WP in position, push 87 Ns on MB and corresponding Ns on RB to WP. Pitch H. Arrange Ns for a 2 x 1 rib cast on. Thread up plating feed, cast on and K3 tubular rows. Rack 1 position to L and transfer L edge st to MB. T3/3 K10[12:14] rows, T4/4 K30 rows.
T 5/5 K10[12:14] rows. Transfer sts to MB.
Join cuff
With wrong sides of knitting facing, hook up sts from first row above WY on main body section, doubling up on every 3rd N. Pull one set of sts through the other and cast off.

Welts
Work 2 alike.
With RB in position, push 133[151:171] Ns on MB and corresponding Ns on RB to WP. Pitch H. Arrange Ns for a 2 x 1 rib cast on. Thread up plating feed, cast on and K3 tubular rows. Rack 1 position to L and transfer L edge st to MB. T3/3 K10[12:14] rows. T4/4 K30 rows. T5/5 K10[12:14] rows. Transfer sts to MB.
Attach welt
With wrong sides of work facing, pick up loops from back or front main body section onto equivalent Ns. Pull one set of sts through the other and cast off.

Neckbands
Work 2 alike.
With RB in position, push 80 Ns on MB and corresponding Ns on RB to WP. Pitch H. Arrange Ns for a 2 x 1 rib cast on. Thread up plating feed, cast on and K3 tubular rows. Rack 1 position to L and transfer L edge st to MB. T3/3 K2 rows. T4/4 K6 rows. T5/5 K2 rows. Transfer sts to MB.

Attach neckband

With wrong sides of work facing, pick up loops from back or front main body section onto equivalent Ns. Pull one set of sts through the other and cast off.

To make up

Neaten ends. Join all ribs using mattress stitch.

Skirt

Skirt panel

Worked in 4 panels from the waist downwards.

Work 2 panels alike then a further 2 panels alike but swapping A and B throughout the chevron patt colour sequence, excepting the pointed hemline sections which are all knitted in B.

Push 66[72:78] sts to WP. Using WY cast on and K a few rows ending CAR. Using MT and A K6 rows. K3 full rep of chevron patt (see patt note).

Pointed hemline

Set carr to HP. Push 3 Ns at opp end to carr into HP and using B K1 row. Cont in this manner until all Ns are in HP. Set carr so HP Ns will K and K1 row. Transfer every alt st to adj N, leaving empty Ns in WP. K2 rows and cast off.

Interim make up

Neaten all ends. Block and press following the measurement diagram. Join centre back and centre front seams using mattress stitch. Press seam.

Waist band

Work 2 pieces alike.

Push 130[142:154] Ns to WP and pick up sts from back or front skirt top onto equivalent Ns, making sure to double up sts at centre '0'. Using A and MT K1 row. B K10 rows. A and MT+2, K2 rows. B and MT, K10 rows. A K1 row. Pick up sts from below first row of waistband onto equivalent Ns. Pull one st through the other and cast off.

To make up

Join side seams and waistband, leaving an opening to insert waist elastic. Stitch remainder of opening.

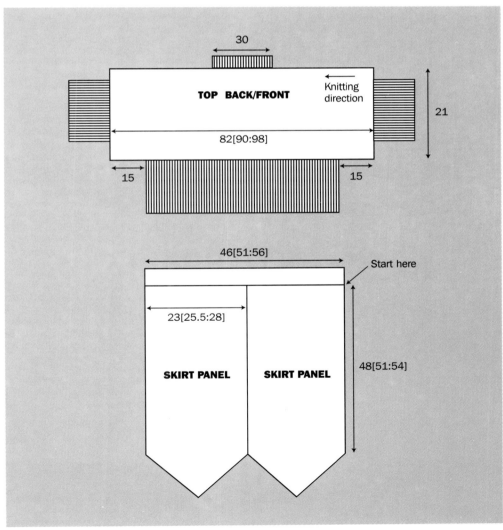

In this *Style File*, we explore alternative design ideas that develop my beachwear pattern *Reef*. This is firstly to encourage you to customise the pattern as written, and secondly to show you how easy it is to create a range of outfits, given a common starting point, by making small modifications to the shape, or by changing the stitch pattern, yarns, colourway or the decoration.

Yarns and Colours

Inspiration for the original outfit was an eclectic mix of Wild West meets Jungle Jane, with the South Seas and tropical colours thrown in for good measure, whilst keeping the beach in mind! Alternative colour stories might include faded denim blues, multi-coloured rainbow shades, sandy browns and tans, or white on white.

For the blue colour story, consider Yeoman Yarns 1ply and 4ply Wash and Fade Indigo Blue range, in three different tones of blue, alongside shades Jeans (167) and Denim (166) in Brittany 2ply, Oxford Blue Janeiro and Citadella ribbon in shade 4 Navy.

Yarns that give a close match to the sandy browns, cocoa and tan can also be found on the Yeoman shade cards. Look at Citadella ribbon shade 10 in Chocolate, Janeiro in Tobacco (shade 7) and Sienna (shade 6) or 2ply Brittany cotton in Brick (shade 110) or Cafe (shade 111).

For the rainbow colours which fade one into the other, look for space-dyed yarns, or dye your own using the dip-dye method. Texere Yarns carry a good range of undyed yarns in silk, cotton and Viscose, along with dye kits for home dyeing natural fibres. Texere also sell Indigo dye kits which contain synthetic Indigo chemicals and equipment if you want something different.

For the white-on-white look you could use the undyed yarns noted above from Texere. Alternatively, consider shades 100 White and 101 Off White in Yeoman 2ply Brittany Cotton, shades Cream (1) and White (11) in Janeiro and White (3) or Cream (7) in Citadella ribbon.

Techniques and knitting know-how

To knit the large chevron designs shown on some of the designs over the page, you could choose any of the following knitting techniques: partial knitting, intarsia, summer jacquards — Pfaff E6000 knitting technique whereby stitches knitted on the front bed are released after every decrease and cast off — standard double bed Jacquard using lightweight yarns or cut-and-sew. Each technique has different characteristics and properties which need to be taken into consideration at the design stage. For example, Intarsia is time consuming but would be best suited to complex or asymmetrical chevron patterns, whereas partial knitting is speedier than the latter and good for bold, repetitive shapes. Both techniques could be knitted sideways or lengthways, and be purl or knit facing.

Summer Jacquards have a different handle to stocking stitch, and tend to produce a more blurred design than intarsia and partial knitting. Standard, double-bed jacquard generally has less drape than the latter, but would work for the body section of the cropped top or the skirt although you would not be able to work in rows of eyelets which follow the peaks and troughs of the chevron pattern as you could with partial knitting.

Cut-and-sew techniques allow you to mix stitch patterns that are normally impossible to knit side by side; for example a textured, single tuck stitch pattern next to a slip stitch pattern. When patching different knitting techniques together, make sure they are compatible in terms of weight, elasticity and tension.

To complement the bold patterns, you could use a small-scale texture in single or double bed knitting techniques, such as racking patterns, slip or tuck stitch.

BEACH BABE!

VARIATIONS ON A THEME; DIFFERENT WAYS TO CHEVRON HEAVEN AND A COLOURWAY FOR EVERYONE

Developing your own styles

To develop the basic garment shape, use the outline diagrams and measurements from my pattern and relate them to your own vital statistics, as a starting point to developing your own styles. Remember, if you alter one part of the pattern make sure that the adjacent pattern pieces are aligned correctly.

If you are developing new stitch patterns, or working a different yarn or tension to the one for which the original pattern was written, you will need to make tension swatches first and then re-calculate rows and stitches for each new variation.

And my favourite hobby horse — save yourself time and brain space by simply drawing out the garment pattern shapes onto your charting device/Knit leader. Make the appropriate tension swatch in the stitch pattern, tension and new yarn before knitting off your own variation on a theme. It couldn't be easier!

Design ideas

The illustrations take my original idea for the beach outfit as a point of departure, showing how one idea can lead to another and another and another! To keep the mood of the collection, certain common elements have been retained and/or modified; the main stylistic features being the low slung skirts and the revealing cropped tops.

Design sheet 1

Short skirts in three different knitting techniques. From left to right partial knitted panels with multi-coloured double-bed slipstitch and sideways-knitted intarsia chevrons with beaded or knotted fringes. The skirts are worn with fitted, cropped cardigans with either a wide boat-neckline, or a 'must-have' revealing V-neck, all based on the pattern draft for the *Reef* cropped sweater.

Design sheet 2

Skirts of differing lengths with beaded and knotted fringes.

The centre design could be made up of cut and sew sections in textured knitting, and is worn with a racked rib, cropped top knitted from the waist upwards. The short sleeves are knitted as an integral part of the body section, with the cuffs and neckband attached separately.

The sweater design on the far left is similar in style, except for a ribbed yoke and a tie front which would be a continuation of the side seam. The ribbed yoke would need a couple of reductions in the number of stitches to ensure a good fit.

The sweater on the far right is similar to the published pattern, except for the fluted sleeves and the revealing slit under the bustline. Start the sleeves off on waste yarn above the fluted cuff. Knit the latter separately, gradually reducing the width of the cuff before attaching it to the main sleeve either by the fully fashioned shapings, or the yoke shaping method.

3

Design sheet 4

The final design sheet shows a development of some of the previous styles, but with added fringes. These can either be knitted as an integral part of the design or, for speed, bought in and stitched onto the outfit along the chevrons or sideways knitted stripes.

You will need to work with purl facing stocking stitch if you intend to add the fringing as an integral part of the knitting process.

If you have already knitted the pattern as written, why not try your hand at making a cropped cardigan to complement the skirt? Accessorise the outfits with tasseled belts or neck pieces, feathers, shells, beads or fringes.

4

Design sheet 3

Here the skirts are long and slim fitting, worked in four panels each the same shape using the partial knitting technique, or designed to be made patchwork-style by cut-and-sew methods. Deep ribbed hip yokes balance out the main panels of the skirts. Of particular interest is the short bolero-style cardigan. This could be knitted sideways using the yoke shaping technique to reduce the number of stitches in three stages, starting from the centre front or centre back and knitted downwards to the cuff. The front and back bodice section is knitted as one, the left and right sections are knitted separately, then joined together down the centre back and along the underarm. The curvilinear shape of the bolero reflects the curved yoke of the skirt.

Crystal

Stunning shaped halterneck dress and gloves decorated with beading, slits and knitted tabs

Texere twisted floss in light (A) 4ply ribbon in Ecru (B), Vision DK ribbon yarn in white (C), Vision in Ecru (D), Ripple Floss light (E2).

Empress Mills 60's
100% white sewing cotton (E1), beading thread in white (F), Empress Mills 7/16's 100% soft white cotton (G) and knitting elastic in white (H). E1 and E2 are threaded up together through tension assembly.

These instructions are written for standard gauge punchcard or electronic machines

Sizes
To suit dress size small and medium
Finished measurement 88[94]cm
Length centre back to hem approx 113cm
Length centre front measured from top of V neckline to hem approx 138cm (dependant upon how short straps are tied).
Please note that the fabric will stretch when hung in storage and in wear, so adjust length accordingly. For small adjustments you can knit a few less rows on the main border pattern (Section A). For more substantial alterations to length then you can omit a complete section from beginning to end of a partial knit section and its equivalent amount on the side panels so that side and centre panels match in length. Remember also to adjust the number of rows between dec on the side panels so that you still end up with the number of sts stated in the pattern. If you knit less rows then the dec will come closer together.
Figures in square brackets [ ] refer to larger sizes; where there is only one set of figures, this applies to all sizes.

Materials
500g in A
100g in each of B, C and D.
1 spool E1 and 100g E2
2 small reels F
1 x 50g cop in G
1 x small bobbin in H.
Small metal crochet hook for beading.
Good quantity of small beads. I used transparent glass beads. You do not necessarily need to use the same style of bead throughout.
Access to a blocking board.

Garment weight
Medium size approx 520g
Gloves approx 50g

Main tension
29 sts and 39 rows to 10cm, measured over st st using A after light blocking and steam pressing (TD approx 6 = MT).
Tension must be matched exactly before starting garment.

Note
Purl side is used as right side. Measurements given are those of finished garment and should not be used to measure work on the machine.

Special notes
Beading technique
You will need a small metal crochet hook which will fit through the hole of the beads. Beading thread is used on the row before and after setting in the beads for strength.

Working method
Make an eyelet at every 4th N. Push the empty N back into WP and K1 row in beading thread. Hook the bead onto the stem of the crochet hook. Next insert the crochet hook under the bar of yarn formed above the empty N, taking it off the N and pulling it through the bead. Using the one eyed transfer tool, transfer the loop of thread on the crochet hook onto the empty N. Do this all the way along the row. K a further row with beading thread. You may find that some of the beads get stuck in between the gate pegs. Carefully push them forward with the end of a transfer tool.
To work this technique efficiently put enough beads for each row into the lid of a jam jar or similar. You should be able to pick them straight out from there with the crochet hook.

Knitting the beaded tabs
Push 15 Ns to WP. Using WY cast on and K several rows ending CAR. Working from L and using B, work a chain cast on. Do not thread B through main tension assembly as you will continue with this yarn for the main knitweave patt. Leave attached.
RC000. Change to F and MT. K1 row from L to R. Make eyelets on every 3rd N. Push empty N back to WP. K1 row. Insert beads over eyelets as working method note. K1 row. Set machine to select Ns using patt A and using A K1 row. Set machine for knitweave. K26 rows in patt using B as weaving yarn. RC shows 30. WK.

Partial knitting
The centre back and front panels are knitted in partial knitting technique with alternating purl or knit faces as right side. Use WY to turn the knitting where indicated in the patt and see Diag 1. Note that it is easier to turn the knit facing panels, after the partial knitting, if you knit the first row of the decoration before turning the work.

Pattern note
Patt A is basic birds-eye patt (usually Card 1 from basic set).

Back and front border pattern
Work 2 pieces alike.
Prepare 26[28] tabs as given in notes and finish on WY.
Push 190[200] Ns to WP. Hook up 13[14] tabs onto these Ns, doubling up sts every 28[20] Ns. Attach claw weight to each tab (clothes pegs will work if you run out of claw weights!).
** RC000. K2 rows in G, selecting Ns on the second row. Using C, hand wrap selected Ns. It is easier to do this if you push the selected Ns to HP. K2 rows E selecting Ns on second row. Hand wrap selected Ns in C. K2 rows E. RC6. Make an eyelet on every 4th N. Push empty Ns back into WP. K1 row F. Attach beads over eyelets. K2 rows F. RC9. K1 row A selecting Ns. Hand wrap selected Ns with B. K1 row F. Make eyelets on every 4th N and push empty Ns back into WP. K1 row F. Attach beads as before. K2 rows F. RC14. * K2 rows E, selecting Ns on second row. Using C hand wrap selected Ns *. Repeat from * to * twice in all. RC18. K2 rows G and WK**.

Slitted section
Push 170[180] Ns to WP. Replace sts from bottom section, doubling up every 8th N 10[0] times and every 9th N, 10[20] times K2 rows G. WK. Working from L to R, pick up first group of 10 sts and knit as for bottom tabs excepting that you only K until RC shows 20. Rep this operation across all sts.

Top border section
Re-hang all 170[180] sts and repeat from ** to ** as before except that C replaces D and vice versa and strip off sts onto three separate sections of WY.
Small size only: side panels are each 55 sts and centre panel 60 sts.
Medium size only: All panels are 60 sts wide.

Centre front panel
Knit and purl facing. Refer to Diag 1 to check orientation of knitting.
Push 62 Ns into WP. With purl side facing knitter, hook up centre 60 sts from border. Inc 1 st each edge for seam allowance.

Section B
Purl facing. See Diag 1. RC000. * Using A and MT, K30 rows. RC30. Set carr for HP. At the opposite end to carr, push 3 Ns into HP and K1 row. Rep this operation 20 times in all. 2 sts rem. RC50 *.
** To knit decorative stripe cancel HP

K2 rows G. Using D 'e' wrap over alt Ns. K1 row E. Make eyelets on every 4th N. K1 row F. Attach beads. K1 row F. K2 rows E and 'e' wrap D over alt Ns. K1 row E. K1 row G. RC 59. K1 row G. RC 60 **. WK. Turn knitting and re-hang sts onto equivalent Ns.

Section C
Knit facing. *** Lock RC. CAL. Set carr for HP. Push all Ns to R and all Ns to L of centre 0 into HP except 3 Ns nearest the carr. K2 rows. Push 3 (more) Ns to UWP and K2 rows. Cont in this manner until all Ns to L of centre 0 are back in WP. Push these Ns back to HP and rep operation on R ***.
Restart RC. K30 rows A. RC90. Rep from * to *. RC110. K first row of decoration. RC111. WK. Turn knitting. Repeat from ** to ** but omitting first row of patt. RC120.

Section D
Purl facing. Lock row counter. Rep from *** to ***. Restart RC. K30 rows A. RC150. Rep from * to *. RC170. WK. Turn knitting. Rep from ** to ** . RC 180. WK. Turn knitting.

Section E and F
Follow Diag 1 for section E which is knit facing and section F which is purl facing. RC300.

Section G
K30 rows A. WK.

Centre back panel
Knit and purl facing. Work as given for centre front until RC shows 300. WK. Re-hang sts doubling up on every 5th N. K until RC shows 320 and WK.

Side front panels
Purl facing throughout. Knit a L and a R side front panel, reversing all shapings for the latter.
Push 57[62] Ns to WP. With purl side facing knitter, pick up 55[60] sts from border. Inc 1 st each edge (for seam allowance). Follow the instructions below for patt details and at the same time dec 1 st on side seam every 8 rows 32 times in all. RC256. K (straight) until RC shows 264. Inc 1 st every 8 rows 9 times in all. RC328. K until RC shows 330.

Yarn and stitch panel
RC000. Using MT and A. K30 rows. * To knit decorative stripe. K2 rows G and 'e' wrap D over alt Ns. K1 row E. Make eyelets on every 4th N. K1 row F. Attach beads. K1 row F. K2 rows E and 'e' wrap D over alt Ns. K1 row E. K2 rows G. * RC40. Using MT and A. K50 rows. RC 90. Rep from * to *. RC100. Rep the last 60 rows 4 times in all. RC 280. **K50 rows. RC shows 330. WK.

Side back panels
Purl facing throughout. Knit a L and a R side back panel, reversing all shapings for the latter.
Follow patt for front side panels until **.

RC280. K40 rows. RC shows 320. WK.
Back bodice
With wrong sides facing the knitter pick up rem sts from centre back panel, and L and R side fronts doubling up on every 10th N. 106[116] sts. T4 K10 rows in A, K2 rows of knitting elastic and 10 rows A. Make a hem and cast off.
For a tighter fit across the back you could additionally dec 1 st both ends first 10 rows of hem rows . 86[96] sts rem. Inc 1 st both ends foll 10 rows 106[116] sts. (This is the working method on sample garment shown).

Front bodice and halter neckline
Push 124[134] Ns into WP. With right side facing knitter, pick up sts from L side panel, centre front panel and R side panel.
Shape armhole
RC000. Cast off 6[7] sts beg next 2 rows. 112 [120] sts. Cast off 3[4] sts beg next 2 rows. 106[112] sts. Cast off 1[2] sts beg next 2 rows. Dec 1 st beg next 4 rows. RC shows 10. 100[104] sts.
Shape neck
WK. Push 50[52] Ns to WP and pick up sts from L side only. Use ff shaping technique to shape the armhole edge and the V neck thus:
Armhole edge: Dec 1 st every alt row 7 times in all. RC14. Dec 1 st every 4 rows 5 times in all. RC 34. K (straight) until RC shows 85. Dec 1 st every 4 rows 12 times in all. RC133.
'V' neckline: At the same time dec 1 st every 3 rows 25 times in all. K10 rows. RC shows 85. Inc 1 st every 4 rows 12 times in all. RC shows 133. 13[15] sts rem. Knit straight for desired length of

strap. Sample garment was an additional 30 rows. Cast off.

To make up
Neaten all ends. Pin out onto blocking board following the measurement diagram and with reverse of garment facing knitter. You will need to pin out each individual tab on the bottom section. Cover with cloth and gently steam press. Wait until completely dry before removing from the board. Viscose is very heavy when wet and creases badly if not left to dry properly. You may find that you will need to work in sections dependant upon length of board. If this is the case then do the bottom border first and then the main section of the dress.
Tack all the long seams together and leave on dress stand overnight to allow for any drop in the length. Mattress stitch side and centre front seams. Do the same to the back. Steam press these seams in the manner described above prior to making up side seams.
Give a final press. Allow to dry thoroughly. Store flat wrapped in tissue paper.

Gloves
To work the blocks of knitweave on the gloves you will need a separate ball of yarn for each triangle, which is used as weaving yarn over Ns programmed/selected into upper working position.
Patt A is standard Birds Eye (as for dress) Patt B is 283 from Brother Stitchworld 2 and is used on reverse setting (punchcard alternative given).

Knit a L and a R glove commencing at upper arm thus.
Section A
Push 78 Ns into WP and cast on with WY. K several rows. Change to A and MT4.

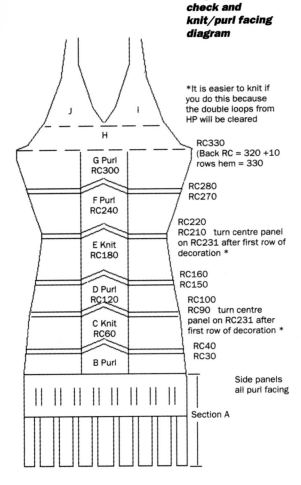

Diagram 1 Row check and knit/purl facing diagram

*It is easier to knit if you do this because the double loops from HP will be cleared

J   I

H

G Purl
RC300

F Purl
RC240

E Knit
RC180

D Purl
RC120

C Knit
RC60

B Purl

RC330
(Back RC = 320 +10 rows hem = 330

RC280
RC270

RC220
RC210   turn centre panel on RC231 after first row of decoration *

RC160
RC150

RC100
RC90   turn centre panel on RC231 after first row of decoration *

RC40
RC30

Side panels all purl facing

Section A

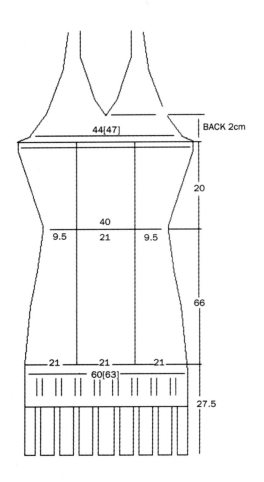

44[47]

BACK 2cm

20

40

9.5   21   9.5

66

21   21   21

60[63]

27.5

RC000. K2 rows A. K2 rows K and 'e' wrap alt Ns with D. K2 rows K. RC 6. Using D 'e' wrap alt Ns. K2 rows each K and E, making eyelets as for dress when RC shows 9. RC 10. K1 row F. Attach beads. K1 row F. RC12. K2 rows each E and K. RC 16. Using C 'e' wrap alt Ns. K2 rows K. RC18. Using C 'e' wrap alt Ns. K2 rows A. RC 20.
Patt B. K1 row to select Ns. RC21. Knitweave 3 complete triangle patts, alternating C and D across the row as described above. RC shows 51. K1 row G. Using C 'e' wrap alt Ns. K1 row each E and F, making eyelets on RC 53 as before. RC54. Attach beads. K1 row each F and E. RC56. K2 rows K. Using C 'e' wrap alt Ns. K2 rows A. RC60. WK.
Push 63 Ns into WP. Replace sts doubling up on every 4th N 15 times in all. K1 row A and 'e' wrap alt Ns with D. K1 row A and WK.

Section B
Knitweave strips: Every alt strip is 10 sts and every other alt strip is 11 sts. Knitweave 20 rows for each individual strip as for tabs, but using B as weaving yarn. WK.

Section C
Push 48 Ns into WP. Replace sts doubling up on every 3rd N 15 times in all.
RC000. K2 rows E and 'e' wrap every alt N with C. K4 rows K and 'e' wrap every alt N with C. K2 rows E and 10 rows K. RC18. Using D 'e' wrap every alt N. K2 rows E. RC20. Using D, 'e' wrap every alt N. K6 rows K. RC26. Using C, 'e' wrap alt Ns. K 10 rows K. RC36. * Using D, 'e' wrap alt Ns*. K2 rows E. RC38.

Section D (increasing for the thumb)
RC000. Inc 2 sts ff every 5 rows 10 times in all. Start the increases on the L and R of the central 3 sts and then cont inc outwards in like manner until RC shows 50. 69 sts. At the same time 'e' wrap alt Ns with C when RC shows 22.

Section E (the thumb)
K2 rows A. Divide knitting into 3 sections each 23 sts. Using WY strip off 23 sts at L and R. 23 sts rem. Using E cast on 3 sts beg next 2 rows. 29 sts rem. Using D 'e' wrap alt Ns. K1 row E. RC3. K7 rows K. RC10. K1 row E and 'e' wrap alt Ns. K2 rows. E. K1 row A. RC14. Cast off.

Section F (hand section)
Replace 23 sts from below WY on the L, pick up 3 cast on sts from L of thumb and then the next 3 cast on sts from R making sure that the thumb is not twisted. Replace 23 sts from R as for L. 52 sts. * Using

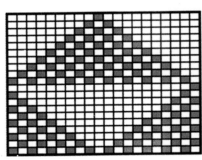

Patt 283 Stitchworld 20sts x 20rows Courtesy of Brother UK

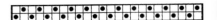

Birdseye pattern

Punchcard alternative for Stitchworld 283 24sts x 24rows

D 'e' wrap alt Ns. K2 rows K *. Rep from * to * twice in all. RC4. K1 row E and make eyelets as before. K1 row F. Attach beads. K1 row F. K2 rows E. RC9. Using C 'e' wrap alt Ns. K2 rows E. K1 row A. RC12. Cast off.

To make up
Neaten all ends and carefully block and press taking care not to let the iron touch the knitting. Use a pressing cloth as a barrier.

Hem for upper arm
Push 60 Ns to WP. Replace sts from below WY onto Ns in WP, doubling up on every 4th N. T4, K10 rows A. Using MT * 'e' wrap knitting elastic over alt Ns and K1 row with A *. Rep from * to * twice. T4 K10 rows A. Hook up first row of hem sts. K1 row A and cast off. Steam press to tighten elastic, taking care not to let iron touch knitting.

Joining underarm seam and attaching tabs.
Push 10 Ns into WP. Pick up 10 loops from one side seam with wrong side facing knitter. Pick up 10 loops from the other side seam with right side facing knitter and onto same Ns as before. 2 loops on each N.
RC000. Using A. Set machine to select Ns using patt A and K1 row. Set machine for knitweave. K20 rows patt using B or C as weaving yarn on alt tabs. RC20. Cast off.

Adapting Patterns

'I'm normal!'

A look at so-called 'non-standard' sizes

Finally, the British fashion industry is waking up to the fact that there is a market for stylish, fashionable and glamorous clothing in size 14 and above. A recent survey came to the conclusion that the average dress size in the UK is now a 14, which is reflected in their new sizing range. It also reported that since the 1920s the average British woman has added approximately 1.25cm to her bust, 2.5cm to her waist and just under 2cm across the hips about every 10 years. This is hopefully a sign of a more inclusive approach towards issues of size across the whole spectrum of body shapes that will encourage designers, stores and the media to accept and work with this diversity.

Whatever our size and shape be it curvilinear, rectangular or pear shaped, the aim of good clothing design should be to accentuate the positive attributes of the wearer and help them feel good about themselves.

In the following pages we will focus on knitting a perfect fit for real women with the emphasis on non-standard figures. Initially, we will look at issues of size and shape generally. How can you assess your body shape and take those vital measurements so you can adapt existing patterns for a customised fit?

Finally, potential design ideas are explored, particularly relating to more structured patterns such as the panelled jacket pattern, *Dizzy*.

Just what is a generous size 14?

During the late 1970s I was designing and making knitwear for stores in the UK and the USA, but also dealing directly with the general public. I would design and knit to order from a range of my own designs, and I made the mistake initially (through inexperience) of simply asking my customers for their dress size rather than taking personalised measurements. The reality didn't always match the information given (what is a generous size 14?).

My experience showed me that few people are an exact match to industry-standard sizes, or of 'perfect' proportion. To complicate matters, a size 14 in one store may not be the same elsewhere; some being more or less generously cut than others. UK sizes are usually a size smaller than those of the

USA, so a USA size 12 is about the equivalent of a UK size 14. Also, many people might be approximately size 14 on top and a size 16 on the bottom. To add to this confusion, sizing in the ready-to-wear industry may not be the same as that for dressmaking patterns; the latter sometimes being one, or even two, dress sizes different. I came across a very interesting article in *Threads* magazine on this subject (*A Look at Garment Sizing*) which explores the links between ready-to-wear sizes and dress pattern sizes. The key is to work from actual body measurements, and to get to know the underlying structure of your body really well, while developing an awareness of the relative measurements of one body part against another. It cannot be emphasised enough that taking accurate body measurements will always help you to get a great fit.

It's all relative

It does take a certain amount of courage to assess our own body shape, but doing this will make it easier to find clothing that flatters (if not flattens!) the wearer by emphasising their strong points, and so help them feel good about themselves. Of course, honesty and a realistic assessment of your body shape and size are vital. There is nothing worse than making clothing a size too small, or too big, and then hoping to look good in it, when realistically the next size up or down would be more flattering. Areas of the body are all relative in size, shape and proportion and vary from one person to another. This is why standard size garments do not always give a perfect fit; for example you might have a full bust compared with the rest of your body measurements; or a long back balance (usually due to a rounded back) and a shorter front balance compared with a set of industry-standard measurements. Generally, women's bodies can be categorised as; pear-shaped, rounded, rectangular or a combination of these elements.

From this, you will be able to see whether you have square shoulders and a wide back in comparison to, say, your hips; or a long back or large bust in comparison to shoulder or waist size. You might be short or long waisted, or your shoulders might be wider or narrower than your hips. The important element, as already noted, is the

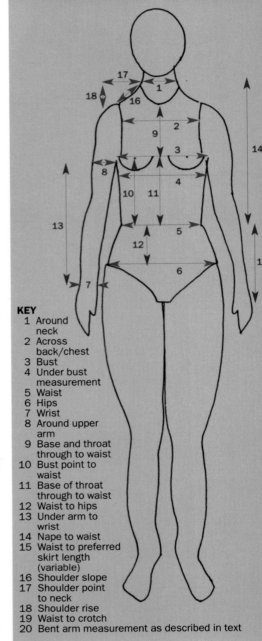

KEY
1 Around neck
2 Across back/chest
3 Bust
4 Under bust measurement
5 Waist
6 Hips
7 Wrist
8 Around upper arm
9 Base and throat through to waist
10 Bust point to waist
11 Base of throat through to waist
12 Waist to hips
13 Under arm to wrist
14 Nape to waist
15 Waist to preferred skirt length (variable)
16 Shoulder slope
17 Shoulder point to neck
18 Shoulder rise
19 Waist to crotch
20 Bent arm measurement as described in text

Measurement chart
Height (purple lines)   Girth (red lines)

relationship of one area of the body to another. From my own experience I know that my measurement from waist to hip is shorter than standard, which in practice means that fitted trouser and skirt waistbands on ready-to-wear clothing generally end up sitting too close to my bust.

Getting down to basics

If you can bear to do it, get a trusted friend to photograph you from the front, back and side in close fitting undergarments, or leotard and tights. Trace an outline drawing of your body from the photos, then superimpose the most appropriate geometric shapes from my sketches over the outline to give an

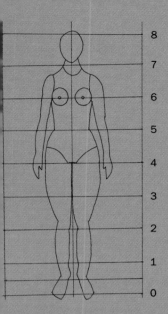

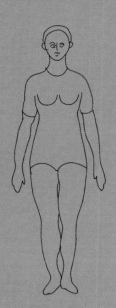

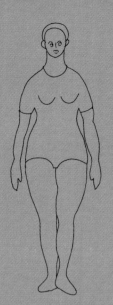

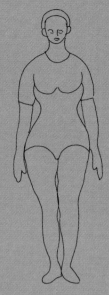

Average proportion of the female figure. 7½ heads

Average height. Rectangular figure shape. Very little difference between hip and bust measurement. eg. bust 98cm Hip 100cm

Average height. Triangular pear shaped figure. Small bust and prominent hips. Approx 14cm difference between hip and bust eg. bust 94cm, hips 108cm

Average height. Curvy hour glass figure shape. About 8cm difference between hip and bust measurement eg. full rounded bust 96cm, hips 104cm

overview of your own body shape. Compare your own body shape and proportions with those illustrated. The illustration shows that the average proportion of the female figure is approximately seven and a half heads high; that is, the head fits into the height of the body seven and a half times, while the head measurement is the same ratio of the whole measurement as is the waist-to-hip measurement or the bust-point-to-waist measurement.

Taking measurements

Always use another person to take your measurements, even if you are only measuring up for a sweater. Then take all the important measurements shown in the illustration. They can be used to cross reference one measurement against another so helping you to see the relationship between areas of the body. Keep a record for future use, particularly if you aim to construct your basic pattern block as a starting point for your own design ideas.

Wear close-fitting, plain clothing as above. Stand normally and resist the temptation to breathe in! It is usual to take girth measurements quite tightly because this is a record of your body size, not the size of garments, which will have different ease allowances depending on the styling. You will notice that the published patterns in the magazine usually give a bust size measurement; for example 86 or 91cm, and also a finished measurement; for example 96cm, depending upon the amount of ease demanded by a particular style. Minimum ease should generally be no less than 5cm even for close fitting styles (unless, for example, you are working with body hugging, ribbed fabrics).

If you take more than one hip measurement, make a note of how far down from the waist you have taken it. Also with regard to full-length sleeve measurements: take the arm length measurement with the arm bent, measured from the shoulder tip, around the back of the elbow, bringing the tape measure forward to just below the wrist bone. Take the underarm measurement as a double check.

Starting from scratch

You might eventually want to draft a basic pattern block based upon your own measurements from which you can then develop your own styles. It really is worth putting in this ground work to ensure a perfect fit at all times; but if you have never tackled this before, I would recommend that, at first, you try drafting a basic block from standard measurements. Book references on pattern cutting, which usually include a set of industry standard size charts, are given at the end of this article if you are interested in doing just that. If you are a dressmaker as well as a knitter, you may already possess a multi-size master pattern to work from; but do bear in mind that knitted fabrics are usually more accommodating to the curves of the body than woven materials.

References

Pattern Cutting books

Nicely Knit Lines: Professional Pattern Drafting for Machine Knitters
by Mary Louise Norman, Published by Nicely Knit, 1310 Clermont St., Denver, Colorado 80220 - 2440.
This is an invaluable source of reference on pattern cutting plus it was written specifically for machine knitters. It is probably out of print but try the sources at the end of this article.

Metric Pattern Cutting
by Winifred Aldrich, ISBN 0 263 061191
This a straight forward and informative text on all aspects of pattern cutting.

Pattern Cutting and Making Up: The Professional Approach
By Martin Shoben and Janet Ward, Heinemann Professional Publishing Ltd. ISBN 0 434 91836 9

Threads
Articles from *Threads* magazine, such as a series on *Fitting Your figure or Fitting Solutions*, are available as compilations from R.D. Franks see below. *Threads* is an American publication with 6 issues per year.

Where to buy

Internet

Amazon.co.uk
The amazing internet book phenomena. (They even had one of my books last time I looked! Ruth)
www.fjwarnes.u-net.com
(Good stocks but quite expensive when compared with the stock I have found in other second hand book shops, however if you are not near a good secondhand book store then it could be worth the extra if they have what you want. Editor of *Machine Knitting News*)

Book shops
R.D. Franks Ltd, Kent House, Market Place off Great Titchfield St, Oxford Circus, London W1N 8EJ
Stockists of an excellent range of fashion/ textile publications for the profession with mail order facilities, Tel 0171 636 1244 Fax 0171 436 4904 email R.D.Franks @BTinternet.com

Knit to fit
part 1

We examined issues of sizing, with particular reference to non-standard body shapes. Here, common fitting problems are discussed and suitable solutions suggested to help you alter existing patterns, including those published in MKN, to your own measurements. Of course, if you have drafted a pattern block based on your own measurements from scratch, this should not be a problem. Small-scale deviations from standard measurements should cause no difficulty, given the accommodating and fluid nature of knitting; although the more fitted a style (for example a close-fitting, classic, set-in sleeve pattern) the more the need to refine existing measurements.

First things.... first
In order to learn how to manipulate pattern pieces for a perfect fit, you will need either access to a basic fitted bodice and sleeve block designed specifically for knitwear, or an existing classic set-in sleeve pattern similar to the shapes shown below. You may have been supplied with a basic set of patterns with your charting device. You will also need thin-ish paper (such as layout or pattern-drafting paper), scissors, pins, sticky tape, a ruler, set square and a pencil. If you are working from a full- or half-scale paper pattern, you might like to scale it down to practice with.
An easy working method is shown below. Draw a series of lines radiating out from the bottom corner as shown, making sure that the lines cross all the important style lines of your pattern. To make a 1/5th or 1/10th scale version, simply measure the length of each line, then divide the measurement by (for example) 5 or 10. Mark off the resulting measurements as shown in Fig 1. Connect the dots for a scaled-down version of your pattern piece. To scale up a small diagram you can do the reverse procedure, or enlarge the image on a photocopier.

Some common fitting problems
As already discussed, there are many different body sizes and shapes which deviate from the industry standard sizes. Before you attempt to alter a pattern, you should check whether it is a figure problem; e.g. a larger-than-average bust, broad shoulders or posture that is causing the fitting fault. Posture issues generally fall into three distinct categories: normal, upright or stooping. For example, a long front balance (see below) might be the result of an upright carriage, a large bust, or a combination of the two. Different corrections are needed in each instance.
Common fitting problems include:
- square shoulders and a wide back.
- sloping shoulders and a narrow back.
- longer or shorter-than-average back or front balance.
- low or high bust.
- large bust or a flat chest.

Other fitting problems include a large bust compared with shoulder and waist size, and shorter or longer hip-to-waist measurement. Do however remember that measurements are all relative to each other and so, for example, if you alter the armhole on the bodice block you will need to refine the measurements of the corresponding sleeve head.

Making alterations in length and width to published patterns
If you sew from ready made, paper patterns, you will be aware that there exist different points on the pattern where you can make simple alterations without causing problems to the fit. You can apply the same principles to published knitting patterns. You will need to make yourself a paper pattern to work on. Most alterations to the pattern involve either pinning and folding the paper to remove excess measurements, or cutting and spreading the original pattern to allow inlets to be made, and the insertion of additional strips of paper to accommodate the difference in measurements. To do this, make copies of the original pattern in a scale you feel happy working with. When you fold in a pattern, the outer edges will need re-drawing to give a smooth, continuous seam line.

Simple alterations
To narrow the back bodice, fold in a vertical tuck on the pattern from half way along the shoulder line to half way along the waist line (see Fig 1). To alter the front bodice use the same principle, except fold down to a third of the way along the waist line measured from the centre front (Fig 2). To widen, use the same reference points, cutting and opening out the pattern instead of folding in tucks. Make a paper inlet to fill the gap, then tape to the original pattern. Re-draw seam lines if necessary (Figs 3 and 4). To shorten or to lengthen the bodice block, make a tuck or an inlet across the pattern halfway between the waist and the bust line (Figs 5 and 6).

Altering the sleeve
The same principle can be applied to sleeves, but as always remember that if you alter the sleeve head then you will need to make corresponding

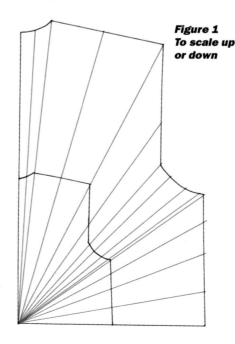

Figure 1
To scale up or down

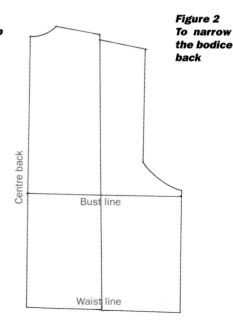

Figure 2
To narrow the bodice back

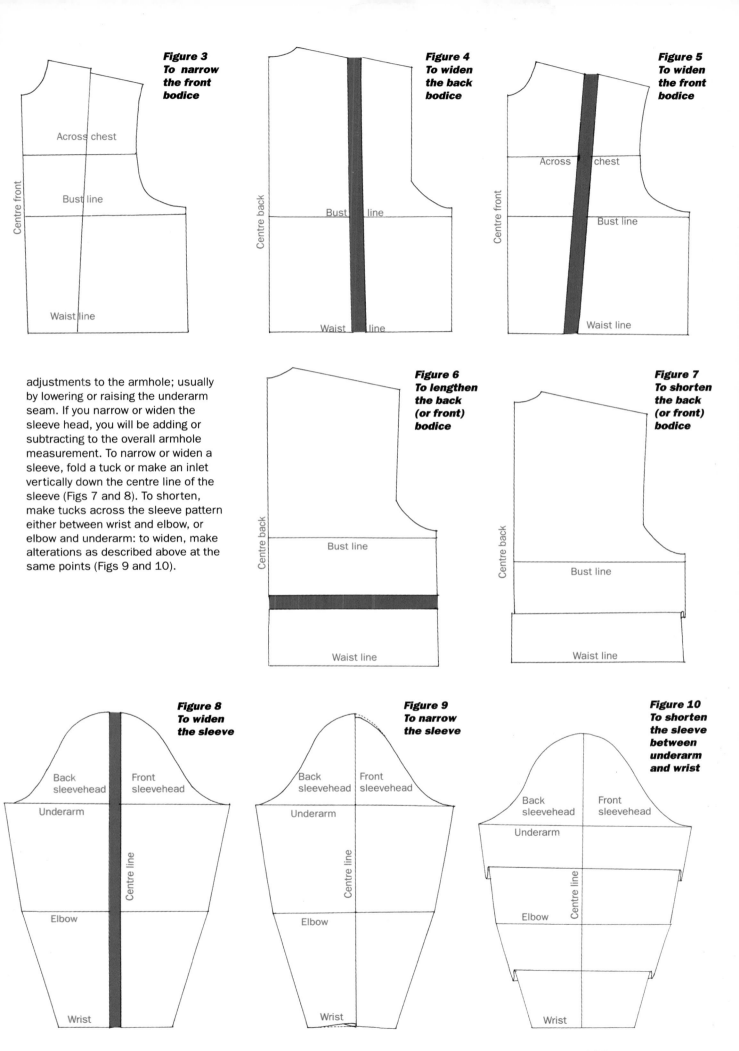

**Figure 3
To narrow
the front
bodice**

Across chest

Bust line

Centre front

Waist line

**Figure 4
To widen
the back
bodice**

Centre back

Bust line

Waist line

**Figure 5
To widen
the front
bodice**

Across chest

Bust line

Centre front

Waist line

adjustments to the armhole; usually
by lowering or raising the underarm
seam. If you narrow or widen the
sleeve head, you will be adding or
subtracting to the overall armhole
measurement. To narrow or widen a
sleeve, fold a tuck or make an inlet
vertically down the centre line of the
sleeve (Figs 7 and 8). To shorten,
make tucks across the sleeve pattern
either between wrist and elbow, or
elbow and underarm: to widen, make
alterations as described above at the
same points (Figs 9 and 10).

**Figure 6
To lengthen
the back
(or front)
bodice**

Centre back

Bust line

Waist line

**Figure 7
To shorten
the back
(or front)
bodice**

Centre back

Bust line

Waist line

**Figure 8
To widen
the sleeve**

Back
sleevehead

Front
sleevehead

Underarm

Centre line

Elbow

Wrist

**Figure 9
To narrow
the sleeve**

Back
sleevehead

Front
sleevehead

Underarm

Centre line

Elbow

Wrist

**Figure 10
To shorten
the sleeve
between
underarm
and wrist**

Back
sleevehead

Front
sleevehead

Underarm

Centre line

Elbow

Wrist

Style File

Knit to fit
part 2

We have seen how to make simple alterations to the bodice block, here we look at altering the skirt block.

Altering the skirt block

The skirt block is easy to alter. The most common problem associated with fitting a skirt is the variation in girth between waist and hip measurements, as compared to standard measurements, and differences between waist and hip lengthwise. For example, if you are short waisted (as I am) then your hip-to-waist measurement is less than average; this manifests itself as skirt and trouser waistbands sitting too high up under the bust. Fold a horizontal tuck half way between the waist and hips. Re-draw the pattern with a smooth seam line.

If your hip to waist measurement is average but you want to shorten, or make longer, the overall length of the skirt, you should make a tuck or an inlet in the pattern halfway between the hips and the hem line (Figs 1 and 2).

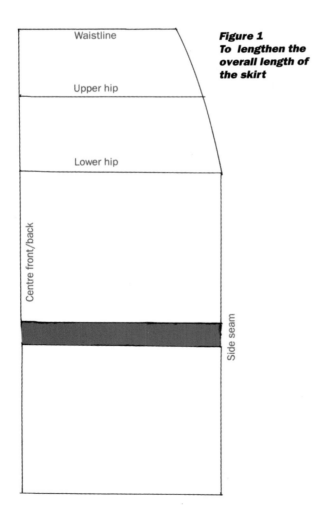

Figure 1
To lengthen the overall length of the skirt

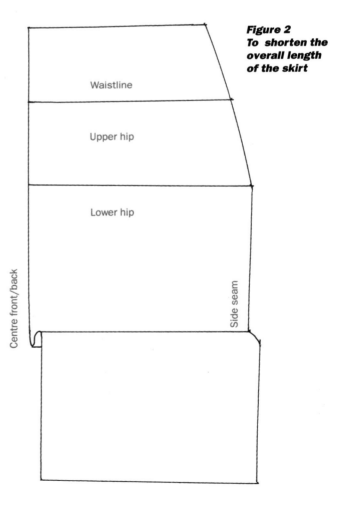

Figure 2
To shorten the overall length of the skirt

For a smaller-than-average waistline in relationship to hip measurement, take in at the waistline and re-draw the seam line from waist to hips (Fig 3).

If the hip measurement is larger than average compared to the waist size, alter the skirt block by adding extra fabric at hip level through to the hemline. To do this, mark and cut a line vertically from half way along the waist line to half way along the hem line. Open out the pattern keeping the waist line closed. Make paper inserts and re-draw the pattern with a smooth seam line (Fig 4).

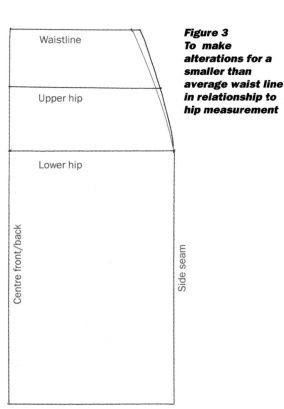

Figure 3
To make alterations for a smaller than average waist line in relationship to hip measurement

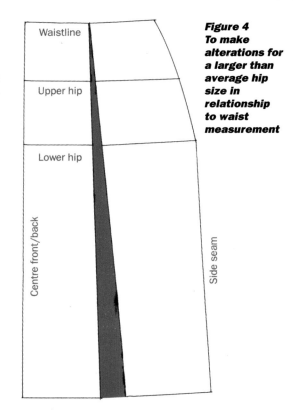

Figure 4
To make alterations for a larger than average hip size in relationship to waist measurement

To narrow (or widen) the skirt pattern, fold in (or extend outward) from halfway along the waist to halfway along the hem line (Figs 5 and 6).

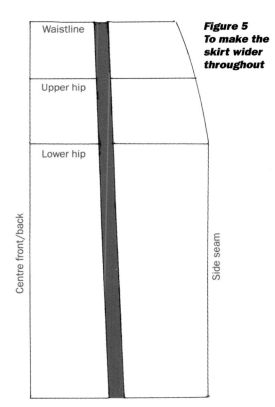

Figure 5
To make the skirt wider throughout

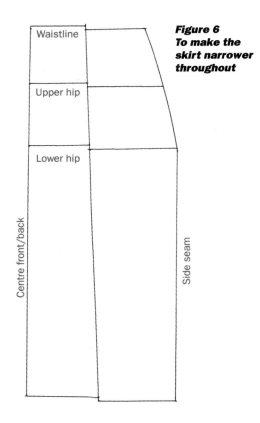

Figure 6
To make the skirt narrower throughout

Testing your pattern

It is a good idea to make a mock-up of the new garment if substantial alterations have been made to the original pattern. A fashion designer would always mock up a newly drafted pattern in calico (this is called a toile) to check for fit before embarking on the sample garment. Similarly in knit design you could cut and sew a mock up in sweatshirt material using a full-scale version of the paper pattern. You can then try it on and make any further adjustments before any knitting takes place. Alternatively copy your pattern draft onto your knit charter or electronic garment shaper and knit a prototype in stocking stitch. You can always cast on and off with waste yarn to speed up the operation as the main objective of the exercise is a perfect fit. I like to keep a version of all my pattern drafts using one or other of the above mentioned methods for future reference. It is much easier to assess changes to proportion and style lines when viewed in three dimensions than as a flat shape.

Style File

Knit to fit
part 3

Adjusting the standard bodice pattern to fit individual/non-standard measurements

Square shoulders and a wide back

To accommodate square shoulders, you will need to straighten the shoulder line by opening out the bodice pattern on a diagonal line through from the armhole to neck point, as shown in Fig 1. Raise the armhole measurement by a corresponding amount.

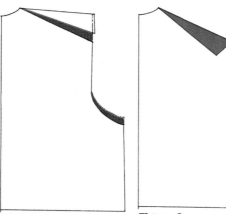

Figure 1
Compensating for square shoulders. Example shows back of pattern

Figure 2
Compensating for sloping shoulders. Example shows back of pattern

Add extra width to the back armhole if the back measurement is wider than average. Wide shoulders will tend to make the garment drag across the shoulders due to insufficient room at the armhole end.

It is also possible to make a similar alteration by taking a wedge-shape out of the bodice. To do this, take a graduated tuck across the front and back bodice from the top of the armhole on a straight line which is at right angles to the centre back or front. This method will straighten the shoulder line without altering the measurement of the armhole, but will

reduce the back length measurement. For prominent front shoulders, add extra height to the front shoulder line only.

Sloping shoulders

Fig 2 shows you how to alter the basic block for sloping shoulders. To do this, overlap the shoulders, taking out a wedge-shaped section from the neck point and increasing the amount gradually to the shoulder point. Lower the underarm by the same amount. The second method involves adding an extra amount across the bodice. Open up the pattern along the same line as for square shoulders, and add an inlet of paper. This will increase the angle of the shoulder line without affecting the armhole measurement. Note that the wedge shape is a mirror image of that used below to adjust for a rounded upper back.

Shoulders in relationship to armhole measurements

To accommodate square, sloping or prominent front shoulders, remember to raise or lower underarm if at all possible so that armhole measurement doesn't change. You will also need to check the armhole measurement in relationship to the sleeve head measurement, and alter accordingly. To do this, stand the tape measure on edge to measure the curved seam lines.

Long back balance or rounded upper back

To adjust the bodice pattern for a stooping figure with a rounded upper back (sometimes referred to as a Dowagers Hump) extra material is needed at centre back, as the average back bodice will hang away from the body at the back and be too short in length. There are two possible places to make alterations and you might only need to alter one or the other. If you need to add more than say 5cm in length, you will first need to open up the pattern about halfway down the armhole edge and open it out by 2.5cm. Insert a 2.5cm straight strip of paper (see Fig 3a). Then follow the instructions outlined below. For under 5cm alterations you will only need to do the latter.

Open up the pattern halfway down the armhole, and pivot until the back measurement is reached. Straighten up the centre-back line as shown in Fig 3b and redraw your pattern. This will result in a wider neckline which can be darted to give a better fit if required.

Once you know where to correct the pattern, this alteration can be achieved in knitting, using the partial knitting technique to work a knitted-in wedge shape: the extra width at the neck line can be eliminated by decreasing stitches regularly across the back neck prior to

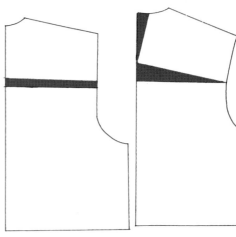

Figure 3a
Step 1. The Dowager Hump (rounded back)

Figure 3b
Step 2. The Dowager Hump (rounded back)

attaching the neckband. To do this, strip off on waste yarn a few rows before the neckline, and replace onto fewer needles as you would for yoke-style shaping.

To lengthen the lower bodice back

Open the pattern up 5cm above the waistline, as shown in Fig 4. Make a graduated wedge shape and straighten up the centre line, noting that this will give additional width to the neckline. If you can use partial knitting to make this adjustment then you will not have to alter the neckline. In this method the side seam is unaltered.

Hollow chest/shortened front

You may find that the figure type described above has a hollow chest. In this example the front length is too long when compared with average measurements, and you will notice that

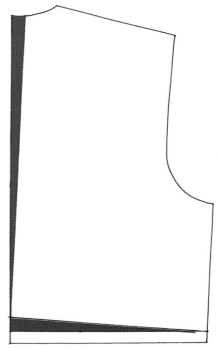

Figure 4
To lengthen lower back

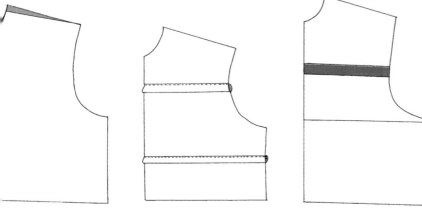

Figure 5
To compensate for a shortened front/hollow chest

Figure 6
To compensate for a shortened front

Figure 7
To allow for a long front balance. Step 1. Extend pattern at chest line

the knit will sag in the chest area. Here you will need to shorten the front pattern at the shoulder, as shown in Fig 5, or make horizontal tucks across the front and back at chest and shoulder blade level, as shown in Fig 6. To alter the front bodice further, you can make an additional shortening below the bust line if necessary. Check that the sleeve pattern matches the new armhole measurements if appropriate.

Long front balance

If your figure type has a long front balance, you will notice that an average front bodice pattern will be too short in relationship to the back bodice, and hang away from the figure at the front. This is generally associated with a large bust, possibly combined with an erect, upright stance. In this example you will need to extend the front bodice pattern at the chest and bust line by incorporating inlets of paper which correspond in measurement to the extra width required, as shown in Figs 7 and 8. You will need to adjust the sleeve head measurement proportionally.

Short back/hollow waist

A person with a long front balance may also have a short back measurement and a hollow waist as compared to standard measurements. Shorten the back pattern by reducing the pattern at the neck and shoulder line. To compensate for a hollow waist, raise the centre back by approximately 1.5cm and taper to the side seam as shown in Fig 9.

Large bust in relationship to shoulder and waist size

To accommodate a larger than average bust size when the rest of your measurements are a smaller size, try raising the underarm seam by 1-2 cm (see Fig 10). You will need to smooth the armhole curve and alter the sleeve head accordingly. If you use this method, select a pattern which corresponds to your waist size.

Alternatively, cut horizontally through the pattern at the bust line, insert an inlet of paper, as shown in Fig 11, and dart the bodice. The extra length at the front can be gradually cut off if required so that the back and front side seams match.

Use partial knitting to make the bust dart if at all possible.

You can also compensate for a large bust in relation to shoulder and waist size by cutting through the pattern from shoulder to waist on the bust dart line and opening the pattern out to the required amount. If your waist line is small, you might only need to open up the top section from shoulder to bust point.

High or low bust line

To make alterations to the bust line, you will need to measure the height of your bust from waist to bust point and compare it against average measurements. This fitting fault will tend to manifest itself more in fitted sweaters and jackets which have a bust dart.

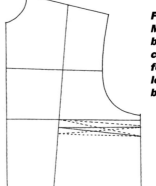

Figure 12
Moving the bust point to compensate for a low/high bust line

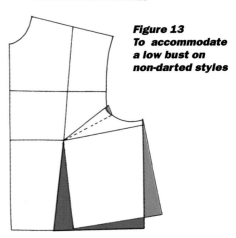

Figure 13
To accommodate a low bust on non-darted styles

A high bust line will cause strains and wrinkles at the high bust line, whereas a low bust will cause excess fullness at armhole level. To make this alteration simply raise or lower the bust point and redraw the dart, as shown in Fig 12. If the style is not darted, then cut the front pattern up from the waist to the low bust level and open out, as shown in Fig 13. Pinch in a dart at the armhole where excess fullness occurs. Re-curve the armhole and redraw the side seam to eliminate any unwanted excess at the waistline.

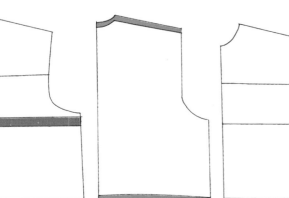
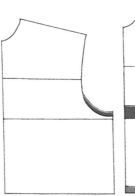
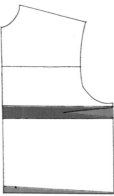

ure 8
allow for a long
t balance. Step
xtend pattern
ust line

Figure 9
To compensate for a short back and hollow waist

Figure 10
To allow for a large bust in relationship to average waist/shoulder measurements

Figure 11
To accommodate a large bust

Style File

Knit to fit
part 4

The Princess Line, or French Bodice as it is sometimes known, is a particularly flattering style with many possible variations and is much used in dressmaking. Long vertical panels which subdivide the bodice into side, centre-front, and back sections can be more easily shaped to fit the contours of individual measurements rather than a single piece pattern. The essence of this type of bodice will translate well into knitting once its construction is understood and suitably refined for knitted fabrics. It is especially suitable for making larger sizes on the knitting machine as the width is divided between many pieces of fabric. To see examples of Princess line garments take a look at my designs, *Dizzy* and *Ice Dreams*.

Shapely Knits
Generally speaking, shapely knits rely either on the fluidity and stretch inherent in knitted structures such as rib and stocking stitch, and have a tendency to cling closely to the body in more fitted styles. Alternatively, multi-piece patterns with a number of seams or fitting darts give great scope for an individual fit. Different amounts of ease and choice of stitch structures will result in a style that is either moulded gently to the body or made to fit like a glove (tight fitting fabric bustiers are often designed on this principle, with boning encased in the seam lines to aid the fit).

Suitable knitted structures
Choose firm, structured stitch patterns that will hold their shape and have properties similar to woven fabrics, such as knitweave, double-bed jacquard and slip stitch, for an elegant yet shapely style line.
Stocking stitch and rib will also work well when shaped, rather than stretched tightly over the body.
It is also possible to design knitting that is wider than the needle bed, and with stitch structures that are proportionally less wide than others, for example, slip stitch as compared to tuck stitch when knitted to the same tension, number of rows and stitches and in identical yarn. This is simply because the style is broken down into a number of subsections which go to make up the whole, rather like a jigsaw puzzle, and can therefore be designed to accommodate a wide range of sizes.

Style and fitting lines
Initially we examine styles that use the look of the Princess line, but without actual shapings (Figs 1 - 4). We then move on to darted and shaped pieces which could form the basis of many exciting and sophisticated styles for all figure types (Figs 5 - 12).
As you can see below, seam lines can be style lines only, or serve a practical function in determining the shape of the finished garment (or indeed both). The long curved seam lines can also be most useful in concealing figure problems such as the so-called dowagers hump, or to accommodate a larger than averaged bust size.

Mock princess style
Figs 1 to 4 show two different methods of subdividing a standard set in sleeve bodice pattern, into vertical panels, to give the effect of a princess line style, but without any dart shapings. The vertical divisions are simply used to divide the pattern into smaller pieces and do not affect the overall shape of the garment. Fig 1 shows the half of the front bodice pattern divided by a curved vertical line through from a point on the shoulder line to the hip line, while Fig 2 illustrates the resulting pattern pieces.
In Fig 3 a similar division takes place, but now the vertical line starts at the point on the armhole were the chest reference line meets the armhole and then curves on through to the hip line.
Fig 4 illustrates the separated pattern pieces, and shows potential for a small degree of shaping from the hip line to the waist line on the side seams, worked in either fully fashioned shaping techniques or knit straight from hip to waist line, then reduced in width using the yoke shaping method (see my yoke sweater *Ice Dreams*). The pattern pieces shown in Figs 2 and 4 could be developed into either sweaters or cardigan and jacket patterns. You can also combine princess-style lines into raglan and yoke patterns (again see *Ice Dreams*). The letters on the pattern pieces indicate where sections are joined one to another.

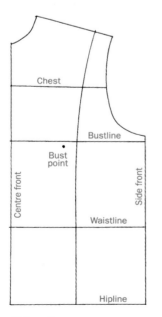

Figure 1

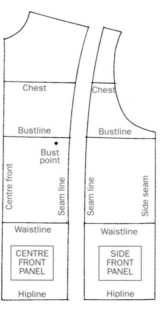

Figure 2

Figure 3

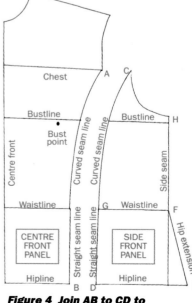

Figure 4 Join AB to CD to complete front bodice

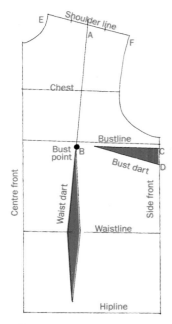

Figure 5

Darts

To achieve a good fit when working with non-stretchy knitting (knitweave, jacquard, slip stitch for example), you will need to incorporate darts into the style lines.

The function of a dart is to dispose of unwanted fullness by suppressing areas of fabric which gives a three-dimensional shape to an otherwise flat piece that will mould to the contours of the body. In knitting, darts can be incorporated into the knitting process through the use of partial knitting and fully fashioned shaping techniques.

In the Princess style, vertical darts are incorporated into the shaped seam lines and are employed in place of the standard underarm bust dart (as shown in Fig 5) and provide a good, inconspicuous method of fitting the garment.

If you are familiar with basic pattern-cutting techniques in dress making, you will know that you can move the position of the bodice darts from the underarm seam to the shoulder, neckline or the armhole seam line (for example). A simplified version of this procedure has been applied in to our basic bodice block in order to develop variations on the Princess style.

To move darts from one position to another on the bodice block, you will need reference lines for the bust, waist and hip line. You should also mark your bust point.

Moving on

Fig 5 is a development of the bodice block for knitwear, with added waist and bust darts. To incorporate the waist dart, the shoulder line has been subdivided into two equal parts at A, and a straight line ruled through the bust point (B) and on into the waist line.

The waist dart is approximately 2 - 2.5cm wide in this example, and is connected upwards to approximately 2cm away from the bust point, and downwards toward the hip line for approximately 12.5cm, tapering to a point in both instances.

Use fully fashioned shaping techniques to make the waist dart when knitted vertically, or partial knitting for sideways-knitted garments. Depending upon the shape of your pattern, you are essentially removing an oval or diamond-shaped piece out of the original pattern. The bust dart is incorporated into the underarm seam line between points C and D. In this example, the top of the bust dart runs parallel to the bust line, and connects the bust point (B) to the side seam. Move the point of the dart approximately 3cm away from the bust point and towards the side seam. The depth of the bust dart will depend on your cup size.

The bust dart can be knitted into the fabric using partial knitting. This will mean that the length of the side seam remains the same as that of the back side seam.

Developing the princess style for knitwear

Figs 6 - 8 develop a style where the long vertical darts work from the shoulder through to the hip line. Figs 9 - 12 show a similar development, except that the darts commence in the armhole seam and curve more radically into the hip line. Fig 6 shows how to move the underarm dart, reposition into the shoulder line and finally incorporate the dart into a curved/shaped seam line. To do this, make a half-scale paper model and mark in the darts as shown in Fig 5.

Now cut down the line A - B as far as the bust point. Close the underarm dart either by folding and pinning, or by cutting away the dart and then joining the two open edges with tape. You will notice that a new wedge shape has opened up on the shoulder line. Cut away the areas marked in red (see Fig 6) to reveal two separate pattern pieces which are now shaped to fit the contours of the body. Finally trace over the shapes (see Fig 7). Curve the seam lines to complete the pattern (see Fig 8).

Fig 9 shows the beginnings of a similar manoeuvre, except that now the bust dart is to be repositioned into the armhole seam. To do this, make another half-scale copy of Fig 5, but this time draw a straight line from the point on the armhole (A) where it meets the chest line through to the bust point (B).

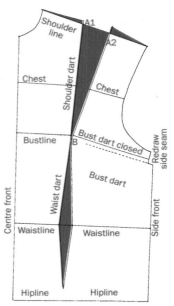

Figure 6 Cutaway areas marked in red (see fig 7 for finished pattern pieces)

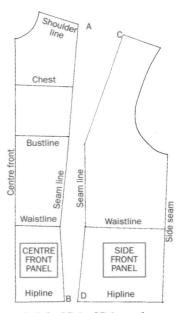

Figure 7 Join AB to CD to make up fitted bodice front

Figure 8

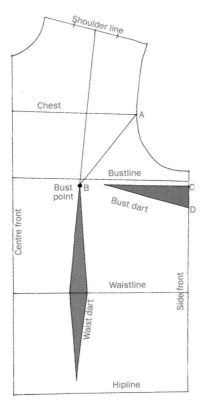

Figure 9

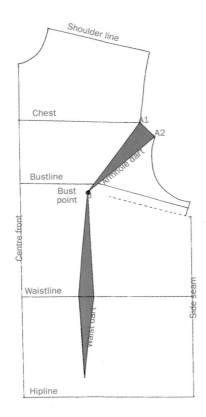

Figure 10

Cut down this line as far as the bust point, and close the bust dart situated in the side seam as described above as shown in Fig 10. Complete the pattern as shown in Figs 11 - 12 in the same way as you did for Figs 7 - 8.

The back bodice pattern

Use the same procedures as for the front bodice pattern to divide the original pattern block with waist darts into two separate sections, but in this case you will not have to incorporate the bust dart into the pattern pieces.

Making a toille

If you have access to a sewing machine it is a good idea to make a mock-up of your new pattern shapes. Use sweat shirt material (or similar stretchy type fabric) for close fitting styles, or a medium weight calico for the more tailored styles.
Alternatively, use your charter to knit up a quick version in stocking stitch, or a similar stitch structure to that of the finished garment. Use bin-ends or ends of cones from other projects. I find that time spent at this stage of the design process helps me to build up an invaluable reference library of garment shapes. If you are knitting for others then these mock-ups will help your customer (and indeed yourself) to see how a particular style works with any given body shape. You can also see what, if any, alterations to the pattern are needed before embarking on the finished piece.

Knitting tips

To ensure a good match on the seams, insert tie markers into the knitting at key points such as waist, bust and commencement of sleeve shaping.
If at all possible, knit the front and back side panels as one until the armhole shaping. At this point strip off on waste yarn and knit the front and back separately.

Using your charting device (knit leader)

This device (my favourite hobby horse) can liberate you from slavishly following published patterns. The advantages of using a visual charting device are so great that I am still surprised to find it so little used. It is so much easier to translate intricately shaped pattern pieces into knitting without having to resort to complex mathematics each time you want to change tension, stitch structure, yarn type and so on.
It is easier to follow, enables you to make simple, visual changes to the pattern shape for individual sizing much more readily, and offers scope for greater creativity; involving the knitter in the decision-making process throughout. Customised knitwear to suit individual sizes and tastes! What more could you ask for!

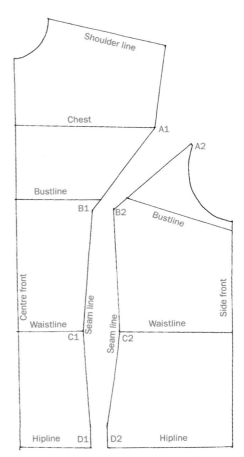

Figure 11 To make up front bodice you will first need to curve lines A1 – C1 and A2 – C2 as shown in Fig 12

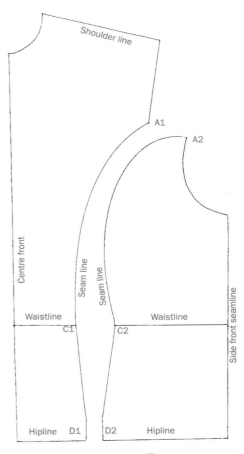

Figure 12 Curved seam lines developed from Fig 11

Style File

Knit to fit
part 5

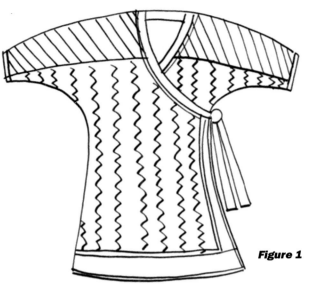

Figure 1

Here we explore the creative possibilities of sideways knitting, and in particular how it can be used to accommodate a range of waist, hip and bust sizes. Sideways knitting is an ideal technique for the design of vertical stripe patterns, worked in knit or purl facing stocking stitch or both. Stripes are very trendy at the moment, whether knitted sideways, horizontally or multi-directional. As you will see, many variations are possible, especially if you utilise your knit charter for the basic garment shapes, introducing variety by simply altering the proportion of one stripe against the other, or the order in which you choose to knit the colours.

Turning the limitations of sideways knitting to our advantage

The overall length of any single piece of knitting is limited by the width of your needle bed and the tension/stitch pattern selected (see below). This can easily be overcome if the limitations and advantages of the technique are carefully considered at the design stage. Take, as an example, multi-piece patterns that are constructed by piecing panels of knit together. A basic Kimono shaped pattern, for instance, could be subdivided into smaller sections (Fig 1) and translated into sideways or horizontal knitting, or a combination. Alternatively extra length could be achieved through the addition of deep welts, peplums and frills, perhaps in a different stitch, gauge or yarn, that could be knitted sideways up or horizontally, depending upon the effect you are trying to achieve. Take a look at Figures 2 and 3 for variations on the *Milan* pattern. You may have made sideways knitted skirts designed around the same principle incorporating a hip yoke to give extra length. Consider a mix of sideways and horizontal knitting techniques, for

example my design *Milan.*
In this design the sleeves are knitted horizontally so that the stripes continue in the same orientation as those of the body section, which is sideways-knitted.

How to do it

If you are designing from scratch you will first need to make a tension swatch in the yarns, tension and stitch pattern you intend to use, but think rows instead of stitches and vice versa. Thus all the horizontal measurements are translated into stitches and all the horizontal measurements become rows. For example, measure the length of the side seam position. Sample measurement is 28cm. If 1cm is 1.7 stitches, then the side seam will be 28cm x 1.7 which is 48 stitches. If half the bust width is 48cm and 1cm is 2.6 rows, then 48cm is 125 rows.
Sideways knitting can be used knit or purl facing, or a combination of both. Use waste yarn or garter bar to turn the work to vary the texture of the knitting and the appearance of the stripe pattern.

Shaping techniques

Partial knitting can be used most successfully to shape the waist, hips or bust, and makes an attractive design feature. There is a bonus in that this method of working eliminates the need for side seams. Partial knit shapings integrated into the stripe patterns make for diamond or triangular shaped patterned insets on the side seam, or from the bust point through to the hips in styles based on the princess-style design (see *Knit to fit, part 4*) .
To calculate for shapings, you will need to know how many stitches and rows there are to 1cm taken from your tension swatch. For example if 10cm is 17 sts and 26 rows, then 1cm is 1.7 sts and 2.6 rows.
To calculate a waist shaping that is decreased by 2.5cm in width, gradually over a 10cm length from above hip to

Figure 2

Figure 3

waist and from waist to underarm which measures 18cm, you will first need to turn the width measurement into rows and the length measurements into stitches. Do two separate calculations for waist to hip and waist to underarm. The amount of rows will be the same, but the number of needles put into holding position will be different (see Fig 3).

Waist to hip calculation: 10cm equals approximately 16 stitches and 2.5cm equals 8 rows. This gives 4 chances to decrease 16 stitches down to zero stitches in 4 rows (every other row). Therefore you will need to push 4 needles to holding position at the opposite end to the carriage on every alternate row 4 times in total.

Waist to underarm calculation: As we noted before, 2.5cm is 8 rows but 18cm equals 30 stitches. In this calculation we need to decrease 30 stitches over 4 rows, and (using the Magic Formula!) this works out as follows:

Decrease 7 stitches twice on alternate rows, and 8 stitches twice on alternate rows. Translated into partial knitting technique this means you will need to push 7 needles into holding position on alternate rows twice, and 8 needles into holding position on alternate needles twice.

Finally, co-ordinate the two shaping instructions (a bit like learning to play the piano, where you finally put left and right hand together!) so that you are shaping at the end opposite to where the carriage is situated on every row, 8 times in total.

Stitch patterns, tension and gauge

Tuck-stitch knits up wider, when compared to stocking-stitch and slip-stitch, if knitted up in the same yarns, tension and number of stitches. Tuck stitch in this example would give the longest piece of fabric, and slip stitch the shortest measurement. Loose tensions in a coarse gauge yarn will give greater width (which of course translates into length when knitted sideways) than a tight tension knitted up in a fine yarn over the same number of stitches and in the same technique. Matching tensions, weights and elasticity is important if you decide to combine horizontal and vertical knitting in the same piece.

A further complication appears if you choose to work across fine and chunky gauge machines. A new trend coming through in knitwear utilises a marked and quite often exaggerated difference between tensions; for example from start to finish of a sleeve. I had toyed with the idea of knitting the cuffs and welts of the *Milan* pattern on the chunky gauge machine moving from a loose tension to a tighter tension, perhaps even double to single strand of ribbon yarn, then moving onto the fine

gauge machine for the main body of the sleeve.

Making up techniques

A great advantage of sideways knitting is the elimination of the need for side seams. The fronts and back are knitted as one with button and buttonhole bands incorporated into the knitting.

Fronts bands can be knitted as one with the main body of the garment. Begin and end the main body sections on waste yarn, blocking and pressing before attaching the bands. Hook up the stitches from below the waste yarn and knit a single bed hem. You may need to drop the tension slightly on the bands so that they lie flat.

The waste yarn will act as a marker so that you can see clearly which line of stitches needs to be picked up. Waste yarn can be used to hold stitches which might need to be picked up onto the machine at a later time, or where you need to graft two different panels of knitting together (for example at the point where the sleeve joins the armhole). The same technique can be used where sleeves or armhole trims are knitted first, stitches for the front and back section of the sleeve are stripped off onto separate pieces of waste yarn and then hooked back up onto the machine after knitting the front or back and cast off (for further explanation see *Linear*).

Peplums, hems, cuffs and yokes can generally be knitted first, stripped off with waste yarn and then hooked back up onto appropriate needles, together with the main body of knitting, and then cast off.

Grafting one section of knitting to the other through open stitches can be daunting but it is worth the effort. Done properly, it should be impossible to tell

where one section is grafted to the other; for example between the top of the sleeve head and the armhole. If you have never tried this technique it isn't as scary as you might think. Try your hand on a chunky gauge fabric, and use non-slippery yarns. I find it easier to work this technique if I strip off the waste yarn before stitching the raw edges together, as long as it is a fairly stable yarn to work with.

It is possible to knit the sleeve from the armhole down towards the wrist, having picked up the armhole stitches from the main body of the garment. You would need either to incorporate side seams in the main body of the knitting, or a seam down the centre of the sleeve. In the crossover cardigan this would give you the option of offset stripes on front and back sleeve linked by a decorative seam line (see Fig 4).

Styles

Work from a basic pattern block to develop a number of different garment ideas. For instance look at ways of dividing up a basic shape such as the Kimono style pattern into smaller panels, jigsaw style. Experiment with different combinations of textures in the same garment, or work a boldly patterned border against a plain knitted or striped front and back.

The crossover cardigan could be knitted so that the fronts only reach three quarters of the way around the body, rather in the manner of crossover-style ballet cardigans. Batwing designs seem to be reviving in fashionable circles and are a good candidate for sideways knitting. Skirts knitted on yokes and princess-style fitted jackets could also be knitted partially or wholly sideways, incorporating knitted-in shapings to give a classy, tailored look.

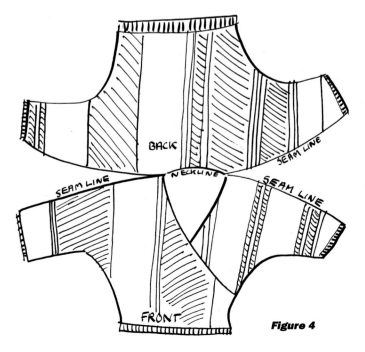

Figure 4

A Note about
Yarns and Colours

You may find that some of the yarns and colours used in the patterns are no longer available. If so, you will need to knit a new tension swatch in yarns and tension of your choosing. Check that the tension is compatible with the pattern. If it is not, alter the number of rows and stitches as appropriate, or copy the outline garment pattern to your charter paper in order to knit alternative versions.

About the Author

Ruth Lee, a textiles and fibre arts tutor, has been designing knitwear for many years. Past clients include the world-renowned department stores Bloomingdales and Harrods. Ruth, a regular contributor to *Machine Knitting News*, combines her writing and teaching with designing for exhibitions, plus a variety of speaking engagements.

Index

TITLES AVAILABLE FROM
GMC Publications
BOOKS

Woodcarving

Beginning Woodcarving   *GMC Publications*
Carving Architectural Detail in Wood: The Classical Tradition
     Frederick Wilbur
Carving Birds & Beasts   *GMC Publications*
Carving the Human Figure: Studies in Wood and Stone
     Dick Onians
Carving Nature: Wildlife Studies in Wood   *Frank Fox-Wilson*
Carving on Turning   *Chris Pye*
Celtic Carved Lovespoons: 30 Patterns
     Sharon Littley & Clive Griffin
Decorative Woodcarving (New Edition)   *Jeremy Williams*
Elements of Woodcarving   *Chris Pye*
Essential Woodcarving Techniques   *Dick Onians*
Lettercarving in Wood: A Practical Course   *Chris Pye*
Relief Carving in Wood: A Practical Introduction   *Chris Pye*
Woodcarving for Beginners   *GMC Publications*
Woodcarving Tools, Materials & Equipment
(New Edition in 2 vols.)   *Chris Pye*

Woodturning

Bowl Turning Techniques Masterclass   *Tony Boase*
Chris Child's Projects for Woodturners   *Chris Child*
Contemporary Turned Wood: New Perspectives in
a Rich Tradition   *Ray Leier, Jan Peters & Kevin Wallace*
Decorating Turned Wood: The Maker's Eye
     Liz & Michael O'Donnell
Green Woodwork   *Mike Abbott*
Intermediate Woodturning Projects   *GMC Publications*
Keith Rowley's Woodturning Projects   *Keith Rowley*
Making Screw Threads in Wood   *Fred Holder*
Turned Boxes: 50 Designs   *Chris Stott*
Turning Green Wood   *Michael O'Donnell*
Turning Pens and Pencils *Kip Christensen & Rex Burningham*
Woodturning: A Foundation Course (New Edition)
     Keith Rowley
Woodturning: A Fresh Approach   *Robert Chapman*
Woodturning: An Individual Approach   *Dave Regester*
Woodturning: A Source Book of Shapes   *John Hunnex*
Woodturning Masterclass   *Tony Boase*
Woodturning Techniques   *GMC Publications*

Woodworking

Beginning Picture Marquetry   *Lawrence Threadgold*
Celtic Carved Lovespoons: 30 Patterns
     Sharon Littley & Clive Griffin
Celtic Woodcraft   *Glenda Bennett*
Complete Woodfinishing (Revised Edition)   *Ian Hosker*
David Charlesworth's Furniture-Making Techniques
     David Charlesworth

David Charlesworth's Furniture-Making Techniques –
Volume 2   *David Charlesworth*
Furniture-Making Projects for the Wood Craftsman
     GMC Publications
Furniture-Making Techniques for the Wood Craftsman
     GMC Publications
Furniture Projects with the Router   *Kevin Ley*
Furniture Restoration (Practical Crafts)   *Kevin Jan Bonner*
Furniture Restoration: A Professional at Work   *John Lloyd*
Furniture Restoration and Repair for Beginners
     Kevin Jan Bonner
Furniture Restoration Workshop   *Kevin Jan Bonner*
Green Woodwork   *Mike Abbott*
Intarsia: 30 Patterns for the Scrollsaw   *John Everett*
Kevin Ley's Furniture Projects   *Kevin Ley*
Making Chairs and Tables – Volume 2   *GMC Publications*
Making Classic English Furniture   *Paul Richardson*
Making Heirloom Boxes   *Peter Lloyd*
Making Screw Threads in Wood   *Fred Holder*
Making Woodwork Aids and Devices   *Robert Wearing*
Mastering the Router   *Ron Fox*
Pine Furniture Projects for the Home   *Dave Mackenzie*
Router Magic: Jigs, Fixtures and Tricks to
Unleash your Router's Full Potential   *Bill Hylton*
Router Projects for the Home   *GMC Publications*
Router Tips & Techniques   *Robert Wearing*
Routing: A Workshop Handbook   *Anthony Bailey*
Routing for Beginners   *Anthony Bailey*
Sharpening: The Complete Guide   *Jim Kingshott*
Space-Saving Furniture Projects   *Dave Mackenzie*
Stickmaking: A Complete Course
     Andrew Jones & Clive George
Stickmaking Handbook   *Andrew Jones & Clive George*
Storage Projects for the Router   *GMC Publications*
Veneering: A Complete Course   *Ian Hosker*
Veneering Handbook   *Ian Hosker*
Woodworking Techniques and Projects   *Anthony Bailey*
Woodworking with the Router: Professional
Router Techniques any Woodworker can Use
     Bill Hylton & Fred Matlack

Upholstery

Upholstery: A Complete Course (Revised Edition)
     David James
Upholstery Restoration   *David James*
Upholstery Techniques & Projects   *David James*
Upholstery Tips and Hints   *David James*

Toymaking

Scrollsaw Toy Projects   *Ivor Carlyle*
Scrollsaw Toys for All Ages   *Ivor Carlyle*

Growing Successful Orchids in the Greenhouse and
    Conservatory   *Mark Isaac-Williams*
Hardy Palms and Palm-Like Plants   *Martyn Graham*
Hardy Perennials: A Beginner's Guide   *Eric Sawford*
Hedges: Creating Screens and Edges   *Averil Bedrich*
Marginal Plants   *Bernard Sleeman*
Orchids are Easy: A Beginner's Guide to their
    Care and Cultivation   *Tom Gilland*
Plant Alert: A Garden Guide for Parents   *Catherine Collins*
Planting Plans for Your Garden   *Jenny Shukman*
Sink and Container Gardening Using Dwarf Hardy Plants
                        Chris & Valerie Wheeler
The Successful Conservatory and Growing Exotic Plants
                              Joan Phelan
Tropical Garden Style with Hardy Plants *Alan Hemsley*
Water Garden Projects: From Groundwork to Planting
                        Roger Sweetinburgh

PHOTOGRAPHY

Close-Up on Insects   *Robert Thompson*
Double Vision   *Chris Weston & Nigel Hicks*
An Essential Guide to Bird Photography   *Steve Young*
Field Guide to Bird Photography   *Steve Young*
Field Guide to Landscape Photography   *Peter Watson*
How to Photograph Pets   *Nick Ridley*
In my Mind's Eye: Seeing in Black and White *Charlie Waite*
Life in the Wild: A Photographer's Year   *Andy Rouse*
Light in the Landscape: A Photographer's Year *Peter Watson*
Outdoor Photography Portfolio   *GMC Publications*
Photographing Fungi in the Field   *George McCarthy*

Photography for the Naturalist   *Mark Lucock*
Professional Landscape and Environmental Photography:
    From 35mm to Large Format   *Mark Lucock*
Rangefinder: Equipment, History, Techniques
             Roger Hicks & Frances Schultz
Viewpoints from *Outdoor Photography*   *GMC Publications*
Where and How to Photograph Wildlife   *Peter Evans*

ART TECHNIQUES

Oil Paintings from your Garden: A Guide for Beginners
                              Rachel Shirley

VIDEOS

Drop-in and Pinstuffed Seats   *David James*
Stuffover Upholstery   *David James*
Elliptical Turning   *David Springett*
Woodturning Wizardry   *David Springett*
Turning Between Centres: The Basics *Dennis White*
Turning Bowls   *Dennis White*
Boxes, Goblets and Screw Threads   *Dennis White*
Novelties and Projects   *Dennis White*
Classic Profiles   *Dennis White*
Twists and Advanced Turning   *Dennis White*
Sharpening the Professional Way   *Jim Kingshott*
Sharpening Turning & Carving Tools *Jim Kingshott*
Bowl Turning   *John Jordan*
Hollow Turning   *John Jordan*
Woodturning: A Foundation Course   *Keith Rowley*
Carving a Figure: The Female Form   *Ray Gonzalez*
The Router: A Beginner's Guide   *Alan Goodsell*
The Scroll Saw: A Beginner's Guide   *John Burke*

MAGAZINES

WOODTURNING ◆ WOODCARVING ◆ FURNITURE & CABINETMAKING
THE ROUTER ◆ NEW WOODWORKING ◆ THE DOLLS' HOUSE MAGAZINE
OUTDOOR PHOTOGRAPHY ◆ BLACK & WHITE PHOTOGRAPHY
TRAVEL PHOTOGRAPHY
MACHINE KNITTING NEWS ◆ BUSINESS MATTERS

The above represents a full list of all titles currently published or scheduled to be published.
All are available direct from the Publishers or through bookshops, newsagents and specialist retailers.
To place an order, or to obtain a complete catalogue, contact:

GMC Publications,
166 High Street, Lewes, East Sussex BN7 1XU, United Kingdom
Tel: 01273 488005 Fax: 01273 402866
E-mail: pubs@thegmcgroup.com

Orders by credit card are accepted